Disenchanting Citizenship

LATINIDAD

Transnational Cultures in the United States

This series publishes books that deepen and expand our knowledge and understanding of the various Latina/o populations in the United States in the context of their transnational relationships with cultures of the broader Americas. The focus is on the history and analysis of Latino cultural systems and practices in national and transnational spheres of influence from the nineteenth century to the present. The series is open to scholarship in political science, economics, anthropology, linguistics, history, cinema and television, literary and cultural studies, and popular culture and encourages interdisciplinary approaches, methods, and theories. The series grew out of discussions with faculty at the School of Transborder Studies at Arizona State University, where an interdisciplinary emphasis is being placed on transborder and transnational dynamics.

Marta E. Sánchez, Series Editor, School of Transborder Studies

Rodolfo F. Acuña, *In the Trenches of Academe: The Making of Chicana/o Studies*

Marivel T. Danielson, *Homecoming Queers: Desire and Difference in Chicana Latina Cultural Production*

Rudy P. Guevarra Jr., *Becoming Mexipino: Multiethnic Identities and Communities in San Diego*

Lisa Jarvinen, *The Rise of Spanish-Language Filmmaking: Out from Hollywood's Shadow, 1929–1939*

Regina M. Marchi, *Day of the Dead in the USA: The Migration and Transformation of a Cultural Phenomenon*

Priscilla Peña Ovalle, *Dance and the Hollywood Latina: Race, Sex, and Stardom*

Luis F. B. Plascencia, *Disenchanting Citizenship: Mexican Migrants and the Boundaries of Belonging*

Disenchanting Citizenship

⸿

*Mexican Migrants and
the Boundaries of Belonging*

LUIS F. B. PLASCENCIA

RUTGERS UNIVERSITY PRESS
NEW BRUNSWICK, NEW JERSEY, AND LONDON

Library of Congress Cataloging-in-Publication Data

Plascencia, Luis F. B.
  Disenchanting citizenship : Mexican migrants and the boundaries of belonging /
Luis F. B. Plascencia.
     p. cm. — (Latinidad : transnational cultures in the United States)
  Includes bibliographical references and index.
  ISBN 978-0-8135-5279-8 (hardcover : alk. paper) — ISBN 978-0-8135-5280-4
(pbk. : alk. paper) — ISBN 978-0-8135-5334-4 (e-book)
    1. Mexican Americans—Ethnic identity.   2. Mexican Americans—Civil rights.
3. Mexican Americans—Social conditions.   4. Mexicans—Migrations.
5. Citizenship—United States.   6. Aliens—United States.   7. United States—
Politics and government.   8. United States—Ethnic relations.   9. United States—
Emigration and immigration—Government policy.   I. Title.
  E184.M5P59   2012
  305.86823'72073—dc23

                                                              2011032962

A British Cataloging-in-Publication record for this book is available from the British
Library.

Visit our website: http://rutgerspress.rutgers.edu

Manufactured in the United States of America

Para Lucia

Con amor y gratitud

Contents

Acknowledgments

Books are like plays. The efforts of visible and less-visible actors make a final production possible. The production of this book reflects such a process. It is in this context that I first want to express my deep appreciation to an important set of actors: all of the migrants who generously shared their time, life stories, and experiences in their quest to obtain U.S. citizenship. My understanding of the opportunities and challenges of citizenship was greatly aided by what they shared with me. Although few if any of them will read this book, it is my hope that I was able to reciprocate their kindness through my effort over two years as instructor in the citizenship/ESL classes they attended. My efforts aimed to aid them in meeting their own goals to acquire citizenship. The many conversations in and outside of the classes, particularly among those with whom I was able to keep in touch over the years as they moved closer to achieving their goal, allowed me to more clearly understand the interplay between citizenship and social hierarchies.

I also want to acknowledge the intellectual presence of individuals who shaped my early scholarship and aided my appreciation of key figures in anthropology and the social sciences at the University of Chicago. In particular, I want to note the importance of the late Victor Turner and the late Paul Wheatley—both of whom shared their intellectual passions with social anthropology and comparative urban geography, respectively. Raymond T. Smith, in particular, influenced my comprehension of classical thinkers in the social sciences—Marx, Weber, Durkheim, Polanyi, de Coulange, Mauss, and others.

At the University of Texas, Professors Martha Menchaca, Henry Selby, James Brow, Kamran Ali, and Gretchen Ritter generously shared their insights and advise on my earlier efforts to interpret the process and construction of citizenship. Our ongoing common interest in Mexicans and naturalization has allowed Professor Menchaca and I to continue our conversation on the historical intricacies of the topic. On a more personal level, I want to express my appreciation for the long-term friendship that Henry Selby and James Brow have shared with me over the years. In addition, I want to acknowledge the support and collegiality that Professors Rodolfo O. de la Garza, Gary Freeman, and David Leal extended to me at the Public Policy Clinic in the Government Department at the University of Texas. Their support allowed me to pursue my exploration of citizenship and naturalization. Mention must also be made of professor and former secretary of labor F. Ray Marshall. Not only did he encourage my involvement with the Center for Study of Human Resources, but I also feel honored that he asked me to collaborate with him on an analysis of the work of Jamaican sugar cane cutters in Florida. I also want to acknowledge the impact of the late Begoña Aretxaga on a theoretical question addressed in the book. Our multiple conversations were instrumental in shaping my interest in examining the question of productivity of discourses—an undertheorized issue in Michel Foucault's work. Finally, Professor De Ann Pendry has proven to be an exceptional colleague and friend; her astute observations and comments made the earlier draft a much stronger and fluid work. She was able to push a fellow anthropologist to clearly express what he was thinking when not articulating those thoughts well enough. I feel fortunate to have benefited from her generous time and insight.

At my current institution—Arizona State University—I have been fortunate to come in contact with a group of colleagues that have encouraged and supported my research. In particular, I want to express my appreciation to Professor Carlos G. Vélez-Ibáñez, director of the School of Transborder Studies, who has fostered my scholarship. Special thanks are due to Professor Gloria Holguín Cuádraz, who has become a close colleague and exceeded all expectations in providing intellectual support and assistance. Professor Cuádraz read and commented on most of the chapters in the book.

Finally, I want to communicate my appreciation to the two anonymous reviewers of the book manuscript. Their insightful comments allowed me to better articulate my arguments. Consequently, any errors that remain are my own. Leslie Mitchner, Lisa Boyajian, and Monica Phillips at Rutgers University Press ably guided the manuscript through the publication process. Their encouragement and support is greatly appreciated. My deep appreciation is extended to my wife, Lucia, who kindly tolerated my long hours in the home office, and who with her humor and supportive nature kept me in touch with the broader reality of life.

Disenchanting Citizenship

because of the foregrounding of citizenship as a contested notion during the election and continuing to the present. It is a high-stakes issue. During the election one question centered on whether Senator John McCain (R-Arizona), if successful in gaining the necessary electoral college vote, could take office given his birth location—the Panama Canal Zone. And, during and after the election, whether President Obama was actually born in the United States and thus legitimately occupies the Office of President. The former issue was somewhat resolved through a Senate Resolution (S.R. 511) in April 2008. The nonbinding resolution recognized Senator McCain as a "natural born Citizen," according to Article II, Section 1 of the Constitution. Ironically, Senator Barack Obama (D-Illinois) was one of the cosponsors of the resolution. In the case of President Obama's birth, many have accepted his Hawaiian birth certificate, but even after the official release of the long form by the White House, some still question the authenticity of his U.S. citizenship and thus the legitimacy of his presidency.

An August 2010 CNN poll reported that 42 percent of U.S. residents believed that President Obama was "definitely born in U.S." The remaining respondents were less certain or were certain that he was born elsewhere.[2] On April 18, 2011, Governor Janice K. Brewer (R-Arizona) vetoed a bill (HB2177) approved by the Arizona legislature that required presidential candidates to prove their U.S. birth to the secretary of state before being included in the ballot. HB2177 was an action on the part of state legislators to address the concern with the question of President Obama's birth and his qualification as a "natural born Citizen."

From 2005 to the present, the notion of citizenship has been salient to national debates on migration and migrant policy.[3] Congressional leaders have sought to forge an acceptable "comprehensive immigration reform." Yet from the 2005 bill sponsored by Representative Sensenbrenner (that became part of the stimulus for the unprecedented 2006 pro-migrant marches across the nation), to the Senate's secure borders bill that came close to passage in 2007, and to the CIR-ASAP Act of 2009 (Comprehensive Immigration Reform for America's Security and Prosperity), citizenship remains a focal point of contention. In addition to the birthright debate, one key concern is whether there should be a path to citizenship for undocumented migrants (whom I label "informally authorized migrants" [Plascencia 2009a]) as part of comprehensive reform. The 2001 to 2011 debate on the DREAM Act is also a contention about whether the United States should provide a path to citizenship to affected individuals, or if it is simply a plot to grant amnesty.

Citizenship, as a form of membership and belonging, has also been central in state and local governments' actions since the mid-1990s to restrict employment, housing, in-state tuition at public colleges, and other resources to citizens (Plascencia 2001; Plascencia, forthcoming; Plascencia, Freeman, and Setzler 2003). By 2007, all fifty states and hundreds of municipalities had enacted measures to exclude noncitizens, particularly informally authorized migrants, from resources deemed to belong to citizens. And for the first quarter of 2011, the National Conference of State Legislatures reported that 1,538 were introduced in fifty states and Puerto Rico, and twenty-six states enacted 63 laws and adopted 78 resolutions (NCLS 2011). In short, since the 1990s citizenship has become a key element within efforts to define the national and local community—who is a member, who belongs, and who is deserving of public resources. The significant proportion of Mexican-origin persons in the U.S. population as a whole and within the informally authorized migrant population, the continued unauthorized entry of migrants from Mexico (albeit at a reduced number due to the U.S. recession) and the unprecedented number of Mexican-origin persons acquiring U.S. citizenship have played a significant role in shaping the national and local debate on migration and citizenship. Consequently, much of the debate about migration is ultimately a debate about Mexican migration and the impact of Mexican migrants on the nation.

The concepts of citizen and citizenship are central constructs in U.S. sociopolitical discourses and remain contested constructs. In the United States they are fundamental. They index a broad set of ideas, such as belonging, membership, identification, social standing, as well as support, and overlap with discourses related to nationality, nationalism, patriotism, loyalty, and others. It is a construct so central to the U.S. national narrative that it occupies a taken-for-granted position in the everyday lives of U.S.-born residents. The nation's Citizenship Day, for example, is a date that many U.S. citizens are not aware exists, nor can they readily note the date it is celebrated. Ironically, most foreign-born persons seeking naturalization know the date; they have to, as it is one of the items they must learn. The date is September 17.

The ubiquity of the construct of citizen/citizenship, however, should not be understood as representing a consensus regarding specific definitions of each, including elusive notions such as "natural born Citizen." "Citizen" and "citizenship" also should not be thought of as having a singular meaning. Both concepts signify multiple meanings. In general, the polysemy of both terms can be divided into three discursive fields: juridical uses, sociopolitical uses, and everyday uses.[4] Under juridical uses, people are exposed to enunciations about the number of persons naturalized (i.e., persons who petition and are granted U.S. citizenship), local efforts encouraging eligible persons to apply for U.S. citizenship, and the granting of posthumous citizenship to noncitizens killed in war, as well as others. The focus of these is on the juridical question of whether an individual is or is not a citizen. In sociopolitical contexts references are made to citizenship as a masculinist concept in Plato's political thought, schools and their role in making tomorrow's citizens, citizen input in proposed municipal policies, and citizen participation in research by political scientists, just to name a few. And in everyday contexts people hear and see multiple references to persons being good citizens, in the expression "second class citizen," organizations with names such as Public Citizen, books with titles such as *Citizen McCain*, projects at universities entitled Citizen Scholars, or corporations being recognized for their positive actions as good corporate citizens. This analytical separation, however, does not mean that the three fields do not inform each other; to the contrary, there is considerable semantic overlap across the three fields.

The openness of the term "citizenship" is important. While some attribute the absence of a clear consensus as contributing to the declining significance of citizenship in the United States, I suggest a different perspective. I suggest that part of the power of the concept of citizenship can be attributed to its lack of cloture. Its very openness allows the state, interest groups, and individual actors to ground their actions on behalf of citizenship—a citizenship that is differentially defined and generates its historical variability. The meaning of citizenship is often contested, particularly in its juridical sense. For example, when Fred Korematsu and other Japanese-descent persons challenged the constitutionality of President Franklin D. Roosevelt's Executive Order 9066 (the 1942 internment order),[5] and Yasir Esam Hamdi and José Padilla challenged the constitutionality of

President George W. Bush's policy on the detention of enemy combatants, they did so on U.S. citizenship grounds.[6] More recently, the legal challenge to the Obama administration regarding the assassination order on the Las Cruces, New Mexico–born Anwar al-Awlaki, the radical leader living in Yemen allegedly linked to the Fort Hood shooting and attempted Times Square bombing, is also anchored on the concept of U.S. citizenship. The legal challenge by the American Civil Liberties Union and the Center for Constitutional Rights to the assassination order addresses a fundamental question: what are the inalienable rights of a U.S. citizen? In other words, can the U.S. government assassinate a U.S. citizen without ever charging the person with a criminal offense or providing the opportunity for the person to face his accusers or defend himself in front of a jury of peers? These efforts to define the primary elements of U.S. citizenship are examples of the openness of the concept and its ongoing contestability in the United States.

Since the early 1990s, there has been a significant resurgence of interest in the concept of citizenship in the social sciences and legal scholarship. Will Kymlicka and Wayne Norman (1994) label this renewed academic interest "the return of the citizen." A voluminous literature has emerged since then on the topic of citizenship. The major contributors have been from the fields of political philosophy, political science, and sociology, with anthropology also contributing to the efforts to understand citizenship.[7]

The resurgence of academic interest on the concept of citizenship has been driven by national and international factors. Some of the key examples include the development of supranational citizenship, particularly the development of the juridical construct of European citizenship, the national policies promoted by Prime Minister Margaret Thatcher and President Ronald Reagan, commonly labeled neoliberal policies (what Pierre Bourdieu refers to as the "abdication of the state"),[8] the unprecedented surge in the number of persons applying for and receiving U.S. citizenship since 1995, and the acrimonious debate on whether a comprehensive immigration reform should include a path to citizenship for informally authorized migrants.

Citizenship, particularly in its juridical sense, is an object of interest to academics and individuals because it is embedded in contexts involving power relations. And its effects within national and local power relations have direct and immediate impact on the political status and material interests of individuals. In particular, in the United States one's ability to assert the identification of U.S. citizens has important political and economic consequences on the well-being of individuals and families. Historically, it marks a position of privilege with reference to political actions (e.g., voting, serving on juries, holding elected office, testifying against accusers); property rights (e.g., owning land, receiving an occupational license, operating a business, being employed by the federal government); as well as a wide range of other privileges, such as receiving a federally subsidized educational loan and the right not to be deported/removed.

The removal/departure of U.S-born Yasir Esam Hamdi to Saudi Arabia on the condition that he renounce his U.S. citizenship, or else remain imprisoned on charges of being an "illegal enemy combatant," however, points to the presence of state exceptions (Agamben 1998, 2000) regarding the privilege of citizenship. Citizenship is also important because it traverses the social facts of race, gender, and sexuality, and historically it has been linked to privileges tied to notions of "whiteness," masculinity, heterosexuality, and ownership of property. Moreover, citizens may hold the same political status but still occupy unequal positions; the historical differences between male and female citizens and suffrage rights exemplify the inequality among citizens. Consequently, the differences between citizen and noncitizen can be characterized as representing more of a continuum than a simple dichotomy.

Citizenship, I argue, simultaneously fosters exclusion and inclusion. In terms of inclusion, it promotes and invokes an imaginary solidarity, in the sense used by Cornelius Castoriadis (1987) and Benedict Anderson (2006), by emphasizing shared membership in a nation-state. Nationalism depends on this. As citizens of a particular nation-state, individuals are expected to have affective ties to that nation, and to be concerned with its well-being, as well as ultimately possess a willingness to kill and die for it, or to support such efforts when the nation confronts an enemy. The discourse of citizenship encompasses ideas and practices that endorse the important common ties that sustain a sense of belonging and of membership. However, as evident from the early Greek city-states to modern democracies, the circle of membership is never universal, and so categories of individuals residing within the territory are excluded from the circle based on criteria that are ultimately arbitrary and at times undefined—the 1790 Naturalization Act's "white person" criteria resulted in over fifty court cases between 1878 and 1944 that led judges to ponder what the authors of the act meant (Haney 1996). It is a political paradox that democracies operating under democratic principles of inclusion, such as the principles of all affected (i.e., all affected by the rules and laws of government) and equality, stress inequality and difference in constructing the boundaries of belonging (Beckman 2006).

Despite exclusionary practices, it must be acknowledged that U.S. naturalization law has, overall, been generous. From 1907 to 2010, 24.6 million foreign-born persons, or 89 percent of petitioners, have been granted citizenship—though the actual number is greater since it is unknown how many were naturalized between 1790 and 1906.[9] Thus the boundaries of belonging have allowed entry to about 90 percent of those wishing to enter into the circle of membership, over 25 million migrants.

This book examines the experience and perceptions of one group of individuals born outside the United States who are in the process of seeking or have been granted U.S. citizenship. It examines the experience of persons born in Mexico who later migrated to the United States— Mexican migrants. It also examines efforts to promote citizenship and provide citizenship classes. I use Mexican migrants as a label that makes neither their nativity nor their experiences in relocating to the United States essential qualities of their lives. Their relocation to the United States and their nativity are viewed as experiences in their lives, and not as an essence that they possess. Hereinafter, the label "Mexican migrant" should be read with this qualifier in mind. The aim within such a framework is to seek to understand how personal perspectives and socially defined options motivate the actions of individuals. Moreover, it accepts the fact that irony, paradox, congruence, and contradiction can and do exist in the efforts of individuals to navigate external demands and internal desires within the multiple power relations that they are subject to and positioned within.

The experiences of some of the individuals examined in the book are unique. Some have traversed the juridical and social categories from informally authorized to temporary resident, then to lawful permanent resident (i.e., having a green card), and eventually to that of U.S. citizen. This migration-citizenship trajectory is unlike that for most naturalized citizens, who generally entered with a work visa; permanent residents; or individuals who married a U.S. citizen, obtained their green cards, and then sought and obtained U.S. citizenship.[10] The uniqueness is based on the fact that they are part of a policy decision that was debated for over fourteen years and then enacted in 1986—the Immigration Reform and Control Act (IRCA). IRCA contained two important provisions: a provision allowing persons who could prove that they had resided in the United States since prior to January 1, 1982, without the formal permission of the government to apply for legalization (also known as "amnesty"); and a Special Agricultural Worker (SAW) provision allowing persons who had performed agricultural work in specified perishable crops for a specified period to also apply for legalization.[11] President Ronald Reagan signed the act into law in November 1986, and the legalization program began on Cinco de Mayo of 1987. My view is that this starting date was not accidental. It was likely aimed at drawing attention to the program and recognizing that the single largest national origin group that would apply would be from Mexico, as over 70 percent of those who applied in Arizona, California, and Texas were of Mexican origin. Close to 3 million persons were granted legalization and given temporary resident status (a red card).[12] These individuals then had to apply within eighteen months for permanent residency. Five years after holding this status, they could petition for U.S. citizenship (three years if they were married to a U.S. citizen, or less if they had served in the military). Thus, based on the IRCA legalization, those who have become U.S. citizens or desire to acquire this status remain unique in the citizen-making history of the United States.

Choice of Labels and Book Title

In order to move away from the common practice of classifying persons as having or lacking documents (*papeles*)—and thus explicitly bringing the state back into not only the formal issuance of authorizing documents but also the management of national economies—I use the labels "informally authorized" and "formally authorized" migrants (Plascencia 2009a). Informally authorized immigrants are—through the discretion of federal authorities (i.e., by not enforcing employer sanctions aggressively)—allowed to participate in the economy. This pattern is, in effect, a "Texas Proviso" writ large.

The Texas Proviso was added to the criminal harboring provisions of the 1952 McCarran-Walter Act, which increased penalties for smuggling, transporting, and harboring illegal aliens, yet explicitly excluded employment as a form of harboring.[13] This in effect signaled that it was admissible to employ such persons and shielded employers from being criminally liable for harboring them at the workplace. The employer sanctions provision of the 1986 IRCA made employment of persons not unauthorized to work in the United States a civil and eventually a criminal act, but the clear lack of interest in implementing the restrictions since its enactment has de facto reinstituted a practice akin to the Texas Proviso.[14] The point is not to suggest employer sanctions as a solution to the problem, but rather to underscore the contradiction between the discourse that blames informally authorized migrants for taking jobs away from U.S. citizens and the practices that facilitate hiring the persons said to be taking jobs away.

The label "informally authorized" is offered as an option to the more clearly pejorative label of "illegal" (*ilegal*) that creates the subjectivity of illegality for individuals and simultaneously exonerates the state and employers from any role in fostering the demand for such labor. Employers are simply referred to as employers, not as illegal employers, even when they are known to hire informally authorized workers and are fined for doing so. "Formally authorized" persons are here defined as those individuals who have been formally allowed to enter and, for the most part, work in the United States. Formally authorized persons include permanent residents, students, parolees, asylum seekers, temporary agricultural workers, NAFTA Treaty workers, athletes, and other visa categories.

The proposal for new terms, while not free of problems, aims to suggest a more complex view of individuals who deploy strategies to meet individual and family goals within unequal economies. More precisely, it aims to highlight the U.S. government's role in authorizing migration that is not formally authorized. A focus on whether or not an individual migrant possesses a document obscures several issues. One is the role of the state in issuing and withholding documents, and through this process determining not only the employment position of individuals but also the labor market competition between those who have documents and those who do not. This is different from the view, suggested by the term "undocumented," that some individuals have chosen to obtain documents and others have not. Another is the passing and enforcing of laws regarding the undocu-mented that favor some interests over others; for example, focusing interior enforcement on workplaces employing males (such as construction sites) instead of raiding high-income neighborhoods in search of females taking care of children of affluent, and potentially politically influential, families. The former is common; the second seems to be tacitly sacrosanct.

The concept of disenchantment as used here draws upon the insight articulated by Max Weber (1973) regarding the long-term impact of ration-alization and intellectualization on culture and society; however, it takes into account the substantial commentary by scholars who have noted the limitations in Weber's formulation, particularly the assumptions about the past and the presence of enchantment within modernity.[15] I use it to draw attention to a perspective discovered among some migrants who have acquired U.S. citizenship (discussed in chapter 6), and to the idea that foundational concepts, such a citizenship, have to be examined in order to make sense of how they may simultaneously enchant and disenchant social processes.[16]

Source of Data and Methods

The primary data examined are drawn from structured open-ended inter-views of Mexican migrants who were either in the process of preparing to petition for U.S. citizenship or had been granted that status. In addition, data were obtained from multiple sources: (1) informal conversations with migrants in citizenship classes I taught voluntarily in two Austin community-based organizations (1997–1998 and 2003–2004); (2) structured open-ended interviews with a U.S. Citizenship and Immigration Services (CIS) official and several local leaders in Austin and Houston; (3) natural-ization ceremonies in El Paso, San Antonio, and Phoenix; (4) observations and informal conversations at several local events encouraging migrants to apply for U.S. citizenship or to complete the naturalization application (Austin and Phoenix); and (5) citizenship classes. Multiple documents on citizenship, including legislation and court cases, and news stories from numerous sources were also compiled and reviewed. Finally, I have also drawn on my own experience of transitioning from a "real green card alien" to a U.S. citizen;[17] giving testimony to federal agencies, legislative committees, and city councils regarding migrant issues; providing staff support to a Texas Governor's Office task force on migration; and serving as chair of the Austin Commission on Immigrant Affairs for four years.

INTERPRETATIONS AND ARGUMENTS

While a substantial literature has emerged that examines what U.S. citizenship is through an author's self-reflection, the analysis of legislative or court cases, or an examination of the different dimensions of citizenship, most authors have overlooked several important issues: What do citizens or aspiring citizens themselves understand as constituting citizenship or being a good citizen? What motivates an eligible person to seek U.S. citizenship? What obstacles do individuals face in seeking U.S. citizenship? By providing some answers to these and related questions, the book contributes to the expansion of our understanding of a historically important concept and process in the United States.

A substantial part of the existing literature on citizenship, particularly the literature focusing on and generated within the United States and Western European countries, is hindered by an universalist assumption: that citizenship as constructed in Western nations represents a universal concept. Based on a brief examination of the concept of citizenship in Mexico, my argument is that greater attention must be given to the conceptual and historical specificity of its use. We should not universalize the concept and assume that linguistic glosses in other languages (e.g., *ciudadanía*) are the same or entail the same meanings as its conceptual translation. As noted above, we also should not assume that citizenship has a singular definition in the United States. Furthermore, we should not assume that the concept in other nation-states necessarily encompasses the many meanings that this term implies in English. Attention must be given to understanding the historically informed contexts of the concepts and investigate the extent of commensurability across nation-states, what I label the "trans-state discursivity" of concepts.

Additionally, as mentioned earlier, even though some writers interpret the absence of a single understanding of citizenship as a weakness in U.S. society, an open interpretation should be considered. Openness undergirds the discursive power of the concept. This book illustrates that the dual nature of exclusion and inclusion in citizenship is reflected in the contestations regarding who can become a citizen (a member) and what privileges should be granted or taken away. I argue that exclusion and inclusion operate simultaneously; they are the Janus faces of citizenship.[18]

The major theoretical question addressed in this book is "How does the discursive formation of citizenship produce the subjectivity of citizen among Mexican migrants desiring U.S. citizenship?" The subjectivity of citizen is produced because (1) the power of the discourse does not rest on its independent operation, but rather on its overlap with parallel discourses that are common in the lived experiences of individuals (e.g., weddings, graduation ceremonies, schooling); (2) multiple entities and individuals are involved in mediating the demands of the state and promoting fidelities to it (federal migration agencies, migrant assistance and advocacy groups, volunteer teachers of citizenship classes); (3) elements in the discourse make sense to them—they recognize the value and privileges associated with juridical citizenship, want to be good citizens, and want their children to be good citizens (i.e., law-abiding persons); and (4) becoming a citizen held out the promise of meeting some of their needs (e.g., to sponsor a relative), and desires—desires to belong (to be a full member in the political community) and to be recognized (to be accepted as a human being and citizen, not just a dominated category). However, that disenchantment can also surface after the acquisition of citizenship.

Theoretical Guideposts

Theoretically, the book relies on insights from the work of Giorgio Agamben, Alain Badiou, Pierre Bourdieu, Michel Foucault, Antonio Gramsci, Jacques Lacan, and Max Weber. The central theoretical framework combines three perspectives. The first perspective sees discourse, or more precisely discursive formation, as central to understanding power relations in the process of the state inculcating a person's fidelity to the state through citizenship, as well as the creation of a person's subjective conception as a citizen (the process of subjectivization). The second perspective recognizes that to produce subjectivities (to be productive) discourses must make sense to the subjects. The third perspective incorporates the notion that the productivity of discourses is enhanced if it meets the desires or needs of the subjects.

The central theoretical concern of the book is Foucault's (1989, 1991) proposition that power not only involves schemes of surveillance, discipline, control, and governmentality; it is also productive. It produces subjects, and subjects are involved in producing the self. As suggested by Foucault: "Governing people, in the broad meaning of the word, governing people is not a way to force people to do what the governor wants; it is always a versatile equilibrium, with complementarity and conflicts between techniques which assure coercion and processes through which the self is constructed or modified by oneself" (1999, 162).

But what is undertheorized is how power and the discourses involved accomplish their production. In the empirical case being examined here, the question is, "How do the discourses of citizenship produce subjects who consider themselves as citizens, or more specifically, good citizens?" I suggest that the productivity/efficacy of discourses is linked to the fact that the discourse makes sense (they want to be good citizens) and meets their needs (they want to vote, want to sponsor relatives, and want to be recognized and belong).

LOCATING THE AUTHOR

While it is not always easy to explain why researchers take up one question and not another, there are several reasons for my interest in citizenship. The first relates to my own migration-citizenship trajectory. As one who was born in Mexico City and then migrated with my parents to the United States at the age of ten, I fall into what Rubén Rumbaut calls the "1.5 generation." I was born outside the United States but arrived in this country before I was eleven years old. It is an odd cohort within sociological thinking regarding immigrant generations. Such individuals are foreign-born (i.e., migrants) but largely socialized in the United States, and so they are from here but not from here. As noted in an Argentinean song: "*No soy de aquí, ni soy de allá.*"[19] It is a close parallel to the "twoness" (i.e., double consciousness) that W.E.B. Du Bois suggests is present among African Americans (1953, 17). This twoness has played a role in motivating my long-term interest to understand Mexican and other Latino migration and migration policies within the United States. Moreover, like the individuals interviewed for this book, I also underwent the process of petitioning and being granted U.S. citizenship. Details regarding my experience with the N-400 (the naturalization application) and my oath taking ceremony are discussed in the book.

In addition, citizenship is a key issue within the broader field of migrant and migration studies in which I have been involved at many different levels for some time. Previous research projects include my first ethnographic field project, which was conducted as part of an undergraduate anthropology class on field research methods while attending California State University–San Diego. I studied a squatter community in Tijuana, Baja California, known as "Cartolandia," a reference to the cardboard used to construct homes in that flood-river basin. All of the families residing in Cartolandia had migrated there from other parts of Mexico, including from some indigenous communities in Oaxaca. Many had tried crossing into the United States but had not succeeded. They eked out a living making and selling papier-mâché flowers to U.S. tourists. The Tijuana city government had for some time been concerned about the community's image in the eyes of U.S. tourists crossing into Tijuana by foot. Cartolandia was adjacent to the main bridge and was the first thing that many tourists saw. Its official reason for its elimination was a proposed flood control canal, a joint public health project with the city and county of San Diego. But the government's main concern was not as much about public health as it was about how "they" see "us."

The focus of the study was to understand the involvement of residents in preventing or delaying the elimination of their community. The Tijuana city government, with the aid of the Mexican military, eventually gave a twenty-four-hour notice to the residents and then proceeded to physically force them out. The fieldwork was tiring and at times dangerous due to flooding and local officials' suspicions of my visits and my camera. I was explicitly told that I should not hang around.

Although not versed in the social theories of discourse analysis and power relations at the time, I came to appreciate the articulation and unequal power of different discourses about the community, one on the part of the residents and the other on the city government's. This ethnographic research experience allowed me to witness the direct consequences of the use of state-sanctioned power on individuals and families and to appreciate the migrants' perceptive analyses of the forces they were confronting. They knew that the government had the upper hand, but they were willing to defend their homes till the inevitable move and they pressured the government to provide an alternative for them.

In the end, the Tijuana police and Mexican military arrived with bulldozers to level the homes, a portion of the families were allowed to buy small cinder-block homes near the old airport (at quite a distance from the downtown area where they sold their flowers), other families relocated themselves and squatted in sections of the canyons at the edge of the city. Some of the families felt that their community was destroyed and that they had suffered a loss of income. Now they had to take one to two buses to get to the downtown area and could no longer walk a block for more flowers once they finished selling the ones they had. Some began to reconsider migrating to the United States. This is an example of how development in Mexico can stimulate emigration.

Another important project was my involvement in Chicago's Pilsen community (the largest Mexican-origin community in Chicago) through the efforts of CASA (Centro de Acción Social Autónoma).[20] The organization, whose leadership included young-adult Chicanos (some being the children of migrants) and Mexican migrants, encouraged informally authorized migrants to defend their rights as workers. The open participation of a significant number of informally authorized persons was quite impressive and led me to appreciate the political skills and energy of persons who at the time and even now were often presumed to be passive and unengaged due to their precarious migration status. Fliers and posters, for example, announcing an upcoming meeting for *indocumentados* were openly distributed and widely posted throughout the community. On the day of the event, a crowd of 50 to 100 persons, and at times much more, depending on the event, would attend and participate.

Although job-related issues tended to dominate the meetings and activities, parents with children were also concerned with the progress and treatment of their children in the local public schools. They saw schooling as the mechanism through which their children would learn English and achieve more than themselves. Their hope, not uncommon among many parents, was that their children would get an education and have an easier life than themselves. The United States was undoubtedly a place of opportunity, and they respected and appreciated this. At times, some mothers were surprisingly forthright with teachers and principals regarding what they saw as just and fair, while other mothers were hesitant to speak up.

Later I had the opportunity to work at the Texas Governor's Office as a policy analyst covering migration and labor issues. This position allowed me to regularly interact with Immigration and Naturalization Services (INS), which later became part of Citizenship and Immigration Services, as well as with related agencies within the Department of Homeland Security, officials, and prominent business leaders, such as Mr. Bo Pilgrim (head of Pilgrim Pride, the second largest poultry producer in the United States and the leading producer in Mexico). Pilgrim Pride is a major employer of Mexican migrants in Texas, leading to a substantial increase in the Mexican migrant population in rural communities near the plants. Even though the company claims that all of their workers have papers, legal assistance staff, organized labor, meat processing researchers familiar with the industry, and Immigration and Customs Enforcement (ICE) personnel involved in factory raids at Pilgrim Pride plants argue differently.

During this time I learned important lessons about how public policies, including state migrant policies, are formed. I also learned about how individuals within such policy bureaucracies can shape the discourse and practices within these "state apparatuses," to borrow a phrase from Louis Althusser (1971). For example, Alan Nelson, former commissioner of INS under President Reagan,[21] formulated a project titled SAVE (Systematic Alien Verification for Entitlements), and set up meetings with governors in selected states (Texas was one) to sell his program as a way to "save" them money, money they were presumably spending unnecessarily on "ineligible aliens" that could be spent on U.S. citizens instead.

The aim of SAVE was to enable the employees of two to three state agencies, such as the Texas Employment Commission (TEC, later renamed Texas Workforce Commission), to determine if a person was eligible to receive a selected benefit by comparing identifying information on a database located on a special INS server. In order to entice governors to adopt the program, Commissioner Nelson directed the INS staff to run a small pilot in another state so that it would show the sizable savings that SAVE could generate. I agreed to compile a briefing document for the senior policy staff in the Governor's Office on the SAVE program. I requested data from INS regarding their pilot program, contacted counterparts in other states where Commissioner Nelson was promoting the program, and compiled other relevant data, such as newspaper articles and court cases filed challenging the program.

My report examined in detail the SAVE program and pointed out that most of the alleged savings were nonexistent. It also questioned the inclusion of the program Nelson had recommended: unemployment insurance (UI) benefits.[22] When the senior staff met with Nelson, they indicated that Texas was reluctant to implement the program, at least in the way it was designed and given its focus on UI benefits. Texas held off for some time, despite intense pressures from Nelson, but eventually Texas agreed to a small pilot. As predicted, the cost of implementing and running the program led to only a small net savings.

This net savings, however, was difficult to calculate after the legal challenge by a Mexican migrant (*Fidel B. Ibarra v. Texas Employment Commission*). Ibarra was a migrant who claimed eligibility on the grounds of his status as a person "permanently residing under color of law" (PRUCOL). He was verbally denied and kept from completing an application at a local TEC office. In the initial settlement, the approximately $1,000 that Ibarra would have been able to file claims against, based on his employment, would have led to the payment of approximately $300,000 to cover the remedies ordered by the Federal Circuit court. The passage of IRCA in November 1986 and its incorporation of the program, and the ruling of the appeals court, made the settlement moot; yet the state already had incurred the cost of legal counsel at TEC, the staff time of the attorneys and assistants at the Texas Attorney General's Office, multiple meetings with the U.S. Department of Labor and INS legal counsel, and travel to Tyler (circuit court) and New Orleans (appeals court).

This example was noted because of its importance, at least in my education, in illustrating how statements create a platform of truth that shape the rules for structuring what is valid and not valid for subject positions to enunciate. It also shows how Nelson's statements about creating savings by providing benefits only to deserving citizens made sense to senior state officials and why ultimately they agreed to a pilot in Houston. Thus, through a process creating a distinction between deserving and undeserving individuals based on citizenship, the exclusion of the ineligible aliens, and an argument about saving public funds, citizens and citizenship accrued an additional degree of privilege. The accrual of privilege can be thought of as advancing the inclusivity of citizenship while simultaneously advancing the exclusion of persons defined as aliens.

Subsequent to my tenure at the Governor's Office, I was involved in a number of research projects at the University of Texas at Austin.[23] Here I will highlight three that are relevant to migration as well as citizenship. The first was a survey of persons in the process of applying for legalization (also known as "amnesty," or *amnistía*) under the 1986 Immigration Reform and Control Act (IRCA). This survey allowed me to visit several locations in Texas that were promoting the legalization program, as well as to talk to individuals who were pursuing that option. One of the questions focused on their interests in pursuing U.S. citizenship once they became eligible to apply. The majority indicated that they planned to do so.

The second project involved implementing group interviews with persons participating in ESL/citizenship classes in several Texas cities. The survey asked more than 500 permanent residents why they were applying for citizenship and what their experiences were with INS (Freeman et al. 2002).

The third project involved the analysis of twenty-three occupations in six major migrant-receiving states from 1977 to 2001. The focus of the analysis was on occupational exclusions based on the lack of U.S. citizenship and the examination of state statutes to determine if U.S. citizenship was still a requirement for a state license to practice (Plascencia, Freeman, and Setzler 2003).

Thus, over the past few years much of my attention has been focused on issues related to citizenship, including the examination of 8 U.S.C. §1440 (the provision that grants U.S. citizenship to foreign nationals in the military, including informally authorized migrants) (Plascencia n.d.a.), the granting of posthumous citizenship, and the deportation/removal of noncitizen U.S. veterans (Plascencia 2010). This background shapes and informs the research focus in this book. I decided to build on my previous research by conducting in-depth and open-ended discussions with Mexican migrants desiring U.S. citizenship. I also wanted to explore how those who have achieved this end feel about this long-sought-after goal of *hacerme ciudadano* (literally, "make myself a citizen").

OVERVIEW OF CHAPTERS

Chapter 1 summarizes the conceptualizations of citizen and citizenship and presents an argument for the need to understand the trans-state articulation of discourses (what is labeled the "trans-state discursivity"). In chapter 2 I address the inclusion side of the Janus face of citizenship, and in chapter 3, the exclusion side. Although they are presented as separate chapters, they should be thought of as constituting a single process. Chapter 2 discusses the component of inclusion through an examination of the K–12 public education system's efforts to provide civics/citizenship education and cultivate good citizens. It also addresses the concern among some prominent academics and journalist that the contemporary naturalization process and the quality of persons being granted citizenship (i.e., Latinos and Asians) are devaluing U.S. citizenship. Chapter 3 explores exclusion from entry, naturalization, and practices of citizenship and then exclusion from livelihoods.

Chapter 4 discusses the promotion of citizenship by several groups in Austin, Houston, and Phoenix and the organization and content of adult citizenship classes, including those that I taught. Chapter 5 presents data related to the views of migrants regarding their aspirations and motivations to acquire U.S. citizenship, an analysis of the naturalization ceremonies, as well as an analysis of the views of those who have gained citizenship. In chapter 6, I present the experience of two individuals who, with much personal effort and cost, achieved their dream: to belong, to be recognized, to become a United States citizen. In the conclusion I highlight the key arguments raised in the book and discuss its contribution to understanding the discourses of citizenship. In the epilogue, I underscore the central and controversial construct of citizenship through a discussion of the contemporary birthright citizenship political debate.

As a final note, I should point out that, in an effort to broaden readership and comprehension, the book's narrative style integrates an ethnographic, ethnohistorical, and public policy style. Additionally, all translations from the Spanish are my own.

❦

CHAPTER 1

Fields of Citizenship

The fundamental concept of citizenship plays a central role in shaping social and political space in the history of the United States.[1] From the colonial period to the present, it is part of a discourse that fosters the bonds and unity among those it encircles. However, the membership circle has never been universal. At different times and across different groups residing in the United States, full membership, in terms of political and social membership, is an aspiration rather than a reality. From the settlement of Jamestown, Virginia, in 1607 to the present, the notions, boundaries, and practices of citizenship have been contested and will likely remain so in the future. The contemporary birthright debate, the debate regarding President Obama's birth, and the recent case of *United States v. Rubén Flores-Villar* (2011), decided by the U.S. Supreme Court regarding the gendered difference in law, are examples of the continued contestability of the concept.[2]

The contestability and complexity of the concept is aptly articulated by Herman van Gunsteren: "When studying citizenship one should not assume that one knows—or after some clarification can know—what citizenship is, but rather treat it as an essentially contested concept that refers to a conflictual practice. Many studies of citizenship . . . obscure the fact that notions and practices of citizenship are variable and conflicting" (1978, 10). Over a decade later, Judith Shklar reiterated the centrality and contestability of the concept when she noted, "There is no notion more central in politics than citizenship, and none more variable in history, or contested in theory" (1991, 1). Despite its longstanding centrality, the academic concern with the concept is fairly recent.

Citizenship, as a topic of general academic concern, ended its relative dormancy at the end of the 1980s. Between the publishing of T. H. Marshall's classic 1950 essay, "Citizenship and Social Class," and J. M. Barbalet's 1988 book, *Citizenship*, the concept of citizenship received scant attention in the social sciences. Stuart Hall and David Held (1990) noted this same paucity in reference to political discourses of citizenship, though they observe its ongoing relevance to the topics of migration and race. Since the early 1990s in the United States and Western Europe, citizenship has become a prominent concern within the disciplines of anthropology, history, political philosophy, political science, and sociology. Political philosophers and political scientists, in particular, have allotted the most consistent attention to the subject. Even though citizenship is a common concern, approaches and specific concerns across disciplines and national academic traditions have varied.

The substantive literature that emerged since the early 1990s can be understood as being located in three discursive fields: juridical, sociopolitical, and everyday. The notion of field used here refers to the dominant concerns within the three approaches. This categorization is a heuristic device to present a broad range of discussions within the discourse of citizenship. It departs from the common formats found in the literature that contrast civic republicanism, communitarianism, and liberalism traditions; or the contrast between the rights and obligations of citizenship; or citizenship in relation to civil rights and human rights; or the concern with whether we have entered a postnational phase leading to global, transnational, cosmopolitan, or world citizenship.[3] My primary concern here is to provide a background to the kinds of issues and questions that scholars have pursued in expanding our understanding of citizenship. Secondarily, I index some of the limitations within these. This information is intended as an introduction on how citizenship has been approached and discussed for the nonspecialist.

The core of the juridical field is the formal construction of the concept of nationality/citizenship and represents, to use Pierre Bourdieu's phrase (1986–1987), the "force of law." It holds a dominant position within the broader discourse of citizenship and has a central role in defining the citizen and the noncitizen. It is one of the mechanisms deployed by the state to construct its sovereignty (Shanks 2001). The second domain, the sociopolitical field, encompasses a broad spectrum of discussions. Included in this category are the multiple contributions by the fields of political philosophy, political science, sociology, anthropology, cultural studies, and feminist writers. The third field is the everyday uses of citizen/citizenship. Somewhat surprisingly, most researchers concerned with citizenship, including anthropologists, have largely overlooked the third domain.

THE JURIDICAL FIELD

Of all the domains, this is the most straightforward. This approach is commonly found in law journals and the writings of legal scholars.[4] Historian James Kettner (1978) and other social scientists also write from this perspective.[5] The primary concern of this segment of the literature is with the specific categories established by legislative and/or judicial decisions. In the case of citizenship, the concern is often with issues related to congressional action, U.S. Supreme Court decisions, naturalization and denaturalization processes, suffrage, jury service, and others.

Frequently authors take an unproblematic view of citizenship, and the general concern falls largely on a dichotomy of citizen and noncitizen (or alien). In general, this means that in the former category the person is recognized as a proper and full member (a recognition of belonging), while the latter category marks a partial recognition and limited access to resources and rights. Thus, under this view, the state either grants a person citizenship or it does not. The primary concern is with the legal/formal definition; in other words, the concern is with an attribute granted by the state.

Although citizenship in the United States is relatively straightforward, I am not suggesting that it is unproblematic in its political history, that it lacks irony, or that the very legal apparatus that it is embedded in is without complexities; on the contrary, it has all of these. The literature on naturalization, located within the juridical perspective on citizenship, is a sizable literature, covering the colonial period to the present, and it addresses a broad number of issues related to race and naturalization;[6] Mexicans,

Latinos, and naturalization;[7] Europeans, culture, and naturalization;[8] and naturalization in general.[9]

Despite the importance of citizenship in the political discourse in the United States, little is actually said about it in the Declaration of Independence and the Constitution. The former uses the term "citizens" once, in reference to "our fellow citizens" taken captive in the "high Seas." The Constitution (excluding the amendments) evokes the term "citizen" in five places: on the qualifications for Representatives (article 1, section 2), on the qualifications for senators (article 1, section 3), on the qualifications for president (article 2, section 5), on judicial powers related to "citizens of states" (article 3, section 2), and in reference to privileges and immunities (article 4, section 2). Consequently, it does not explicitly define national citizenship (U.S. citizenship), what constitutes "natural born," the relationship between state citizenship and national citizenship, how citizenship is acquired, or who is responsible for granting national citizenship. The closest approximation to defining a form of citizenship is article 1, section 8, clause 4, wherein it specifies that Congress shall develop "a uniform Rule of Naturalization," yet it does not provide what guidelines should be considered.[10] Not until close to eighty years later, in the Fourteenth Amendment (1868), is there a definition of who is to be considered "a citizen of the United States."

The formal construction of juridical citizenship is found in the Immigration and Nationality Act (INA) and is codified in Title 8 of the United States Code. The INA is organized under three broad categorizations of persons: immigrant, nonimmigrant, and citizen/national/alien. The INA defines an "immigrant" as a person formally authorized to enter the territory, to permanently reside; a person granted lawful permanent residency (LPR)—that is, a person with a green card. Such persons can later petition for U.S. citizenship if they meet the required criteria. Nonimmigrants are formally authorized to enter, allowed to remain for a specified period, and granted varying degrees of employment authorization. This category includes over fifty types of visas (e.g., student, tourist, temporary nonagricultural worker, skilled professional).

The categories of "citizen" and "national" merit some comments. It is generally not noted that the United States has both of these juridical categories, and that the phrase "I am a U.S. national" or "I am an American national" are perfectly correct, albeit rare, statements. They are correct because all U.S. citizens are U.S. nationals; though not all U.S. nationals are U.S. citizens. Persons born in American Samoa and some other U.S. possessions, for example, are granted U.S. nationality, not citizenship. Moreover, in the case of persons born in Puerto Rico after 1917, they are granted citizenship but do not have the full political rights granted to citizens in the continental states.

Conceptual Limitations within Juridical Constructions

A central taken-for-granted assumption in juridical discussions of the concept of citizenship is the notion that the U.S. or Western European construct of citizenship has universal application and consequently can be accurately glossed into a non-English language and vice versa. Thus one commonly finds the English term "citizenship" translated as *ciudadanía* in Spanish. The linguistic gloss assumes commensurability. A recent document produced by the U.S. Personnel Management Office exemplifies this problem. In *Citizenship Laws of the World* (2001), the authors introduce the compilation as a straightforward effort requiring no qualification or discussion about distinct national interpretations or linguistic translation problems.[11]

The case of Mexico points to the importance of understanding the historical specificity of nation-states and their respective formulation of who is a citizen. In the absence of an everyday discourse of citizenship, the use of a phrase such as *"soy ciudadano Mexicano"* (I'm a Mexican citizen) stems from Mexico's own history, both its history of legal constructs and its political history.

Mexico's legal concepts are not drawn from English common law, as took place in the United States, but instead are based on Spanish law.[12] The Constitución de Cadiz de 1812 incorporated a juridical notion of *vecino* (roughly translated as "resident of a recognized political/geographic community," or *vecindad*, such as a *municipio* or parish) as well as *ciudadano* (citizen), and was applied to Mexico and other colonies of the Spanish Empire (two years after the call for independence and prior to Mexico's formal independence in 1821). Consequently, the notion of citizen surfaced not with the emergence of a new Liberal democracy, as is generally assumed in most of the literature on citizenship, but rather as an imperial act—an act that transformed an empire, at least on paper, into a nation and converted subjects of the Spanish Crown into *vecinos*-citizens.

The adoption of the 1812 Constitution, partially aimed at counteracting the *criollo* (Creole) inspired independence movement, fostered a de jure egalitarian ideology—most colonial subjects were granted the political status of citizens of "*la nación española*" (literally, the Spanish nation, though representing the Spanish empire)—and a language for indigenous and agricultural communities to assert their communal and collective agendas against local and provincial authorities representing the Crown. Thus, local communities could and did assert their *vecino*-citizen status to assert their own interests based on their membership in the *vecindad* (i.e., their residency/membership in the recognized political/geographic community). Elements of the 1812 Constitution were incorporated in subsequent Mexican constitutions.

What is important to note here is that for most colonial subjects being labeled and considering oneself a citizen (having citizenship) did not mean the automatic possession of fidelities to the Spanish Empire or to a nation-state. A *vecino*-citizen status allowed the maintenance of local ties and interests. The *pueblo* and *pueblos* (the people and local communities, particularly the indigenous communities), as *vecinos*-citizens, could abstract concessions and pursue some measure of autonomy from the colonial power and later the Mexican state.

Fernando Escalante Gonzalbo's *Ciudadanos Imaginarios* (1992, 66) offers a detailed and insightful account of the development of citizenship in Mexico's history and argues that "*Los campesinos no eran, ni querían ser ciudadanos*" (agriculturalists/indigenous persons were not, nor wanted to be citizens). It also describes the ongoing tension between elites and rural/indigenous communities. The elites did not care much for the uncivilized indigenes, who they saw as a burden to modernization, but they could not proceed with their national project without them. After all, they were an important political resource that could be mobilized against an opposition. The indigenous communities did not care much for the elites, but they recognized the unequal power relations that they held and so knew they could not ignore them.

At times indigenous and local agricultural communities used national issues to promote local interests, their interests as citizens. Escalante

Gonzalbo, for example, quotes a January 1848 document from the small town of Tantoyuca (Veracruz) during the U.S.-Mexican War: "Given that the war that the United States has brought upon us aims to dominate and appropriate our territory, which will not be recovered unless all Mexicans cooperate, therefore: we declare that all lands in the nation will be collectively held by citizens of the Republic" (1992, 71–72).[13]

The local townspeople of Tantoyuca asserted their own collective land interest—an issue generally opposed by modern nations wedded to private property principles—in the context of national security, and with language that recognized the Mexican nation and the political category of citizen. While not an explicit quid pro quo, the townspeople appeared not to be driven by an abstract national zeal to defend the nation-state, the Mexican *patria* (fatherland). They saw the importance of protecting Mexico from the U.S. invasion but did not lose sight of their local interests. Their willingness to kill and die for the state had to be factored within their everyday local concerns about their economic well-being and their ability to plant and harvest their foodstuffs on the limited land base available to them.

The fostering of Mexican nationalism in the late 1800s and early 1900s, particularly between 1910 and 1940, became a central force in unifying the nation as a dominant social reality. It was a unity grounded more on *forjando patria* (the forging of a fatherland) than on *forjando ciudadanía* (the forging of citizenship), to borrow Manuel Gamio's phrase. The promotion of education, flag, national anthem, national heroes, monuments, and national patriotic days, while at times carried out with a vocabulary of citizenship, emphasized the construction of the *patria*, *nación* (nation), and *nacionalidad* (nationality).

As Gilbert Joseph and Daniel Nugent observe, "the state's subjects . . . consistently sought to refashion liberal and 'revolutionary' discourses of citizenship when these proved threatening to local forms of identity" (1994, 22). The elites were successful in creating the Mexican nation and nationalism, but less so in creating a dominant Mexican citizenship. This distinction and its relevance to understanding what adult Mexican migrants lose and gain in seeking U.S. citizenship is one that has drawn limited attention, and one that I will return to in the discussion of the desire for U.S. citizenship.

In January 1994, at the same time that the North American Free Trade Agreement (NAFTA) came into effect, the EZLN (Ejército Zapatista de

Liberación Nacional) announced its position and began its campaign to improve the socioeconomic status of indigenous and other marginalized communities. What is noteworthy in the initial and subsequent political proclamations (Declaración de la Selva Lancadona) is the general absence of citizenship rhetoric.

In the first declaration, the concepts of citizen (*ciudadano*) and citizenship (*ciudadanía*) are absent. Instead, the declaration's primary notions are *pueblo* (the people): *el pueblo* (the community), *del pueblo, pueblo mexicano, los pueblos, nuestro pueblo,* and *pueblo de México.* And while the document makes reference to democracy, *patria* (fatherland), justice, peace, and equality, and implies a rights discourse, it does not specify these as citizenship rights. Instead, it speaks about *nuestra nacionalidad* (our nationality).[14]

The written text of the second declaration repeats the emphasis on *pueblo* and *mexicanos.* Yet it is noteworthy that the single usage of *ciudadanos* is not in the text written in 1994, but in the quoted text written eighty years before and used as a preface and legitimating text. The 1914 text, written by Emiliano Zapata, states the following: "It is not only those that brandish swords that hemorrhage blood and fire fleeting bolts of military glory, those chosen to lead the government of the people who want democracy; that right also belongs to the citizens who have fought in the press and tribunals, who identify with the ideals of the Revolution."[15]

The 1995 third declaration, while continuing the emphasis on *pueblo,* marks a departure. In the cover letter to the declaration the Zapatistas make a reference to *ciudadanos,* and in the text of the declaration there are three references to the concept of citizenship: the first as a form of address for Cuauhtémoc Cárdenas Solórzano ("al ciudadano Cuauhtémoc"), the second in reference to citizen participation ("participación ciudadana"), and the third a demand related to the autonomy and citizenship of indigenous groups ("Que reconozca las particularidades de los grupos indígenas, reconozca su derecho a la autonomía incluyente y su ciudadanía." [The individuality of indigenous groups must be recognized, their right to their inclusive autonomy and citizenship should also be recognized.]).

The language chosen by the Zapatistas to refer to Cuauhtémoc Cardenas in 1995 is instructive and reiterates the importance of appreciating the historical specificity of keywords. *Ciudadano* as used is an honorific applied to notables and marks a hierarchical distinction between citizens (i.e., respected, notable citizens) and common persons—*los de abajo* (the lower classes). Mexican social scientists that have written about citizenship and nationality, including Claudio Lomnitz (1993, 1996, 1999), have for the most overlooked this usage, despite its long history. In my maternal grandmother's birth registry document filed in Guadalajara in 1896, for example, the government official certifying the birth is introduced at the top of the form as "El Ciudadano Lic. José Andrade González Srio. General De Gobierno, Certifica," and then below are listed the names of the parents and witnesses. The latter are simply named, not even addressed as "Sr." or "Sra."—the notable is recognized as a citizen, the common people are simply people.

Historians and others have generally suggested two reasons for the priority placed in fostering nationalism in Mexico. First, the historical diversity of Mexico (multiple indigenous groups and languages) led elites to emphasize creation of a unified *México* and *lo mexicano* (Mexicaness), a creation of Mexicans by consent and force. Second, the overriding concern on the part of elites with the integrity and unification of the territory, due to external and internal tensions regarding sovereignty and political control, also reinforced the importance of the nation. In other words, the emphasis on creating and maintaining the nation-state meant that citizenship was present in the political discourse, such as under President Benito Juárez, but remained secondary in its materialization.

Consistent with an emphasis on nationalism was the elevation of juridical nationality over citizenship. Consequently, who is a national is formally defined in Mexico's Nationality Law but is not equated with citizenship in the way it is in the United States. The legal scholar Manuel Becerra Ramírez summarizes this as follows: "Nationality and citizenship are distinct concepts under Mexican law. Nationality binds an individual to the Mexican state; citizenship, one aspect of nationality, signifies the eligibility of nationals to participate in governance through the right to vote and hold office. Mexican nationality is established at birth or through naturalization. Citizenship is acquired automatically at the age of eighteen" (Becerra Ramírez 2000, 314). Chapter 2 of the current Mexican Constitution is titled "De los Mexicanos" (Regarding who is a Mexican) and consists of three articles (30, 31, and 32). Article 30 specifies that "La nacionalidad mexicana se adquiere por nacimiento o por naturalización" (Mexican nationality is acquired by birth or naturalization). It is in chapter 4, "De los Ciudadanos Mexicanos," that citizenship is specified (articles 34–38). In this discussion, article 34 is the most important: "Son ciudadanos de la República los varones y mujeres que teniendo la calidad de mexicanos, reúnan ademas, los siguientes requisitos: I. Haber cumplido deciocho años; y II. Tener un modo honesto de vivir." (The citizens of the Republic are those men and women who have the quality of being Mexican, in addition to the following requirements: I. Have reached the age of eighteen; and II. Have an honest mode of making a living.)

Thus, Mexican citizenship is granted by the nation-state to persons who are eighteen years of age or older, those younger than eighteen are nationals, not citizens. The obvious contrast to the United States is that persons under eighteen years of age are thought of as citizens, though not as full citizens since they cannot vote, serve on juries, or be elected to office; but, irrespective of age, all U.S.-born persons are nationals and citizens.

Although the stress of the above discussion has been on the importance of nationality and nationalism in Mexico, it should be noted that since the mid-1990s the notion of citizenship has received greater attention. This has been evident in two political issues. The first is the increasing pressure by politically engaged Mexican migrants in the United States who, with support in Mexico, pressured the Mexican congress to formally allow the electoral participation of Mexican electors residing in the United States ("el voto extraterritorial") (Castañeda 2006; Ross Pineda 2000). The rationale is that the Mexican constitution does not remove the citizenship of its nationals residing outside of Mexico (the expatriates); in fact, they argue, it protects their citizenship, thus their electoral participation has to be guaranteed. Citizenship was central to this debate, and the Mexican congress approved the external balloting process starting with the 2006 presidential election.

The second issue is the national changes to civic education in *secundarias* (secondary schools) (Levinson 2004). The Mexican government began implementing the new curriculum, Civic and Ethical Formation, in 1999, and by 2001 almost all *secundarias* had implemented it. A major theme in the new curriculum is *formación ciudadana* (citizen formation). The notions of citizen and citizenship are thus central to the new initiatives.

Both of these events, however, have not played an important role in shaping the views of the Mexican migrants interviewed regarding nationality and citizenship.[16]

In summary, the discussion of Mexican citizenship and nationality illustrate the limitations in the juridical citizenship literature in the United States and Western Europe. It highlights the taken-for-granted universalism that is found in the literature on juridical citizenship. The discussion of Mexican context suggests that attention must be given to understanding the historically informed context of the concept of citizen and citizenship, and their commensurability across nation-states, what I label the "transstate discursivity" of fundamental concepts. Analyses of citizenship involving more than one nation-state should explore the trans-state discursivity of the concept rather than begin with an assumption of commensurability.

THE SOCIOPOLITICAL FIELD

A voluminous literature is found in the sociopolitical field of citizenship, and it encompasses multiple academic disciplines. The aim of this section is to summarize the types of questions and approaches found in that literature, and to cite some relevant works for each theme. Given the sheer size of the literature under the sociopolitical rubric, it is beyond the scope of this book to discuss the many insights found in that literature, thus the discussion is limited to summarizing the issues and questions that scholars pursue when examining citizenship.

Prior to summarizing the major themes, it is useful to note an important complexity in discussing the citizenship literature: there is no clear boundary to the sociopolitical literature on citizenship. While a large core of works explicitly focus on or invoke citizenship, there is a larger literature that focuses on broader topics—such as democracy, sovereignty, nationalism, education, military history, product marketing—and invariably includes a discussion of the role of individuals as citizens or the role of citizenship. Simultaneously, there are major bodies of work that are relevant to understanding notions of citizenship, yet they are generally not noted by authors discussing the topic. The aim of what follows is to provide a background to how citizenship has been conceptualized, beyond the juridical uses, in order to better understand the discourses of citizenship that most of us, including the Mexican migrants interviewed, are embedded in. The discussion that follows is divided into four themes: histories of citizenship, political-philosophical perspectives, feminist perspectives, and anthropological perspectives. The partitions between themes are not fixed; each is intended to mark a general distinction among overlapping topics.

Histories of Citizenship

Over the past decades scholars have generated important general histories of the development and politics of citizenship. These histories have focused on the notion of citizenship in Western Europe and the United States, have tended to adopt the terms "citizen" and "citizenship" as unproblematic concepts, and have often taken juridical constructions as the starting point when discussing contemporary citizenship issues.[17] Some of the notable efforts include Engin Isin and Bryan Turner's *Handbook of Citizenship Studies* (2002); Engin Isin's *Being Political: Genealogies of Citizenship* (2002); James Kettner's *The Development of American Citizenship, 1608–1870* (1978); and Cheryl Shanks's *Immigration and the Politics of American Sovereignty, 1890–1990* (2001). Each of these, in varying degrees, draws attention to the development and transformations of citizenship and the articulation between citizens and the nation-state, principally in the context of the United States and Western Europe. An important dimension raised in these, though framed differently, is the changing nature of citizenship— how the boundaries and content of citizenship have been transformed by the decisions of political elites, and by pressures from the affected residents of the nation-state.

Political-Philosophical Perspectives

Political-philosophical discussion of citizenship can be divided into three broad groups: (1) those focusing on what can be labeled the "big six" political philosophers (Aristotle, Hobbes, Locke, Machiavelli, Plato, and Rousseau); (2) discussion and debates regarding the positive and negative aspects of political structures of citizenship; and (3) typologies of citizenship. Numerous dissertations and books can be found that discuss these central thinkers' views on themes such as democracy, the state, individual rights, education, and the role of armies. Peter Riesberg's *Citizenship in the*

Western Tradition: Plato to Rousseau (1992) exemplifies the discussion of political-philosophical formulations in the context of Western Europe.

The second set of works can be placed within debates about the political structure of citizenship. A central concern of these works is with the characterization of notions or schemes of citizenship within nation-state political structures. Here one finds characterizations that are dichotomous (liberal versus republican), tripartite (liberal, communitarian, and republican), or otherwise. Michael Mann (1987) suggests that industrial nations have followed five schemes, or strategies: liberal, reformist, authoritarian monarchist, fascist, and authoritarian socialist. Herman van Gunsteren (1998) argues that liberal democracies have opted for three varieties of citizenship theory—liberal, communitarian, and republican—though he expands this by offering his own addition: "neo-republican." Peter Kivisto and Thomas Faist (2007), on the other hand, propose inclusion, erosion, withdrawal, and expansion as the four dimensions within which citizenship has been conceptualized.

The essence of these formulations is the attempt to capture the orientation of each strategy and to suggest how the particular strategy allows cohesion within the political system and the broader society. Under the liberal format the emphasis is on the rights of individuals; under a communitarian orientation the emphasis is on the strong bonds that membership in a community provides; and under the republican notion the focus is on the direct involvement of the individual in the democratic process and the greater concern with obligations. While the frameworks are presented as distinct, most discussions seem to accept the fact that there is an intrinsic overlap, particularly in the fact that communitarian and republican formulations assume the presence of citizenship rights, and liberal views presume the existence of a political community and the need for some degree of involvement of individuals in the political process.

The third approach identifies typologies of citizenship, and encompasses two broad endeavors. In the first broad endeavor, emphasis is placed on T. H. Marshall's (1950) tripartite scheme of civil, political, and social elements. Numerous references are made to this set of distinctions and are generally based on the outline suggested by him.[18] For Marshall, citizenship is "a claim to be admitted to a share in the social heritage, which in turn means a claim to be accepted as full members of the society, that is, as citizens" (8). Citizenship is then conceptualized as comprising civil, political, and social elements:

> The civil element is composed of the rights necessary for individual freedom—liberty of the person, freedom of speech, thought and faith, the right to own property and to conclude valid contracts, and the right to justice. . . . [The] "political . . . [is] the right to participate in the exercise of political power, as a member of a body invested with political authority or as an elector of the members of such body. . . . [The] "social element . . . [is] the whole range from the right to a modicum of economic welfare and security to the right to share to the full in the social heritage and to live the life of a civilized being according to the standard prevailing in the society. (10–11)

Each element is associated with a particular institution and a time period. The civil element of citizenship is associated with the courts and is said to have experienced its formative period in the eighteenth century. The nineteenth century, parliament, and councils of local government are associated with the political element. The social element is associated with educational systems and social services, and with the twentieth century.

Even though Marshall has been criticized for limiting himself to England and for creating a framework that is state- and rights-centered, evolutionary, and male-oriented, his liberal framework has been highly influential (Turner 1993a). One strand of his influence is evident among those who have abstracted the civil-political-social scheme of elements and have transposed it into types of citizenship: civil citizenship, political citizenship, and social citizenship.[19] The second strand can be found among those who have sought to capture the implicit dynamic process that Marshall incorporates in his discussion of the elements of citizenship, and the dynamic tension between capitalism (with its tendencies to foster inequalities) and citizenship as an institution that seeks to promote equality (Turner 1986). The third strand encompasses efforts by researchers to identify important elements that condition the status of citizenship; these are generally posed as qualifiers to citizenship and follow the formula of "X citizenship" (the X serving as an adjective/qualifier of the noun citizenship). Table 1.1 presents a sample of types of qualified citizenship that have been suggested over the

TABLE 1.1

QUALIFIED CITIZENSHIP

Citizenship concept	Source
Social, political, civic	T. H. Marshall 1950
Organizational	Bateman and Organ 1983; Farh, Earley and Lin 1997; Organ 1988; Organ and Ryan 1995;
Cultural	Benmayor 2002; Benmayor, Torruellas, and Juarbe 1992; Berlant 1993; Rosaldo 1992, 1994; Rosaldo, Flores, and Silvestrini 1994; Flores and Benmayor 1997; Ong 1995, 1996; Strong 2004
Infantile	Berlant 1993
Sexual, homosexual, dual, trans, embryonic sexual	Evans 1993
Flexible	Ong 1993, 1999; Visweswaran 1997
Transnational	Bader 1997; Bauböck 1994
Deep	Clarke 1996
Diasporic, transnational diasporic	Laguerre 1996, 1998
Fetal	Mason 2000
Symbolic	Schneider 2000
Local	Pak 2001
Postnational	Tambini 2001
Necro	Castronovo 2001
Diasporic cultural	Siu 2001
Management	Hodson 2002

past sixty years, if we include T. H. Marshall's, though most of these have been suggested over the past two decades.

The adjectival forms of citizenship suggested by the various scholars above draw attention to important processes regarding how individuals are included or excluded within national communities; however, they also have limitations. An observation made by the Mexican historian Enrique Krauze

(1986) on democracy in Mexico and Latin America raises the question of "una democracia sin adjetivos" (a democracy without adjectives) and the issue of what is gained by the addition of a qualifier to democracy.[20] Rather than discuss the limitations of each one of the suggested qualified citizenship forms, I want to draw attention to the common limitation.

It is a limitation that results from the unintended shift in focus and the assumptions made in conceptualizing citizenship. Several of the above constructs incorporate a notion of citizenship as a given or already understood concept, and they tend to give greater weight to a juridical construction or to a generalized notion of membership or belonging. In doing so, they overlook the variability of the concept, that citizenship is a politically contested category and its meaning cannot be assumed; it has to be examined. Once the assumption is made about the concept of citizenship (the noun), much of the focus of the discussion shifts to the qualifier and explaining why the new label marks a distinct form of citizenship, rather than first engaging the concept of citizenship. In this book I seek to shift the attention back to the noun, to make sense of how the concept fosters both inclusion and exclusion, and to specifically understand the experience of a group of migrants pursuing a path to U.S. citizenship.

Feminist Perspectives

Dating back to the nineteenth century, there has been a long history of U.S. feminist writers who have addressed issues related to citizenship. Since the 1980s the literature has become sizable.[21] My aim here is to summarize the major patterns in that literature and highlight the contributions of feminist scholars of citizenship. I should note that by "feminist literature" I mean the academic writing of scholars who have made gender a central concern in their examination of citizenship-related topics.

The work of feminist scholars on the notion of citizenship can be divided into two broad groupings: analyses of key political-philosophical questions, and analyses of specific topics associated with citizenship, such as suffrage, jury service, electoral participation, and military work. Under the political-philosophical category, there is the work of scholars who have analyzed the gendered writings of key figures in political philosophy such as Machiavelli (Pitkin 1984), and Plato (Buchan 1999), as well as key political notions such as democracy. Analyses of these two figures, as well as Locke, Hegel, Marx, and others, alongside broader discussions of political theory and democracy, appear in collections edited and written by Seyla Benhabib,[22] Wendy Brown,[23] Judith Butler and Joan Scott,[24] Mary Dietz,[25] Chantal Mouffe,[26] and Carole Pateman.[27]

Feminist analyses developed by authors such as the above have made significant and important contributions to our understanding of citizenship. Through the careful analysis of the writings of Aristotle, Hobbes, Locke, Machiavelli, Marx, Plato, and Rousseau, as well as those by Hannah Arendt, Jurgen Habermas, and Michel Foucault, and others, feminist scholars have argued that the standard readings of these writings, and of key concepts such as democracy, social contract, men, individuals, and citizens, must be read differently. These concepts, it is argued, are not neutral, universal categories; they are explicitly or implicitly embedded in masculinist and patriarchal political structures. According to Carole Pateman,

> Feminism challenges the patriarchal construction of modern political theory. . . . The feminist challenge is particularly pressing in the case of radical democratic theory which argues for the active participation of all citizens, but has barely begun to acknowledge the problem of women's standing in a political order in which citizenship has been made in the male image. Democratic theorists have not yet confronted the implications of the patriarchal construction of citizenship. (1989, 14)

Commenting on the contribution of feminists, Iris Marion Young observes: "Feminists in particular have analyzed how the discourse that links the civic public with fraternity is not merely metaphorical. Founded by men, the modern state and its public realm of citizenship paraded as universal value and norms that were derived from specifically masculine experience: militarist norms of honor and homoerotic camaraderie; respectful competition and bargaining among independent agents; discourse framed in unemotional tones of dispassionate reason" (1998, 266). Before moving to the second grouping of research, it should be made explicit that although there is a general consensus on interpreting citizenship as a masculinist category, this does not mean that political theory arguments building on this understanding are uniform.

The second grouping in the feminist literature regarding citizenship encompasses a diverse and sizable set of writings. Most of these can be characterized as historical or historically oriented research. This literature can be framed as encompassing five broad topics: (1) the French Revolution and the role of women as included and excluded subjects and citizens (Melzer and Norberg 1998; Melzer and Rabine 1992); (2) constitutional law, suffrage, and jury service (Constable 1994; Kerber 1998; Kraditor 1981; Ritter 2000, 2006); (3) U.S. nationality and citizenship of women (Bredbenner 1998; Gardner 2005); (4) articulation between gender and the formation of the United States as a nation (Burgett 1998; Kann 1991, 1998; Nelson 1998); (5) military work and the development of a masculinist citizen-soldier (Salas 1990; Snyder 1999, 2003).

Together these feminist writings represent an important expansion and supplement to political-philosophical discussions of gender and citizenship. However, one limitation within both segments of the feminist literature is the tendency to exclude the dimensions of race/ethnicity and class within the otherwise rich and insightful discussions. Although it is certainly understandable that addressing gender is not an easy task in and of itself, we nonetheless would have even richer discussions if we could integrate these two dimensions, since in reality they are already present within the characteristics associated with the women and men being discussed.

Anthropological Perspectives

Although the topic of citizenship within anthropology is generally perceived as a recent interest, this view is only partly correct. In 1893 the Anthropological Society of Washington (later renamed the American Anthropological Association) issued a special circular in the *American Anthropologist* announcing its "Citizenship Prize Essay" (Anthropological Society of Washington 1894). The solicitation asked its readers to submit an essay on "the elements that go to make up the most useful citizen of the United States." A notable panel of judges convened to evaluate the essays: Daniel G. Brinton (anthropologist at the University of Pennsylvania),[28] Daniel Gilman (president of Johns Hopkins University), Melville W. Fuller (chief justice of the U.S. Supreme Court), Adlai E. Stevenson (vice president of the United States), and Dr. Robert H. Lamborn (affiliation not specified). The two winning essays were printed in the October 1894 issue of the journal. Even though the contents of the essays are of interest and much can be observed in them, what is important here is that the journal editors formulated a discourse about the useful, or "good/virtuous," citizen.

Approximately fifty years later Australian anthropologist A. P. Elkin published *Citizenship for Aborigines: A National Aboriginal Policy* (1944), which explored why the Australian government should grant full citizenship to the indigenous community, rather than maintain a sort of second-class citizenship status for them. Given that the intended audience was government officials and policy makers, Elkin used the concept of citizenship as an already understood notion that involved a dimension of rights in the context of the Australian state.

Between the mid-1940s and early 1990s, the concept of citizenship sometimes appeared in the anthropological and ethnographic literature, though at times it was addressed as part of transnationalism, globalization, and other topics. One exception is Roberto DaMatta's insightful work (1991) on the construction of a hierarchic *cidadania* in everyday interactions in Brazil, as observed in the common Brazilian expression of "Você sabe com quem está falando?" (Do you know who you're talking to?). In this work he examines the everyday interactions through which a middle-class or elite Brazilian individual asserts their hierarchic *cidadania* over a fellow plain/common *cidadão brasileiro*.[29] DaMatta's (1985) analysis of street (*rua*) and house (*casa*) as distinctions signaling a social difference between citizen and individual, respectively, is an earlier discussion of citizenship. In her well-known *Sojourners of the Caribbean: Ethnogenesis and Ethnohistory of the Garifuna* (1988), Nancie L. González makes several references to citizenship, including this one: "Many Garifuna today have become U.S. citizens, yet they think of themselves as members of two (or more) societies" (10). She references "citizens of the world" and a "sense of citizenship," yet she provides only a limited discussion of her important observations.

During the 1990s, anthropologists began to give greater attention to the topic of citizenship. This anthropological interest emerged within the context of academic engagements with globalization, transnationalism, diasporas, dual nationality/citizenship, and post-coloniality, as well as the significant media and policy debate on the creation of a European citizenship. Building on the extensive work by anthropologists on little communities, then on rural-to-urban migration, several anthropologists began to explore the sociocultural dimensions of transnational migrations (Kearney

1986, 1995). Several important works emerged that examined dimensions related to the transnation migratory process. Among the key works reflecting this new interest are Rouse (1992), Lowe (1996), Laguerre (1996, 1998), and Ong (1996, 1999, 2006). These researchers intervened by suggesting the need to conceptualize the transnational dimension of belonging and identity, and they also coined new labels for forms of citizenship. With the exception of DaMatta's initial effort, the everyday discourse related to citizenship is a field that has received limited attention.

Everyday Uses of Citizenship

Despite the ubiquity of the uses of citizenship in everyday life, anthropologists and other scholars have largely overlooked them. After I began to examine juridical and sociopolitical uses of citizenship, I found myself spotting new manifestations of everyday uses of the notion of citizen. Similar to the situation of persons who have a particular collection of something, even if they did not themselves initiate the collection, I began to notice numerous evocations. This is parallel to the experience of a Catholic priest I interviewed regarding the Catholic bishops' "faithful citizenship" campaign. He was once given a small Snoopy doll in appreciation for something, and now he has hundreds of Snoopy objects in his office that have been given to him by people who want to contribute to his collection—a collection that they think he initiated.

The term "citizen," significantly more than that of "citizenship," is invoked across a broad number of settings and objects, including books, films, newspapers, banks and businesses, nonprofit organizations, social categories, and others. I will list some of these and then turn to a discussion of their relationship to the juridical and sociopolitical uses, as well as their importance within the discourses of citizenship in the United States. I should add that the reason for listing multiple categories and examples within each category of everyday uses of citizenship is to underscore the multiplicity of such manifestations, despite their absence in academic discussions of citizenship.

Under the category of books, it is noteworthy that a particular genre within biographical titles has emerged and continues to be used. The form of the genre is generally "Citizen X," it tends to be reserved for notable persons, and in most cases only the last name is used—the titles take for granted that readers know the referent. An earlier and similar format is found in Charles Hendell's *Citizen of Geneva* (1937), which is a book about Rousseau's correspondence, but it did not get repeated like the aforementioned format. Some of the examples of the biographical genre are *Citizen Toussaint* (1944), *Citizen Tom Paine* (1959), *Citizen Hearst* (1971), *Citizen Nader* (1972), *Citizen Machiavelli* (1983), *Citizen Hughes* (1986), *Citizen Perot* (1996), and *Citizen McCain* (2002). In addition, there also exists a long list of books that invoke the term "citizen" but use a different format, such as Paul Loeb's *Soul of a Citizen* (1999) and Senator Orin Hatch's autobiography, *Square Peg: Confessions of a Citizen Senator* (2003).

The well-known 1941 film by Orson Wells—*Citizen Kane*—is an example of a popular form that deploys the above pattern. Orson Wells and Herman Mankiewicz wrote the screenplay based on the life and politics of newspaper tycoon Randolph Hearst. Although it is not known for certain, it seems that Wells's popular film may have influenced the genre. A more recent film drawing on Wells's format is Alexander Payne's *Citizen Ruth* (1996). Payne's (or Miramax's) title choice is somewhat odd in the context of the film. The only explicit link to citizenship is a line that Ruth Stoops (played by Laura Dern) makes more than halfway into the film: "I'm a citizen."[30]

There are a number of newspapers across the United States, most of them serving smaller metropolitan and nonmetropolitan areas, that have citizen in their name. They include *Tucson Citizen, Citizen* (Auburn, New York), *Citizen-Times* (Asheville, North Carolina), *Citizen* (Key West, Florida), and *Waco Citizen* (Texas).

Some financial institutions also invoke the term: Citizens National Bank (Austin), Citizens State Bank (Austin), First Citizens Bank (North Carolina, Virginia, and West Virginia), and Citizens Bank (Rhode Island). And some even seem to fetishize the word: Citizens Bank is part of the Citizens Financial Group, located at One Citizens Plaza. Many other types of businesses, some well known, others not, have adopted the same term. The multinational corporation Citizen Watch Company, maker of Citizen watches, is probably the best known. According to the history on the company's website, in 1924 the "founding fathers selected the name CITIZEN so it would be 'Close to the Hearts of the People Everywhere.'"[31] Despite the reference to "people," it seems that the Citizen "founding fathers" most likely had male customers with some means in mind, since they would be the ones more likely to wear a vest watch that would be "close to the heart" in Japan in the early 1900s. Moreover, the Citizen Watch Company, as part of its "Corporate Citizenship" program, has since 1990 granted a "Citizen of the Year" award to "ordinary people." Examples of less well-known corporations adopting the concept of citizen include the Citizen America Corporation (maker of commercial thermal printers) and Citizens Insurance Company of America (Austin).

Several nonprofit organizations also invoke the idea of citizenship. In fact, some have even adopted the same name, even though they hold opposite political positions, such as the two groups named Citizen Soldier (discussed below). Public Citizen, founded by Ralph Nader in 1971, is probably the best known nonprofit organization in this category. In addition, there are also hundreds of state and local efforts that incorporate the term "citizen" in their name and cause.

Two issues that seem to stimulate the invocation of citizenship within local activist causes are taxes and migration. Citizens for an Alternative Tax System in Austin is an example. The Arizona Taxpayer and Citizen Protection Act (a Proposition 200 initiative) is another. Protect Arizona Now (PAN) is a group concerned with the economic and social threat of informally authorized persons to "citizen taxpayers" and the abstract "Arizona." According to their discourse, noncitizen taxpayers, including the informally authorized, who pay all of their taxes and reside in Arizona are excluded from the category of "taxpayer" and "Arizonian." Thus, they are simultaneously included as actual taxpayers in the tax collection process, but they are excluded from the group's category of taxpayer; they are included as residents of Arizona, but excluded from the imagined Arizona (an example of the Janus face of citizenship, an exclusion/inclusion process). It is also an example of the surfacing of the socio-juridical distinction between citizen and noncitizen.

An example that also links citizenship and migration is the creation of the Citizens Patrol in Arizona, which has taken it upon itself to "protect" the United States against the entry of informally authorized migrants from Mexico. The members wear military-style clothes, arm themselves with military-style rifles, and sell their services to local ranchers (Chávez 2008). The Minuteman Project subsequently replaced the Citizens Patrol effort.

Citizen Soldier (1) and Citizen Soldier (2) represent the odd example of oppositional organizations noted above. The first is promilitary and seeks to assist active soldiers and veterans; the second is antimilitary and seeks to assist active soldiers and veterans. As expected, the first supports President Bush's spread of democracy in Iraq and the expansion of troops in Afghanistan by President Obama. The second opposes President Bush's and now President Obama's occupation of Iraq and the expansion of the war in Afghanistan. Both organizations invoke the historical notion of citizen soldier.

In the case of social categories, two frequently invoked forms are senior citizen and citizen soldier. The first is so ubiquitous that it has become part of our "doxic common sense" (Brow 1996, 180). It is not difficult to find daily senior citizen specials at many restaurants, movie theaters, airline companies, city buses, pharmacies, and other private and public entities. Although they may use a different age threshold, they nonetheless conjoin the notion of citizen to older persons, and they do not extend the social logic to young persons or infants. No one offers a junior citizen, child citizen, teen citizen, or infant citizen discounts. The closest parallel is the student discount; however, it is not the student citizen discount.

The second common social category is the citizen soldier. In addition to being incorporated in the name of some organizations, such as the two noted earlier, the category is frequently used in books and articles related to military issues, as well as recruitment posters by the Army National Guard. R. Claire Snyder's aptly articulated analyses of the construct of citizen-soldier (1999, 2003) presents the development of the social category of citizen soldier, as well as the masculinist constructions embedded in the concept. In brief, the concept is said to date back to the Roman Empire and ancient Greece and represents the conjoining of military work and citizen-ship, and the creation of a masculinist notion of citizenship. The male soldier was constructed as the ideal citizen; this early construction not only gave citizenship its masculinist dimension, it also diminished the citizen-ship of women. Elements of these notions still persist today despite the presence of women in the military. Moreover, although not fully discussed by Snyder, there is the implied heterosexuality of the masculine subject. Thus masculinist indexes more than maleness.

The final grouping of the everyday uses of "citizen" and "citizenship" are the miscellaneous uses, of which I present five examples. The first example is the invention of the concept of the "citizen brand" in the marketing industry. Marc Gobé's *Citizen Brand* (2002) frames his discussion around the "ten commandments for transforming brands in a consumer democracy." According to Gobé, consumers are attracted to products not only because of their expectations of the quality of the product, but also because of their emotional valuation of the company producing the item (e.g., Ben & Jerry's Ice Cream). Thus, his book is a list of suggestions for corporations on how to develop such branding through the elevation of the citizen as consumer, and how to improve the public image of the corporation.

The second example is the short-lived PAX Cable Network's show *Model Citizens*.[32] The show's plot was to have high-fashion models (females and males) carrying out a good deed in a community. The segment I observed involved five models conducting a garbage pick-up drive on beaches in the Northeast, with the aim of encouraging average persons to join them in their activity (they did not have much success in this effort). The message conveyed at the end of the segment was that if models were willing to do such unpleasant things, certainly the average person could model the models.

The third example is *Citizen Dog*, a cartoon series by Mark O'Hare that portrays one or two dogs that treat humans like dogs. In one episode two dogs verbally harass a firefighter who has connected a water hose to their fire hydrant. One of the dogs disconnects the hose and tells the firefighter: "Nope! Nuh-uh. I'm a taxpayer! I don't have to put up with it!!; Go on! And take your hoses with ya! Ya bums!! Ya filthy mongrels! Go!" We should note here that O'Hare not only invokes the notion of citizen for his cartoon dogs, but also associates it with taxpaying, an activity that good citizens are expected to honestly comply with.

The American Kennel Club's Canine Good Citizen (CGC) Program is a fourth example. Started in 1989, "CGC is a certification program that is designed to reward dogs who have good manners at home and in the community." Dogs that "pass the CGC test receive a certificate . . . and . . . they are automatically recorded in the AKC's Canine Good Citizen Archive." In addition to fostering good citizenship for dogs at home and in the community, the second part of the program "stresses responsible pet ownership for

owners." Although only partially articulated, it seems that the program ultimately uses the dogs as the vehicle to encourage the dog's human partner to
become good citizens. Thus, by paying AKC the required fee, the dog's
companion is able to presumably become a good citizen through the recognition of the dog as an AKC good citizen.

The final example is a controversial issue involving a popular alien:
Superman. In its 900th issue Action Comics included a story titled "The
Incident," which focuses on a private conversation between Superman and
Gabriel Wright, the president's national security adviser. Wright repri-
mands Superman for his involvement in a protest rally in Tehran's Azadi
Square. Superman explains that it was a nonviolent resistance and that he
remained in the square for twenty-four hours in support of the protest, but
only stood there and did not take any action. Wright accuses Superman of
causing an international incident and notes that the Iranian government
accused Superman of acting on the president's behalf. Superman responds:
"which is why I intend to speak before the United Nations tomorrow and
inform them that I am renouncing my U.S. citizenship . . . I'm tired of
having my actions construed as instruments of U.S. policy. 'Truth, Justice,
and the American Way'—It's not enough anymore. The world is too small.
Too connected. I'm an alien, Mr. Wright. Born on another world. I can't
help but see the bigger picture. I've been thinking too small. I realize that
now" (Action Comics 2011).

News of Superman's plan to renounce his U.S. citizenship generated
many comments on the Internet and news media, particularly from conservative segments that expressed disgust with Action Comics and their story
line regarding the renunciation of U.S. citizenship by a comic book character. Former Arkansas governor and *Fox News* host Mike Huckabee commented: "Well it is a comic book, but, you know it's disturbing that
Superman who has always been an American icon is now saying I'm not
going to be a citizen. . . . I think it is part of a bigger trend of Americans
almost apologizing for being Americans. . . . I'm disturbed by this whole
globalist trend. I think we ought to be teaching young Americans that
they're young Americans, that it means something to be an American. . . .
There is something great about this country."[33]

The dialogue on Superman's proposal is extraordinary. Governor
Huckabee and others offended by the story expressed their position as if the

person involved was an actual national leader or celebrity, not a cartoon created in the Depression by a Canadian artist and U.S. writer. It also overlooks the fact that it was in an episode in 1974 that the United Nations granted Superman honorary citizenship in all of the UN nations.[34] So although he is considered an U.S. icon, his super-deeds were rewarded with *international* citizenship. But more important for the discussion here is how the construct of citizen/citizenship is part of our doxic common sense. It is so taken-for-granted that we even engage in acrimonious debate when it involves its representation in a comic book about a fictional alien who comes from a fictional planet but whom we have included in the imagined nation as one of us—an American alien.

All of these everyday examples do not exist in a vacuum. While some might argue that they do not address the real issues of citizenship, such as the controversy regarding birthright citizenship, or the long-standing debate on citizenship within civic republicanism and liberalism traditions, or feminist critiques of the exclusion of women within these two traditions, their nuanced position should not be overlooked. The everyday uses of citizenship are informed by, and embedded within, the juridical and sociopolitical uses of citizenship, they are part of the discourses of citizenship in the United States, and citizens and noncitizens are exposed to all three discursive fields. The multiple meanings invoked in the everyday uses rely upon meanings found in the other two uses, as well as the general social aspects in the United States, and inform and support these.

In the case of the biographical books, for example, the reader may have observed that all of the notables are males. Moreover, though it was not highlighted earlier, all of the authors, with the exception of Elizabeth Drew (*Citizen McCain*), are males. In the approximately thirty biographies within the "Citizen *X*" genre that I have identified, only two were of females, and, oddly enough, they had the same title: *Citizen Jane*.

Thus, taken together the genre reinscribes the dominant position of males, both as subjects and authors in the society—a genre largely about males written by males, about the great deeds of great men—as well as reinforcing the link between citizenship and masculinity. Even the two books on females were written by males. This is not to imply that important biographies have not been written about notable females by females, but rather that the genre invoking citizenship is largely a masculinist project. Women hold a secondary position in the genre, similar to the secondary position they held on suffrage, and the secondary position they held regarding their loss of citizenship due to marriage to a person "ineligible to naturalization" prior to 1931, and the secondary position they hold in the present regarding many political and economic positions.

In subtle and not so subtle ways everyday uses of citizenship underscore certain social ideas, such as gender hierarchies, asymmetric countercon- cepts (i.e., citizen versus alien/noncitizen or taxpayer versus nontaxpayer), class hierarchies, and modes of belonging.[35] In addition to the gender hier- archies related to the biographical genre and citizen soldier, the contrast between *Citizen Kane* and *Citizen Ruth* also reinforces this. Whatever one may think about Randolph Hearst's politics, the fact remains that the film recognizes him as a successful male who built a newspaper empire. Ruth Stoops, the female "citizen," stands in contrast to Hearst, starting with the character's last name, not generally considered a positive term, and her role as a drug-taking, irresponsible mother who is pregnant. Ruth may assert that she is a citizen, but she is not portrayed as a positive citizen. Moreover, her irresponsible behavior, taking drugs and again getting pregnant from a relationship to a man she was not married to, reinforces her second-class citizenship vis-à-vis the activist women who want her to have a choice about having an abortion and the ones who, on religious grounds, want her to have the child and put it up for adoption.

The TV show *Model Citizens* incorporates a class hierarchy. The actors are portrayed (which they are paid for) as elite models who do not need to do what they do, such as pick-up garbage, clean fish, or help build a house for a low-income family. They are simply good citizens modeling their citizenship so that the average Jane, Joe, or José, who are ultimately more fitted to do what the models are showing them they can do, will emulate what they see. The elite models are acting as elites to be modeled by the common people. The presumption appears to be that if the average Jane and José was actively involved in the range of activities suggested by the models, then there would not be any need for the models to be model citizens. They could go back to just being fashion models. Citizenship in this context seems to be an attribute that high-fashion models, and presumably other elites, possess and are conscious off, while average persons may or may not be aware of it and so need to be shown how they can exhibit citizenship in appropriate ways. The show conjoins citizenship and class.

The Canine Good Citizen program illustrates an important element regarding the everyday use of citizenship—the everyday practices that are continually performed, and that play an important role in fostering a notion of a common good, belonging, and people as considerate of other people. Constance Perin's (1998, 107–141) discussion of dogs in the construction of community in the United States is informative. She describes how dogs can either help or harm relationships with neighbors, transforming strangers into friends or adversaries. Noting that "dogs are the most worrisome population of the invisible neighborhood," she quotes one of the neighbors in her study: "Dogs, like children, can be the glue or the solvent of the neighborhood" (108). Although she does not explicitly link it to citizenship, her discussion of how belonging is created or diminished in small and everyday instances captures the frequent comments about good neighbors, responsible dog owners, and responsible parents as good citizens. Conversely, those perceived as inconsiderate neighbors, irresponsible dog owners, or irresponsible parents are not considered good citizens. We can thus see why the AKC's Canine Good Citizen program would stress "responsible pet ownership for owners" as part of inculcating "good citizenship for dogs at home and in the community." It is the good citizenship of the dog's human partner that is being promoted and that humans pay for.

What is key here is the notion of "good citizen" in day-to-day interactions with neighbors, coworkers, and strangers, which creates feelings of belonging, of being part of the community. It is precisely in such contexts that abstract notions about juridical and sociopolitical conceptualizations of citizenship get incorporated in assessing whether or not a neighbor is a good citizen. Perhaps it is in these local settings that ultimately the most important actions of citizenship get evaluated: Is the neighbor considerate in terms of their children and dogs; the volume in their TV or stereo (particularly in apartments); the frequency that they park in your parking space or block your driveway; the frequency of noisy parties; their care of their lawn and trees; their neighborly assistance in a crisis or emergency? These are situations that most of us confront in our everyday lives, and so we can generate a perception of our neighbors and behave in a way consistent with those assessments. They also can shape how neighbors define us and how they act towards us.

An instance that I once observed illustrates some of these elements. An apartment complex opposite to the set of buildings where I lived was occupied by a significant number of Latino, mostly Mexican, migrant families (most likely composed of migrant parents and U.S. citizen children). One weekend one of the families was celebrating an event, probably a birthday or baptism, and were playing Pedro Infante and Vicente Fernández songs loudly. The day after the event, I was outside and overheard the comments by a Euro-American woman in her thirties who lived in a building adjacent to mine. She said to another neighbor that she was upset about the previous day's "noise" from those "illegals." She asked, "How would they like it if I played American music as loud as they were?" Her statement illustrates her evaluation of inconsiderate neighbors, the categorization of noncitizens and citizens (i.e., the U.S.-born children) as "illegals," and the implication that she was a "citizen" (an American). The noisy neighbors were framed as noncitizens, with the implication that they did not belong there—she had the right to be there, they did not. She placed herself within the circle of national membership and located all of the Mexican-descent neighbors living on the other side of the complex's wire fence outside the circle. This everyday instance revolving around inconsiderate actions became the social space wherein juridical, sociopolitical, and everyday notions of citizenship surfaced.

In the case of banks, it is noteworthy that even though the name of the institution may invoke the idea of "citizen," it does not mean that noncitizens cannot deposit their money there. Starting with the initiative of Second Federal Savings in Chicago in March 2001 to accept the IRS-issued Individual Taxpayer Identification Number (ITIN) and the Certificado de Matrícula Consular (consular identification cards), major banks such as Citibank, Wells Fargo, and Bank of America have followed this lead (Freeman, Leal, and Plascencia 2003). Consequently, most banks, and presumably including those with "citizen" in their name, have been part of what I refer to as the battle of the banks, a battle to drum up deposits from Latino noncitizens because of their large financial potential, as evident from the billion dollar remittance market that they fuel and Western Union monopolizes. The battle of the banks is aimed at capturing as large a share as possible of the citizen and noncitizen consumer base, including the informally authorized migrant. Their action was inclusive, as noncitizens were welcomed as customers.

Finally, we can return to the quotidian peculiarity of the everyday uses of citizenship. As was suggested above, academics have overlooked the everyday uses of citizenship despite, as evident from above, the numerous instances where the notion is invoked. In all of the books and articles that I have reviewed, I have not found a single author who examined their presence. The closest reference is the general notion of "belonging." However, all of these, with the exception of Perin (1998) and Berlant (1993), discuss "belonging" in broad terms and tend to focus on the juridical dimensions of inclusion and exclusion.

The oversight of the everyday uses of citizenship may be linked to three elements: (1) the hegemonic position that juridical and sociopolitical uses of citizenship occupy within the citizenship literature; (2) a doxic common sense that has veiled their presence and their relationship to juridical and sociopolitical uses; and (3) the tendency of social anthropologists and ethnographic-oriented sociologists to focus solely on the juridical or sociopolitical aspects of the local discourses of citizenship. In short, the everyday uses of citizenship remains a topic that deserves greater attention than it has received.

CHAPTER 2

The Janus Face of Citizenship

THE SIDE OF INCLUSION

Citizenship is a decisive political marker in the United States. It is a highly prized distinction that demarcates the boundaries of political and social membership. Possession of U.S. citizenship reinforces the imagined circle of membership and belonging, and it fosters the ties of group membership among those who can claim it. Thus it functions as important sociopolitical glue that binds individuals to one another and to the nation-state.

U.S. citizenship is granted through five juridical processes. The three common principles are *jus soli* (right of soil), *jus sanguinis* (right of blood), and naturalization. The first refers to the granting of citizenship based on birth, what is commonly referred to as birthright citizenship, and the second indicates the granting of citizenship based on the citizenship of the individual's parents (also referred to as derivative citizenship). Naturalization is the process that allows an eligible migrant to be granted the status of a "natural born" person, a citizen. In addition, there are two other mechanisms that determine the entry into the circle of membership. The first is congressional action, other than naturalization laws, that confers citizenship to individuals who meet a specified condition. The granting of posthumous citizenship to noncitizens, including informally authorized migrants, killed during defined conflict periods is an example of this. Congress also grants citizenship through private bills; these are legislative bills sponsored by a member of Congress that grant the individual named in the bill a particular privilege, including U.S. citizenship. The second mechanism is the granting of collective citizenship. Congressional ratification of treaties—such as the 1803 Louisiana Purchase Treaty, 1848 Treaty of Guadalupe Hidalgo, and Gadsden Purchase Treaty of 1854—and nonratified treaties—such as the Treaty of Annexation of Hawaii of 1897—granted U.S. citizenship collectively to individuals remaining within the acquired territories. Collective citizenship represents an important exception to what is commonly associated with the granting of citizenship: there is no individual application, no fee, no required oath of fidelity, no language or historical knowledge required, nor is a document issued to the individual noting the award of citizenship. And there is no exact count for the number granted citizenship.

The United States has welcomed millions of migrants from most other nations and gradually reduced many of the past obstacles to entry and to full political and juridical citizenship. Although the number of persons granted citizenship before 1907 is unknown, between 1907 and 2010, the United States granted citizenship to over 24 million individuals, or 89 percent of those who filed a petition, and their minor children. Throughout most of the twentieth century, prominent individuals and national political leaders have expressed concern with the overlapping issues of how best to integrate foreign-born persons and instill "good citizenship" among U.S.-born children. In both instances, schools have been perceived as essential sites to achieving both ends. Because the issue of Americanization of migrants in general, Mexican migrants, Native Americans, and Puerto Ricans have been amply examined by other scholars (Bogardus 1919; Camargo 2003; Carroll 1997; Cooper 2005; A. García 2002; M. García 1978; Hartman 1967; Press 2009; Prucha 1973; Sánchez 1990; Shaver 2004; Van Nuys 2002; Walsh 2008), this chapter focuses on the less examined issue regarding the link between schooling and the production of so-called good citizens.[1]

The Schooling of Good Citizens

Education has become an almost universally valued process. Even if it is qualified as being more appropriate for one gender, one class, or a specified age, it is still, in and of itself, valued as a process for individuals and for its contribution to modernization or, as argued by some, a human right. Despite this broad consensus, education, or more precisely the process of schooling, is a contested field. Established nation-states as well as postcolonial nations have had ongoing debates regarding multiple issues related to the political dimensions of education; debates that range from local to national concerns. Some of the more salient political issues that national education systems confront are the language of instruction, textbook selection, extent of centralization of control, funding structure, citizenship of teachers, and explicit and implicit goals of schools.

A local-level issue that has received some attention is the political representation of noncitizen parents with children in the district. In California, for example, there are at least twelve municipalities where noncitizens constitute 50–63 percent of the adult population, and another eighteen where they constitute 40–49 percent. This translates to at least thirty school districts where a majority or substantial shares of adults are disenfranchised. This issue, which some have labeled "political apartheid" (Avila 2003), stems from the fact that in an increasing number of school districts, a significant number of the households with children in the district pay school property taxes, directly or indirectly, and yet are not allowed to vote in school-related elections because they are noncitizens. Although it is not often acknowledged, renters also pay property taxes, though they pay them indirectly through the rent they pay to property owners. The result is that noncitizens as taxpayers and parents of children in the district are juridico-politically excluded from electing the individuals who make decisions about the schooling of their children, the setting of property tax rates in the district, and bonds proposed for the district. The resultant situation of "taxation without representation" serves to remind us of the inherent simultaneity of exclusion and inclusion: included in the requirement to pay taxes, yet excluded from taxpayer involvement in tax policies.

The issue of pluralism/multiculturalism is particularly relevant in the selection of textbooks because of its overlap with questions related to defining who is part of the nation, and, borrowing Georg Simmel's term (1950), who is a "stranger"—that is, distinguishing between citizen and noncitizen. Students, both citizen and noncitizen, are equally exposed to the selected textbooks and their contents regarding "our" English ancestors who established the thirteen colonies, "our" Thanksgiving holiday, "our" Founding Fathers, Francis Scott Key and "our" national anthem, Betsy Ross and "our" flag, and numerous other themes. They are exposed to the importance of

the Reverend Martin Luther King Jr. and his role in the civil rights movement and in making the United States a more inclusive nation.

A national schooling concern of interest here is the issue of "civic education" and citizenship. Some legislators, educators, social scientists, and
others have expressed their concerns that contemporary public schools are
not cultivating good citizens. Framed differently, this concern is about their
perceptions regarding the weakness in the effects of current school curricu-
lums in creating particular kinds of subjects, subjects who possess the
desired subjectivity of a good citizen in reference to the state and its institutions, as evident in specific fidelities and practices deemed to be important
to democracy, such as character, loyalty, discipline, patriotism/nationalism
and voting, and community service.

Constructing Citizenship

The sizable literature on civic/citizenship education makes it clear that the
U.S. public school curriculum has been central to making good citizens and
promoting good citizenship for years. The citizenship catechesis in older
textbooks sought to inscribe a set of fidelities to the state, such as obedience
to authority (the law), loyalty, patriotism, morality, duty to defend it,
and personal responsibility (i.e., self-support, self-reliance). Most or all of
these continue to be considered as important qualities of a good citizen.

From the 1920s to the 1950s, numerous social studies textbooks were
published that addressed the importance of citizenship for youth and the
critical role of schools in ensuring that students acquire desired citizenship
qualities.[2] In the interest of space, I will summarize the perspectives of two
books that exemplify the themes discussed.[3] The first is a textbook written
in 1937 by high school educators Louise Capen and Melchor Montfort
(1937) for high school level students. In the section devoted to citizenship,
the authors specify the duties of American citizens:

> He should respect his country; He should love its flag; He should be loyal
> to it in time of peace and be prepared to defend it when it needs his help;
> He should know the Constitution; He should respect and obey the laws of
> the community in which he lives and the authority of the officials set up
> in office; He should respect the rights of all other persons; He should pay

his taxes; He should live an exemplary life; He should desire education; He should be self-supporting; [and] He should cooperate with local, state, and national projects which stand for progress and are dependent for their success upon cooperation of the citizen body. (286–287)

This passage and others like it in the text explicitly note the desired actions and attitudes of the good school citizen, more precisely the good male school citizen. The good citizen, however, is not framed as simply a quality that should be present in schools, it is also suggested that the qualities fostered in school can contribute to the desired subjectivity of a disciplined and good employee, a disciplined and good soldier, and a disciplined and good national citizen. Thus, the production of a good citizen is associated with qualities that should persist into adulthood and are related to the nation and the state.

A text aimed at educators and policy makers, and written in the early part of the Cold War, laments the low participation of Americans in becoming knowledgeable and active in elections, and making democracy survive (Myer and Coss 1952). The authors suggest that unless citizens become "citizen-politicians" and "wake-up," the United States and democracy in general will be lost. They further warn that there are dire world political consequences of continued low involvement in the practices of democracy: "Uninformed and lazy citizens may not realize it, but they are actually assisting the communists" (11). Myer and Coss propose that schools do a better job of promoting citizenship. Specifically, they endorsed a nationwide "compulsory five-days-a-week course devoted to the study of current issues and political ideas" for junior high, high school, and college students.

Other similar textbooks illustrate an ongoing concern among educators regarding the important role of schools in making good citizens and teaching the importance of citizenship. Several texts also expressed concerns about youths not having the proper qualities or being sufficiently engaged in practices associated with good citizenship. This brief review suggests that current concerns about instilling good citizenship are not new. At various moments in the past, observers have regarded a lack of citizenship as a situation approaching a crisis. Furthermore, prior to the 1960s, there was a general consensus that students (as citizens) needed to possess a combination of attitudes, affects, and work-oriented inclinations. These are the types of qualities that some educators, policy makers, and neoconservatives have in mind when they call on schools to re-embrace their "historical role" of cultivating citizenship.

REDISCOVERING THE CITIZENSHIP CRISIS

Over the past sixty years, several leading educators, policy makers, social scientists, and foundations have argued that contemporary schooling is falling short in cultivating good citizens. They also note that schools, as the most universal institution in society, can and must do more to inculcate good citizenship in the next generation of individuals. From 1942 to 2006, policy makers and educators issued multiple reports regarding the crisis in the nation's public schools, particularly the issue of citizenship qualities among youth.[4] One of these was the report issued by the Center for Information and Research on Civic Learning and Engagement and the Carnegie Corporation of New York: Civic Mission of Schools (2003).

The Civic Mission of Schools report conveys a sense of crisis about instilling good citizenship in youth. The task force members recommended that the schools must take up the burden of citizenship education (since other institutions, such as the home, community, and church, have seen their roles eroded) and develop effective civic education programs. At the core of their recommendations are the "values and skills required in a democracy," the teaching of the concepts of "justice, liberty, and equality," "moral-education concepts," and "community service." The report suggests the crisis is located in the schools and in youth themselves. A more recent report regarding higher education and citizenship emphasizes that the failure of colleges and universities to teach U.S. history and institutions will lead to a future national crisis (Intercollegiate Studies Institute 2006).

Despite the interval between 1942 and 2006, what is apparent in the reports released is the consistent concern with the weakening or devaluing of citizenship, and the view that schools have not done a sufficient job of inscribing values and attitudes that translate into an active engagement on the part of young persons with voluntary organizations and public issues in general and the electoral process more specifically. An important unstated premise within the reports is that citizens have to be made—that is, individuals are not born citizens (in terms of possessing the desired fidelities). In defining "Americanism," Theodore Roosevelt alluded to this same notion when he commented that it is "not a matter of birthplace," but rather that "children" and the "average citizen" must be "trained" to adopt and implement the nation's "democratic ideals" (1956, 14–15, 59). The educational reports, however, exhibit a notable irony: they criticize schools for not producing the desired citizens, yet place the onus on schools to start producing such citizens through a new curriculum that gives appropriate attention to the needed values, skills, and knowledge.

There are four problems with the emphasis on a new curriculum: (1) it ignores the fact that some type of civics/citizenship curriculum has always been taught, so it is not clear how a new citizenship curriculum will address their concerns; (2) some of the empirical research on high school students suggests that political knowledge may not be acquired through government and civics classes (i.e., curriculum), though it is not clear where politically knowledgeable youth acquire their information (Niemi and Junn 1998); (3) the addition of a strong citizenship curriculum in a political context driven by preoccupations with testing, measuring achievement, and comparison of teachers, schools, and districts, particularly in the wake of the Leave No Child Behind Act, is not likely to elicit much support from school administrators or teachers, irrespective of the valuation of citizenship; and (4) the focus on curriculum ignores the importance of the everyday and routinized practices performed inside and outside of school that are important in fostering citizenship.

The Devaluing of U.S. Citizenship

The discourse of a weakened or devalued citizenship confronting the United States is not limited to national leaders concerned with education. A parallel perspective is found among academics and journalists starting in the 1980s—for example, Peter Brimelow (1995), Georgie Anne Geyer (1996), Arthur Schlesinger Jr. (1992), and Peter H. Schuck (1989). A common thread among these authors is the view that U.S. citizenship has lost much of its past meaning and value. The arguments presented by these authors share a particular concern regarding the acquisition of U.S. citizenship by Latinos, specifically Mexicans.

The foreign-born journalist Brimelow reiterates the concern with multiculturalism and goes some steps further to call for (1) modification of the Fourteenth Amendment, specifically the provision granting U.S. citizenship to those born in the United States, irrespective of the citizenship status of the parents, so that children of "illegal" parents would only be granted provisional citizenship (a proposal earlier suggested by Schuck and Smith [1985]); (2) an "Americanization" campaign aimed at assimilating migrants (from the context of his comments, he seems to have Latin American migrants in mind as the targets of this campaign); and (3) a national English-only statute. With specific reference to citizenship, Brimelow concludes that there has been a "systematic attack on the value of citizenship, by making it easier for aliens to vote, receive government subsidies, etc.," and suggests that "today American citizenship is being acquired in much the same spirit as a driver's license" (1995, 219, 265).

Through her weekly column, the nationally syndicated journalist Georgie Anne Geyer reaches a broad audience, and thus her views about the devaluing of citizenship and dangers of migration have an ongoing impact on the public debate. In her book *Americans No More* (1996), Geyer's central argument is that citizenship is being "demeaned and destroyed," that there is a "silent but real death of American citizenship," and that because of its importance as the "cornerstone of all other commitments—marriage, baptism, school, university," the United States is facing a serious crisis.

For professor Arthur Schlesinger (1992), mass migration (particularly from Latin America), the emphasis on multiculturalism, and the debates about school curriculum "belittles *unum* and glorifies *pluribus*," and has led to a fundamental questioning of "what is to be an American." The effect, for him, has been the "disuniting" or "decomposition of America."

Peter Schuck, as a legal scholar, offers a more academic perspective. The core of his argument is that the principles of equality and due process in the "pursuit of liberal values" have expanded to the point that the fundamental juridico-political difference between U.S. citizen and "legal resident alien" has largely disappeared. For Shuck, "these changes have reduced almost to the vanishing point the marginal value of citizenship, as compared to resident alien status" (1989, 52). The expansion of the application of the principles of equality and due process has impacted the interest on the part of permanent residents to seek citizenship, and the net result has been a "devaluation of American citizenship." He argues that the courts have been central to this process.

A common thread in the reports by educators and the writings by Brimelow, Geyer, Schlesinger, and Schuck is the perception that schools are failing to create good citizens and that the liberal interpretation of courts regarding the principles of equality and due process have resulted in the devaluing of U.S. citizenship. Despite some differences in emphasis and level of detail, the authors suggest two main causes for the problem. The first cause is the social changes experienced in the United States during the 1960s, principally changes in gender and family relations (due to the feminist movements), changes in racial/ethnic relations and resultant pressures for diversity in schools and the workplace, and changes in the respect for traditional values and institutions. The second cause is the changes brought about by the passage of the 1965 Immigration Act (which eliminated existing quotas and led to more migrants from Asia, the Caribbean, and Latin America) and the increase in unauthorized entries and visa overstays that began in the early 1970s. The net effect has been the perception that the United States is no longer what it used to be, and that the "social fabric" of the nation, the body politic itself, is being degraded and weakened due to the changes.

From the 1960s to the present, the nation experienced numerous conflicts and debates regarding issues related to the two general social transformations noted above. The polarization of opinions is evident in ongoing debates regarding a woman's right to an abortion, use of race/ethnicity in university admissions, the rights of disabled persons, the rights of gays and lesbians, the promotion of English-only legislation, efforts to eliminate bilingual education, the promotion of school choice/vouchers, and the rise of conservative Christian groups and their influence in public policy. All of these issues are part of the context within which the concerns about the failure of schools to cultivate good citizens and about the devaluing of citizenship have been articulated.

What is being suggested seems to be a return to a time when the United States was homogeneous (similar to President Theodore Roosevelt's desire for a United States where there are only "Americans," with "no place for the hyphen"); when women stayed home and took care of house and children while the husband went to work; when African Americans,

Mexican Americans, Asian Americans, and American Indians knew their place; and when we all respected the institutions of (heterosexual) marriage, family, school, church, and government. This can be rephrased as a time when we all possessed the right subjectivities and fidelities as citizens, and masculinity and whiteness were accepted privileges, or at least only marginally contested. What this glosses over is that the same principles that schools are being expected to instill, such as democracy, equality, freedom, liberties, voting, serving on juries, being engaged citizens, and others, were only partially available to women and racial/ethnic minorities. It was a time when Jim Crow statutes were in place, miscegenation laws existed, lynching occurred, separate-but-equal principles allowed the segregation of public places and schools, poll taxes were used to prevent voting, military units were segregated, and many other forms of exclusion of citizens and noncitizens existed. In short, educators and authors seem to adhere to an enchanted form of citizenship that excludes the historical tensions that have persisted within citizenship practices in the United States.

In addition there is a historical limitation concerning the devaluing of citizenship. There are implied, broad assumptions about how migrants have obtained citizenship in the past. First, there is an assumption that all migrants who have sought citizenship in the past did it out of a sense of loyalty to the United States, not out of material interests. Second, it is commonly assumed that migrants who were granted citizenship took time to learn English and to study the history and institutions of the United States. Third, it is assumed that those who were granted citizenship must have been eligible to receive it. Fourth, there is an assumption that courts—the "temples of justice"—approving naturalizations petitions simply carried out the letter of the law. The actual history of naturalization is more complex and includes problematic elements generally ignored.

Examples of the multiple problems in the granting of citizenship are found in various segments of the historical literature (e.g., on political machines in large cities in the late nineteenth and early twentieth centuries), federal agency reports, and congressional documents.[5] A particularly noteworthy document is the 1905 report issued by the Commission on Naturalization. The commission was created by President Theodore Roosevelt and was charged with examining reported irregularities in the granting of citizenship. Two common terms found in the report are "fraud" and "corruption" (e.g., "extensive fraud," "colossal naturalization fraud," "gigantic frauds," "corrupt state courts"). The included extract of a report by C.V.C. Van Deusen, special naturalization examiner with the Department of Justice, indicate that many types of fraud were found in naturalization: false impersonation (including entry into the United States with another person's naturalization certificate), perjury by applicant and witnesses, sale and use of fraudulent certificates, court clerks issuing certificates without authorization, unlawful issuance of certificates by courts, and fraudulent issuance of certificates of intention to naturalize. An example cited by Van Deusen (1905, 88) is the case of the examination of 496 certificates of naturalization issued by the St. Louis Court of Appeals; he reports that 400 (81 percent) of these were fraudulent.

The commission also reviewed a report by Joel Marx, special assistant U.S. attorney. Marx provided a table summarizing 791 complaints filed between April 18, 1903, and May 27, 1905. The table shows 685 convictions for the complaints filed, and that 418 of the convictions involved migrants granted citizenship based on the applicants' statement that they had arrived in the United States before the age of eighteen (Commission on Naturalization 1905, 78). Marx notes that the most common form of fraud was the aforementioned invocation of the "Minor's clause."

The core problem identified by the commission centered on the role granted to "common law courts of record" under the nation's first naturalization statute, the 1790 Naturalization Act. This provision allowed federal, state, and local courts to grant citizenship. Thus state and local court clerks and judges became participants in materializing what Van Deusen refers to as the "political value of naturalization," particularly starting with the 1844 presidential election (i.e., James Polk versus Henry Clay). In the first presidential election during Reconstruction, a single judge in New York issued 2,500 certificates of naturalization in a single day in 1868. While the New York judge's actions probably represent an extreme case, numerous federal, state, and local courts throughout the nation were characterized as citizenship mills that dispensed citizenship for financial and political gains. The partisanship of judges fostered their role in contributing to their party's electoral success and the collection of fees. What emerges in the commission's report is a clear image of migrants who were granted U.S. citizenship irrespective of their actual eligibility, understanding of the English language,

knowledge of U.S. history and institutions, or loyalty. The localized granting of citizenship produced a juridical oddity: a state or local court could
de facto override the Supreme Court by granting citizenship to individuals
with a characteristic that the latter court had deemed necessary to exclude a
person from citizenship.

Although it could be argued that the above fraud and corruption in
granting citizenship is a thing of the past, and that subsequent legislation,
starting with the 1906 Naturalization Act, must have taken care of the problem, the actual evidence of the extent or absence of problems after 1906
remains a topic to be empirically examined. And although most individuals
assume that naturalization has been an exclusive federal action for many
decades, it was the enactment of the Immigration Act of 1990 that finally
removed state and local courts from the naturalization process. The act
stipulated that the "sole authority to naturalize persons as citizens of the
United States is conferred upon the Attorney General" (Title V, Section 401).
Federal preemption in naturalization is thus a fairly recent development.

REFLECTIONS ON SCHOOLING AND CITIZENSHIP

As described above, considerable energy and ink has been spent in discussing the essential elements of good citizenship and advising teachers on
effective practices for making good citizens. Most of the civic/citizenship
promoters take for granted that public schools have a central role in creating good citizens. The general argument is that good schooling makes a
good citizen, and a good citizen makes a good democracy. Thus, the logic of
the argument is that schooling is central to a democracy, as well as to
imparting the skills and knowledge defined as important in society. These
arguments, however, encompass important limitations.

One historical limitation in producing good citizens is prioritizing a religious and disciplined subjectivity in students; another is the assumption
that the schooling of good citizens is an exclusive concern of liberal democracies, when monarchial and fascist regimes have also promoted the production of good citizens. An important premise of these arguments is that
schools have always had a universal mission to cultivate good citizens, and
that the meaning of "good citizen" has remained the same. Derek Heater's
(2004) discussion on the history of civic education makes it evident that

these are idealized and limited interpretations of the history of education in the United States. He points out that proposals for education in general by early proponents of public schools ("common schools"), such as Thomas Jefferson, Benjamin Rush, and Noah Webster, were at times controversial and were largely oriented to producing moral, religious, virtuous, disciplined, and obedient subjects. The emphasis in schooling in the eighteenth and nineteenth centuries was on the four "Rs": religion, reading, arithmetic, and writing.

Even though we can see traces of some of the same concerns in the present, during the eighteenth and nineteenth centuries the emphasis was not in creating active, engaged, politically knowledgeable voters. Widely used textbooks instead reinforced the four "Rs." The McGuffey Reader textbooks, for example, dominated the classroom until about the end of World War I. They not only drew from great Western authors such as Daniel Webster, Jefferson, Shakespeare, and Byron, but also contained much from the Bible about Jesus and St. Paul, among others. The explicit inclusion of religion gradually receded in school textbooks, though debates about the religious content of textbooks has continued to the present.

According to Heater, some of the founders of U.S. schooling, such as Benjamin Rush, were more explicit about the role of schools in the embodiment of citizenship in youth, what he labeled the production of "republican machines" or "public property" (Heater 2004, 59). In his 1786 proposal and other writings on public schools, Rush laid out his prescription for the role, focus, and technologies of schooling:

> To assist in rendering religious, moral, and political instruction more effectual upon the minds of youth, it will be necessary to subject their bodies to physical discipline. To obviate the inconveniences of their studious and sedentary life they should live upon a temperate diet. . . . I consider it as possible to convert men into republican machines. . . . Let our pupil be taught that he does not belong to himself, but that he is public property. Let him be taught to love his family, but let him be taught, at the same time, that he must forsake even forget them, when the welfare of his country requires it. He must watch for the state, as if its liberties depend upon his vigilance. . . . In the education of youth, let the authority of our masters be as absolute as possible . . . [and] arbitrary. . . . I am

satisfied that the most useful citizens have been formed from those youth who have never known or felt their own wills till they were one and twenty years of age. (Heater 2004, 58–59)

Citizenship education, for Rush and others, was thus aimed at creating disciplined, obedient, religious, and moral subjects in service of the state— not at increasing knowledge about principles of government, or about the principles of liberty, justice, equality, and community service.

Moreover, education was and still is not guaranteed by the U.S. Constitution, so it was left up to states to develop their systems of schooling. Schooling did not become a large-scale project until after the Civil War. It was fundamentally a political project; a project to embody the virtues and responsibilities required by the state. Drawing on Michel Foucault (1990) and Giorgio Agamben (1998, 2000), it was a biopolitical project that aimed to create specific and embodied subjectivities among male youth, which were expected to continue into adulthood. Consequently, the assumption that schools have always been involved in promoting things such as knowledge about the principles of government, or an engaged citizenry, certainly does not fit the pattern of schooling in the eighteenth and nineteenth century, or even in the early part of the twentieth century.

This historical construction of an idealized past also ignores the political role that schools had to assume, particularly between the end of World War II and the 1960s. The work of historian David Caute (1978) regarding the political inquisition begun by President Truman (1945–1953) and continued by President Eisenhower (1953–1961) against communists and disloyal Americans during the late 1940s and 1950s discusses how schools became central political actors in the fight against communism. The creation of loyal and patriotic young citizens was regarded as an important weapon in accomplishing the war against defined evils; and the enactment of loyalty oaths for teachers was a way to ensure that only loyal teachers taught. The American Political Science Association, Columbia University, the Carnegie Corporation, and other groups played central roles from the late 1930s to 1960 in persuading policy makers and schools about the necessity to prepare youth for citizenship and in arguing that inscribing civic responsibility was one of the main objectives of schooling (Heater 2004, 121). Their mission, however, was by the 1960s placed in the backburner of the public policy arena.

Yet it was not feminism, the antiwar movement, Black Panthers, the Chicano movement, or the sex-drugs-and-rock-roll crowd of the 1960s that accomplished this, as much as Brimelow, Geyer, and Schlesinger find these to be likely suspects. It was anticommunism itself that accomplished it. D. W. Robinson summarizes the events as follows: "But the good intentions of the work of the three or so decades preceding the 1960s seemed to have been all but lost in the rapid changes that followed. In the late 50's the emphasis was shifted to science, mathematics and foreign language, with the passage of the National Defense Education Act. . . . Emphasis upon education for citizenship was reduced to a weak voice in the loud roar of the call for scientific effort" (Heater 2004, 122). Thus by the early 1970s educators and policy makers were now alarmed that significant proportions of America's youth could not, for example, name the Senate as the second body in Congress (ibid.).

The assumption that schools in the past had a universal mission and coverage is also problematic. On the issue of gender, for example, we know that Benjamin Rush and Noah Webster recognized the importance of educating females. However, the primary purpose for educating women was different from educating men. Rush wrote "our ladies should be qualified to a certain degree, by a peculiar and suitable education, to concur in instructing their sons in the principles of liberty and government" (Heater 2004, 62). The education of women was not to make them "republican machines," scholars, or active and engaged citizens, but rather to have them become appendages to the functions of schools in creating good male citizens. In the case of American Indians, African Americans, Asian Americans, and Mexican Americans, their schooling has a long history of being unequal to that of white students (San Miguel 1987; Valencia 1991, 2008). Thus, the history of schooling in the United States has not been one of continuous equal educational opportunity for all.

Lastly, in contrast to the assumption of educators and neoconservative authors that the practices of a good citizen have remained constant, historical sociologist Michael Schudson has pointed out these practices have undergone significant changes. According to Schudson (1998), there have been four distinct phases of what is considered a good citizen in relationship to political participation and democracy. He labels the first phase, from the colonial period to the early nineteenth century, as a "politics of assent" based on "personal authority." The second phase, from the early nineteenth century to the progressive era, is characterized as "interpersonal authority" and represents a "politics of parties" and "impersonal authority." The third phase is based on a "politics of information," starting in the progressive era, and the fourth phase, the present period, is referred to as the "rights-bearing citizen" model.

The changing missions of schools, changes in the definition of "good citizen," and the structural changes regarding who received schooling, as well as who was allowed to exercise their rights and responsibilities related to citizenship, bring into question the assumption that schools were once effective in cultivating good citizens among all school-age children. How could this be argued when a significant number of U.S.-born children (i.e., U.S. citizens) were de facto and de jure excluded from the settings where the cultivation of citizens was being emphasized?

The educational reports and authors discussed here invoke a notion of "in the past," but they do not fix their point of reference in the past, and the present is represented as lacking a citizenship that existed in a nostalgic and enchanted moment. Susan Stewart's insight, drawing on Lacan, regarding "lack" and "nostalgia" is applicable here: "Nostalgia . . . is always ideological: the past it seeks has never existed except as narrative, and hence always absent, that past continually threatens to reproduce itself as a felt lack. . . . [N]ostalgia wears a distinctly utopian face, a face that turns toward a future-past, a past which has only ideological reality" (1984, 23).

What I suggest is that the discourses about wanting contemporary schools to conscript good citizens as they did in the past, and for citizenship to be valued like it was in the past, are ungrounded notions about an ideological past, and they are based on perceptions about a felt lack in the present. The authors of this discourse seem to be longing for a time, at least an ideologically perceived time, when masculinity and whiteness were normatively privileged; when women, for the most part, accepted the aforementioned privileges; and when the nation was perceived as homogeneous or, as expressed by President Teddy Roosevelt, a time when there were only "Americans"—that is, when African Americans, Asian Americans, Latinos, Native Americans, and other hyphenated groups were present but not as visible.

Processes That Devalue Citizenship

As noted earlier, educators, policy makers, and others concerned with citizenship education take a position that U.S. citizenship has been devalued. Since Geyer's devaluation perspective has circulated more than the narratives of other authors, I will focus on it. The gist of her argument is that in the past U.S. citizenship had a greater value than it does today. Her approach is to focus on the contemporary period and then assert that today's citizenship has a lower value than in the past. Yet she does not provide any evidence about the past. The closest she comes to illustrating how citizenship was more valued before are two brief notes. The first is a short description about her parents, who migrated from Germany and Poland, worked hard, and felt like "Americans" (Geyer 1996, 146–148).

The second is a reference to Leo Buscaglia's *Papa, My Father: A Celebration of Dads* and a brief summary of how Papa passed his INS exam and was sworn as a U.S. citizen. Geyer presents the following story from Buscaglia's book: "Papa was disappointed that he had not been asked enough questions. After all his studying, anxiety, and worry, only three things were asked of him: What is the highest court in the land? Who was the third president of the United States? What is a democracy? . . . The swearing-in ceremony was all that was left to make Papa, at last, a real citizen. With hundreds of others, he was required to take the oath of allegiance. We all dressed in our Sunday-go-to-church outfits, squeezed into our dilapidated car, and drove to the courthouse downtown, where the final ceremony was scheduled" (Geyer 1996, 186–187, 188).

The points she presents do not support her argument about the devaluation of citizenship. Furthermore, her allusions to how citizenship was valued in the past fails to take into account a multitude of historical instances that suggest that the granting of citizenship to European and other migrants in the past was at times part of economic and political strategies on the part of individuals and certain institutions (as summarized earlier). For example, in the past local political parties and judges would recruit migrants, grant them citizenship, and then guide them to local voting locations (Tammany Hall in New York City being one well-known story). Van Deusen's report (1905, 12) in the 1905 Commission on Naturalization document notes that two important motivators for migrants seeking citizenship were state and municipal laws regarding the exclusion of noncitizens from occupations and labor union restriction on membership to citizens. Thus material interest led migrants to seek citizenship as a means to securing better jobs; in some cases, even if it meant obtaining the status by fraud or corruption. Moreover, according to sociologist Joseph Lopreato (1970, 115), many Italian migrants in New York in the 1920s and 1930s sought U.S. citizenship as a means to gain access to public jobs (such as those held by Irish Americans), as avenues of social and economic betterment, and, for some, as protection for their businesses (such as the business opportunities made available by Prohibition in 1919).

Being a U.S. citizen/voter and becoming active in local party politics facilitated political protection to take advantage of the supply and demand factors of the market at the time, one of these being the liquor market. Thus the acquisition of citizenship in the 1920s and 1930s by some individuals was based on personal and household material interest, not necessarily on an idealized and abstract notion of fealty toward the United States. Italian migrants in the first quarter of the past century who sought social and economic improvement for themselves and their families are not that dissimilar from Mexican migrants seeking such improvements in the present.

External forces also shaped the citizenship of noncitizen soldiers on active duty in World War II. They were granted citizenship without petitioning it. One such story was shared with me in Houston. Two men had formally migrated to the United States from Mexico, and at the start of World War II they decided to enlist in the Army and defend their adopted nation, though they were not U.S. citizens. Both had similar stories, but I will focus on one.

This man was resting in his barrack when an officer informed him that he was being summoned by the commanding officer. When he got to the office, the commanding officer handed him a pen and told him to sign a piece of paper. Even though he did not know what he was signing, he did so on order from the officer. The officer then told him: "Congratulations, you are now a U.S. citizen, and now you can go back to what you were doing." The man thanked the officer and left the office. Although puzzled by what had just transpired, he appreciated the gesture and felt good about his new status. Yet he wondered why the Army had made him a citizen, since he was planning on staying in the Army until the war was over. He had not enlisted to acquire citizenship. This story illustrates the point that the petitioning and granting of U.S. citizenship in the past was not always idealized and romantic, such as the experience of Papa.

It is also important to understand how the federal and state governments at times devalued citizenship through the deportation of U.S. citizens of Mexican descent during the Repatriation efforts of the 1930s, the internment of U.S.-born Japanese Americans during World War II (an action upheld by the Supreme Court), the deportation of Mexican American citizens during the 1954 "Operation Wetback," as well as numerous suffrage obstacles. The case of Native Americans in Arizona is one such event. Although the 1924 Indian Citizenship Act had granted citizenship to the remaining Native Americans who had not been previously granted citizenship, the state of Arizona did not allow them to vote until their legal victory in 1948 (Meeks 2007, 173).

The point of the above discussion is not that the individuals did not value U.S. citizenship, but rather that they found themselves in situations where external interests were determining the value of citizenship and using it or ignoring it based on their own ends. Some of these instances could be construed as the devaluing of citizenship; yet these are not the kinds of examples that Brimelow, Geyer, Schlesinger, or Schuck included in their arguments.

Geyer's argument also fails to take into account the high valuation that citizenship has for the people she presumes do not value it as much as European migrants did in the past. She did not take the time to talk to people who desire U.S. citizenship and are struggling at significant personal and financial costs to become U.S. citizens. The closest she comes to this is the brief mention of her lunch with Cecilia Coder ("Ceci"), who is married to "the son of my dearest friend Mary McDermott Coder," was born and raised in Peru, and is "an immensely talented, decent" human being (Geyer 1996, 188–189). Coder told her of the simple test she was given and the unceremonious oath-taking event that she experienced at the INS office. Geyer then takes Coder's story and compares it to the Papa story: "In place of the charm and civil manners of Papa's citizenship experience, disappointment from the greatest nation in the world and even suspicions because it asks so little of citizenship petitioners that something seems not quite right! In lieu of the message that Papa got from America, Ceci got the message that, really, you haven't joined very much" (189).

Moreover, she misses the irony of her own argument. Her own labeling of citizenship as a "commodity" or "citizenship-as-carnival" itself devalues citizenship (56). Geyer is also making a major assumption about how easy the naturalization is based on Ceci's experience. Geyer overlooks that the simplicity of the naturalization test for Ms. Coder's may be related to her likely class and educational level. Ms. Coder's good fortune with the test and the INS examination officer may not be shared by others with less education, different class positions, and perhaps different racial/ethnic characteristics. Moreover, Geyer also overlooks the wide variance that actually exists in the oath-taking ceremonies, from simple swearing-in ceremonies conducted at INS (now CIS) offices to more formal events with color guard bands, speeches, and video messages from the sitting president.

Geyer also overlooks the fact that acquiring U.S. citizenship is a costly process, in both money and time. In 2011 cost for the N-400 application and the fingerprint record processing is $680 ($595 for the application, and $85 for the biometric record). For many households this is a substantial sum—Geyer does not say how much it cost in Papa's day. Then there are costs such as the citizenship class, getting the necessary photographs, paying someone (a notary public, attorney, or local organization) to assist with the application process, the cost of sending the application as certified registered mail, and transportation and meal costs related to traveling to the nearest CIS office (which, depending on the state, may be up to a ten-hour drive). These costs do not include what economists call the "opportunity costs"—the foregone income from time allocated to the process rather than on income-generating activities. Low-income persons, such as those I interviewed, tend to work at jobs that do not provide vacation days or sick leave, and so any time taken from work means a direct loss of income. Ceci, if employed, may have been able to take personal time off work and so may not have experienced a loss of income for the day of her naturalization exam.

THE PRODUCTION OF GOOD CITIZENS

The calls for renewed attention to the promotion of citizenship in schools also misrecognize education's other functions, such as reproducing

occupational, gender, and class distinctions found in society. Other scholars have demonstrated the role of schools in fostering such distinctions. The
result of this omission is an incomplete view of the schooling process and its
contradictory practices: "Ironically, schooled knowledge and disciplines
may, while offering certain freedoms and opportunity, at the same time further draw students into dominant projects of nationalism and capitalist
labor formation, or bind them even more tightly to systems of class, gender,
and race inequality. On a more personal level, subjection to the schools'
ministrations can yield a sense of self as knowledgeable, as 'somebody' . . . ,
but it also may encourage a sense of self as failure" (Levinson, Foley, and
Holland 1996, 1).

In the specific case of the production of good citizens, the ministrations
of schools aimed at creating such subjects overlaps with other aims and with
institutions beyond the school walls. It is an overlapping twofold process:
the production of good citizens simultaneously involves the production of
social hierarchies, and the production of good citizens within the schools
overlaps with efforts outside the school, in both school-sponsored and
non-school-sponsored activities.

Proponents of a curriculum fix, such as the educators and policy makers
discussed earlier, fail to recognize that noncurriculum (i.e., non-textbook
based) activities within, as well as outside the school, also play important
roles in promoting good citizens. The most obvious is the daily recitation
of the pledge of allegiance to the U.S. flag in schools across the nation.
Not insignificantly, an average student will have recited the pledge close to
a thousand times upon completion of the sixth grade. The intensity of such
a practice suggests a symbolic embodiment of the pledge's statements and
the physical motions involved in enunciating it.

In Texas, for example, every noncitizen and citizen student is required
to recite the pledge of allegiance daily, as mandated by the Texas legislature
in 2003, unless a parent or guardian submits a written request to exempt
her/his child. The mandated enunciation, it should be noted, accomplishes
two important aims: (1) it is not limited to elementary school, thereby
ensuring that all students must recite the pledge; (2) inserting religion
into the process of developing state-oriented fidelities, which was accomplished by adding a provision for the observance of one minute of silence
after reciting the pledge. The adoption of the "one minute of silence,"

represented, in an important sense, the victory of Christian conservative elements within the Texas legislature to reinforce the fourth "R" (i.e., religion) within public schools, along with the production of good citizens. Religion has been a point of controversy in other states, such as the controversy in Georgia regarding the addition of a sticker, in response to local religious groups, in biology textbooks that indicates evolution is a theory, not a fact.

In 2006 Arizona's legislature took a similar measure aimed at promoting patriotism. Enacted by Governor Janet Napolitano, it directed public educational institutions to display the U.S. flag, Constitution, and Bill of Rights in every classroom. The legislature, however, did not allocate any funds for their purchase; the hope was that private entities would donate the items or the money for their purchase.

The pledge, however, is not restricted to the mandated enunciation and is commonly repeated in after-school sporting events. It is also repeated in professional team sporting events, Boy Scout and Girl Scout meetings, and other instances. Although the direct target may be the student, it should also be noted that the presence of parents at these events, including noncitizen parents, means that this practice of citizenship also hails the parents.

The presence of the U.S. flag in schools is not timeless or accidental. According to Stuart McConnell (1996), in 1890 North Dakota and New Jersey were the first states to mandate the flag in schools; other states followed. The adoption of the pledge of allegiance, however, was slower. Prior to 1890 U.S. residents rarely saw the flag, except during wartime and on ships. However, the last decade of the nineteenth century saw a dramatic rise in patriotism: the flag, the pledge of allegiance, and the national anthem gained prominence. Private groups such as the Grand Army of the Republic, the American Flag Association, Sons and Daughters of the American Revolution, and others made it part of their mission to insert the symbols of patriotism into everyday life. McConnell (1996, 103) reminds us that in "little more than a decade, then, the United States saw the invention—or at least the major retooling—of many of its patriotic traditions."

My own practice of verbalizing fidelity to the U.S. flag was mimetic and gradual. As a newcomer to the United States and to the fourth grade class to which I was assigned, and with limited knowledge of the English language, I simply mimicked what I saw and heard. During the initial weeks of my

U.S. schooling, I repeated a string of sounds that I thought approached what other students were saying, placed my right hand over my heart, and looked directly at the flag. My version of the pledge ran something like the following: "aiplechalichenstudeflagodeunaitedstetsofAmericaantuderipubli caforwichitstanswannacionandergadindibisibelwitalibertianchustisforol." Gradually I began to make sense of the gaps in the string of sounds and match what I heard in speech acts to the segments of sounds. Thus, gradually I began to repeat something like, "Ay plechalichen to the flag." By the end of semester, I had more or less made sense of what I was supposed to say. Of course, like most fourth graders, I was not clear what terms such as "allegiance," "for which it stands," "republic," and "indivisible" meant.

Thus, by the end of the fourth grade I had learned an important practice of U.S. citizenship and began to accept and respect the U.S. flag, yet I was not a U.S. citizen. What is important is not the understanding of what the pledge signifies, but rather that students, noncitizens, and citizens perform the required daily routine. The routinization was the priority and became the practice of a good citizen, rather than the meaning of the pledge and its importance or the importance of the flag.

I did not learn, nor was I taught, anything about the pledge's ironic history—that it was written in 1892 by a Christian Socialist Baptist minister, Francis Bellamy, who advocated socialism over the evils of capitalism; that its author excluded the word "equality" (similar to the French trilogy— *liberté, egalité, fraternité*) because it might be too controversial for public schools due to the implication that it would apply to women and African Americans; that Congress did not formally adopt it as part of the U.S. Code until June 1942; that placing the right hand over the heart replaced the straight arm salute during World War II as a way to differentiate our salute from Hitler's; and that "under God" was inserted in 1954 by President Eisenhower under urging from the Knights of Columbus. Several observers have noted that the insertion of the phrase "under God" explicitly converted the pledge into a statement of civil religion.

Francis Bellamy's reflection on his creation offers an important insight. Bellamy observed that "this little formula has been pounding away on the impressionable minds of children for generations, awakening a daily enthusiasm for the flag, driving in the idea of loyalty, giving them a notion of the great republic, reminding them of a liberty and justice for all,—thinking

those thoughts for them" (2005, 69). He recognized that it was not important that children understand the words; the repetition was more crucial.
For Bellamy the pledge operated similarly to the catechism, the Lord's
Prayer, or Ten Commandments—"the words instill, by repetition, a
religious feeling which in after years becomes a basis of belief" (2005, 69).
I estimate that I probably have repeated the pledge close to 3,000 times
since fourth grade.

"The Star-Spangled Banner," while not mandated that it be sung daily, is
taught in schools as part of social studies and/or music courses. In my own
experience, it was taught as part of a music class in elementary school. Like
the pledge of allegiance, it is frequently heard at school events, as well as
commercial sporting events (baseball, football, and others). International
Olympic events not only prominently display national flags but also incorporate the national anthems. The media also plays an important part in
not only broadcasting the anthem in sporting events and the Olympics, but
it is also used to mark the end of the broadcast day. National anthems, as
discussed by George Mosse, are also sites where states disperse important
statements:

> The national anthem was part and parcel of a whole network of symbols
> through which the new nation sought to present itself to its people and
> to engage their undivided allegiance. The flag, the anthem, and most
> national festivals always retained something of the nation-in-arms about
> them, even in times of peace. Within all of these national symbols, but
> especially in national anthems, waging war was an essential ingredient of
> national self-representation. Studying national anthems means examin-
> ing how war was built into most nationalisms, which in turn formed a
> bridge through which the acceptance of war became a factor taken for
> granted in modern life. (1989, 87)

Noncitizen and citizen students are taught about Francis Scott Key, who
wrote "our" anthem in 1814 based on his eye-witness acount of the British
attack on Fort McHenry. Mosse's observation regarding the link between
anthem and war holds true for "The Star-Spangled Banner." As with the
pledge of allegiance, noncitizen parents with children in school are also
exposed to the anthem. As part of their preparation for the citizenship
interview at the CIS office, they must also learn its name and author.

Students in school learn about a tacit form of citizenship that is not often discussed but, nonetheless, is learned and fosters both inclusion and exclusion. I am here referring to what is generally known as school spirit. From my own experience as a student and parent, I believe that the pressure to participate in activities demonstrating school spirit start in elementary school, become more marked in high school, and are even stronger in college. School spirit is a kind of proto-nationalism that encompasses many of the same material representations that we associate with nationalism: a flag or banner, a ritualized salute, an insignia, and an anthem. It also serves to divide members among those who have it and those who don't—meaning those loyal subjects who express their fidelity by actively participating in events that represent the school/college; or the good from the bad citizens.

The body occupies an important role in the display of the school insignia and colors through the use of clothing and/or paint directly applied to the body. Moreover, the events considered most important are generally those involving an enemy (i.e., an arch rival) and the testing of the physical prowess of male members. Metaphors of war, such as "fight," "battle," "kill," "revenge," "terror," "victory," and others are used to characterize these confrontations (and some even use military-style canons as part of the spectacle). Like war, the confrontation between men is at times framed in rhetorics of domination and gendering of the opponents as female, a kind of allegorical misogynism.[6] At the college level, public universities, such as those in Arizona, Arkansas, Illinois, Ohio, Oklahoma, and Texas, best exemplify the aforementioned. In the second half of the nineteenth century, school spirit and the production of loyal, patriotic, and manly men was also an important concern at Yale University and Harvard University (Higgs 1987). What I am suggesting here is that "school spirit" seems to simultaneously replicate and support the broader discourse regarding the link between being a good citizen and the state: a "good" subject possesses and embodies the desired fidelities—for one's school, for one's nation. Thus, school spirit should also be seen as an element in the production of good citizens and a practice that impacts both noncitizens and citizens.

Another example of a nonschool institution that reinforces the role of schools in conscripting good citizens is the Boy Scouts of America. The history and discourse of the Boy Scouts offers an informative narrative regarding the link between the military, masculinity, and citizenship. The

Boy Scouts founder, Robert Baden-Powell, was a career soldier who served in the Boer War in South Africa. After returning to England, he was assigned to inspect cavalry forces. After that assignment, and based on that experience, he set out to redraft an earlier manual, *Aids to Scouting*, to address the "boy problem" and formulate a program that would turn them into "real men" (which he saw as some combination of military scout, trapper, and colonial frontiersman). The result was *Scouting for Boys: A Handbook for Instruction in Good Citizenship* in 1908 (Baden-Powell 2004), which remains the central text of the Boy Scouts. Baden-Powell enunciated his rationale as follows: "God made men to be men. . . . We badly need some training for our lads if we are to keep up manliness in our race instead of lapsing into a nation of soft, sloppy, cigarette suckers" (Warren 1987, 203). As noted in the subtitle, the goal was to produce good citizens.

Throughout Scout Law one finds references to being loyal, obedient, brave, clean, and reverent. Recent editions of the Scout Handbook in the United States explicitly address the importance of respect for the flag, learning the duties of an "American citizen," and the "meanings and history of the national anthem and pledge of allegiance" (Higashi 2002). Moreover, an explicit objective of the organization is the following: "Scouting is based on life skills education, leadership development, citizenship, and values training. Its unique methods of program presentation are designed to help build youth with strong character who are physically fit and prepared to be good citizens" (http://www.scouting.org).

Baden-Powell's military background influenced the choice of uniforms, as well as the link between good citizenship and soldiers, which is further reinforced through the awards and badges, such as the Citizenship in the Nation award. The elements of the oath and the Law provide a good fit between masculinity, being a good citizen, and being a good soldier (Ferguson and Turnbull 1999). President Theodore Roosevelt recognized this link: "It [Boy Scouts] does not try to make soldiers of Boy Scouts, but to make boys who will turn out as men to be fine citizens, and who will, if their country needs them, make better soldiers for having been scouts. No one can be a good American unless he is a good citizen" (Higashi 2002, 236).

The Girl Scout program dates back to 1912 and was partially modeled on the Boy Scouts. Juliette "Daisy" Gordon Low, after meeting Sir Robert

Baden-Powell, founded the effort in Georgia, with its purpose "to inspire girls with the highest ideals of character, conduct, patriotism, and service that they may become happy and resourceful citizens." Although its mission invokes citizenship, the activities are not as focused on it as those of the Boy Scouts and they seem to retain a marked gender difference.[7] The 2005 annual World Thinking Day, for example, focused on "cooking in various cultures" as a way for girls to understand the role of food and nutrition in the global community; in 2010 the theme was "together we can end extreme poverty and hunger"; and in 2011 it was "empowering girls will change our world." Moreover, despite the early emulation of a military-style uniform for girls (1912–1927), the organization does not explicitly link its activities to military service, nor does it emphasize morality to the degree found in the Boy Scouts.

The multiple narratives and practices that operate beyond the text-book based activities of the curriculum, both within and outside the school, foster citizenship and its concomitant fidelities, and supplement the curriculum-based activities aimed at producing good citizens. Yet educators, policy makers, academics, and journalists critical of the contemporary cultivation of good citizen youth overlook them, suggesting that they underestimate the overlapping and supplemental role that multiple institutions have in fostering citizenship in youth and in their parents.

The Importance of Practices

The meanings and practices involved in producing good citizens are found not only in the curriculum and activities related to the flag or anthem, but also in classroom routines, school activities, and documents generated by schools. My own experience as a migrant, noncitizen (or perhaps more precisely a migrant metic) entering the Los Angeles City Unified School District—Oxnard St. Elementary School in the San Fernando Valley—illustrates how the interpellation and subjectivization process are manifested through the meanings and practices of citizenship in school.[8]

After my family settled in an apartment in the San Fernando Valley, my parents inquired with neighbors about the assigned elementary school. I, on the other hand, had not given much thought to school or how long it would be before I would begin. My preoccupations were centered more on trying to make sense of the strange new place. People actually spoke English all the time, rather than in short segments such as in television commercials or tourists talking to vendors. I began to see novel things on television, including roller derby with male and female teams that went around in endless circles and hit each other in the process, and with referees who seemed relatively clueless to most of the bad team's dirty tricks against the good team. I discovered gigantic red ants building large mounds in the sand, which I had never seen before, and which I learned quickly, the hard way, to avoid while walking around; there were so many things that I had not seen or experienced in Mexico City.

Shortly before my first day I was told that I would be going to school. Though in some sense eager to start school, I was also apprehensive. My main concern was language. How was I going to understand what the teacher or other students said to me? How would I read books in English? Upon arrival at the school we went to the office, my parents signed some papers, and I was quickly escorted to the class that I had been assigned: Mrs. Skahill's fourth grade class. Although I wondered why I had been placed in the fourth grade, since I already had completed that grade in Mexico, I was later told that it was because of the language barrier.

The woman from the office who escorted me to the class said something to the teacher. The teacher responded and then pointed to an empty chair in the room. I took it that she meant for me to sit there and so proceeded to sit in the indicated chair. During the pointing-sitting exchange, the other students stopped what they were doing and watched the interaction. Whether they said or did not say anything, I do not recall. What I recall is that once Mrs. Skahill returned to the lesson she was in the midst of when I arrived, I simply sat and observed the rest of the day. That first day and for a time after that, I simply mimicked what the other students did.

The daily routine consisted of the following: students must arrive early and be in their seats before the first bell rings. When the second bell rings, it's "recess." You get up from your seat and line up, waiting for the teacher to authorize the exit; you walk outside in an orderly way, go to the cafeteria, and if you have money, you buy a small carton of milk and perhaps a cinnamon roll. Another bell rings and you return to the room in a quiet and orderly way. Then another bell rings, and you repeat the exit strategy and eat your lunch in the cafeteria/auditorium or outside of it (those with money ate inside, those with limited or no money, like myself, ate outside). A bell rings and you are allowed to play strange games in the playground (a kind of soccer but with bases, a game where you hit a ball that goes around a metal pole, a game where someone tries to hit you with a ball, etc.). Boys play the games for boys and the girls play the games for girls. Yet another bell rings and you repeat the reentry routine. After a final bell rings, you clean up your desk and quietly wait until the teacher signals her authorization for you to leave.

To function properly in school one had to learn a set of behaviors: following orders, respecting authority, being quiet, being patient, standing quietly in line, keeping your hands to yourself, being attentive to bells and their meaning, interacting primarily with the same sex/gender, staying in your seat unless the teacher orders differently, responding to the teacher's questions, taking tests, doing homework, etc. My limited English language ability and my status as a noncitizen did not limit my learning the everyday practices of being a student in an elementary school in the United States.

I began to tacitly learn how to be a good citizen at school. My ability to behave as expected by the teacher, by incorporating the noted set of behaviors, meant that I was on the road to becoming a good citizen. In addition to the routinized behaviors, I also began to develop respect for the U.S. flag and the national anthem, as well as to relate to the difficulties that our ancestors faced while settling the new land, the struggles colonists faced in defending themselves against the "wild Indians," the principles in the Declaration of Independence and the Constitution, as well as the many other hegemonic narratives about the history of the United States. It was not until high school and early part of college that I was exposed to the contradiction and limitations of the narratives I had read about many times before.

One also learns an important lesson related to social class distinctions, that one becomes bound more tightly to systems of class and inequality. While students who brought their lunch in a brown paper bag or lunch pail could go into the cafeteria to buy milk, they were required to exit the cafeteria after their purchase and find a place to eat outside; those who had lunch money ate their lunch inside the cafeteria—generally a much cooler and comfortable setting. The process made it evident that some students almost always ate in the cafeteria; some ate there once in a while; and a bulk ate outside, including me. The entire process was taken for granted and accepted as natural, or was due to some self-selection on the part of students rather than the resources of the student's family. I, and presumably the other students who ate outside, came to accept that privilege was associated with some of the citizens in the school. It was a tacit acceptance of both the classroom lessons about democracy and equality, and the actual inequality that was observed—a tacit acceptance of a contradiction as not contradictory.

Expected behaviors and accompanying attitudes were graded on report cards, where they appeared in a separate section from the 3 R's and other subjects. On my report card, these behaviors were framed in terms of "citizenship." At the time, the Los Angeles City Unified School District divided the card into three sections. The upper section was titled "Qualities of Citizenship" and listed the following qualities in the left-hand column: (1) Effort, (2) Accomplishment, (3) Obedience, (4) Dependability, (5) Promptness, (6) Cooperation, (7) Courtesy, (8) Enthusiasm, (9) Habits of thrift, and (10) Habits of good health. The second section listed grades for subjects, such as reading and arithmetic; and the third section was the "Record of Attendance," which reported the number of days absent, present, and tardy.

Although the report card does not define or give the criteria for each quality of citizenship, I presume that teachers in the district must have received some training or a handbook that defined each. Yet for the student, and ultimately for the parent who had to sign the report card, no clues were given. The reverse side of the report card merely indicated that "qualities of pupil citizenship, as observed by the teacher, will be indicated for pupils of kindergarten and all grades." Each of the ten-week grading periods had columns labeled "Outstanding," "Satisfactory," and "Unsatisfactory." Thus, teachers evaluated me and other students on our qualities of citizenship, and our ability to embody and exhibit good citizenship even as noncitizens.

In my first report card Mrs. Skahill did not assign grades to me for the twelve subjects (Reading, Language, Handwriting, etc.); instead, she wrote "not receiving grades because of language barrier." However, she did evaluate my citizenship. She assigned an "Outstanding" check for "Effort" and a "Satisfactory" check for the remaining nine elements. In the second ten weeks, she graded me for the twelve subject areas and added: "has made good progress with understanding and using English." More important, my citizenship had also improved in the second ten weeks. She gave me four "Outstanding" check marks and six "Satisfactory" marks. Mrs. Skahill was evaluating my citizenship as a noncitizen, and the report card was interpellating me as a citizen, and I had begun the subject-making process of constructing a subjectivity of citizen.

The school district's report card offers a relatively clear definition of a "good citizen." A good citizen would be a student deemed by her or his teacher as having "satisfactory" or "outstanding" evaluations for most of the ten qualities of citizenship, while a bad citizen would be a student who received "unsatisfactory" on most of the ten qualities. The two extreme positions are a student judged as "outstanding" in all ten qualities (the truly good citizen) and a student judged as "unsatisfactory" in all ten qualities (the truly bad citizen).

A student could also boost her or his good citizenship by enlisting to serve in school roles outside the classroom. The school district distributed certificates of "Service Award" in "recognition of outstanding service to the school" to students who volunteered to take on work tasks such as safety patrol (helping the street crossing guards), bathroom monitor (surveilling fellow students in the bathroom), and ball monitor (distributing the appropriate playground balls and other equipment to fellow students during lunch break). As an enlistee in each of these three services, my role was to carry out the required tasks and report student misbehavior to the proper authority. As a noncitizen, I monitored the behavior of citizen students. But perhaps more important, the link is forged early between good citizenship and the monitoring and surveillance of fellow citizens—programs such as Silent Witness, Neighborhood Watch, Crime Stoppers, various federal and state tip efforts, airport security policies, and the war on terrorism operate on the same principle as that of bathroom monitors. Individuals who, to borrow Benjamin Rush's phrase, "watch for the state" and report "suspicious" individuals to authorities would be considered good citizens.

The report card raises some important issues. One, the discourse of the form selected qualities of citizenship and thus constructed what constitutes citizenship for elementary school students. With the exception of "habits of thrift" and "habits of good health," the qualities were directly linked to issues of authority and the relation of the subject to authority.

In other words, they were about fidelities and power relations. The success of schools in promoting these qualities, and in students accepting these qualities as their own and as important for their own socioeconomic mobility, has an important utility beyond elementary school and the other grades; they are qualities sought by public and private employers and the military.

The processes described by Willis (1977) in discussing "the lads," by Foley (1990) regarding the "*vatos locos*," and by Luykz (1999) for Aymara students wishing to become teachers point to the dual nature of (and the contradictions entailed in) the processes by which schools participate in creating good citizens (obedient, dependable, hard-working individuals) and students make decisions regarding their own trajectories and relations with authority. As suggested by Levinson, Foley, and Holland (1996, 1), schooling simultaneously offers "certain freedoms and opportunity" and "draw[s] students into dominant projects of nationalism and capitalist labor formation." The discourse and practices of citizenship are an important medium through which schools are able to foster both aims. A student able to embody qualities such as the ten listed earlier can become a good citizen student in academic terms, and a good citizen in terms of the necessary fidelities toward the employers, nation, and the state.

In summary, schooling is central to the discourse and practices of citizenship, and in schools individuals are the object and subject of the technologies of citizenship. Students, both noncitizens and citizens, are exposed explicitly and implicitly to a menu of prescribed subjectivities and fidelities. Through the multiplicity and frequency of enunciations students experience the embodiment of citizenship. The routinization of practices, such as the daily pledge of allegiance, as well as the fostering of obedience and respect for authority, all support the school's (and the nation's) construction and definition of good citizenship.

Educators and policy makers critical of the effectiveness of schools in producing good citizens, as well as neoconservative critics concerned with the devaluation of citizenship, provide weak arguments about the role of schools in fostering citizenship and about the diminished practices of citizenship. Ultimately, they seem to be expressing a perceived lack in the present—a lack informed by an ideologically imagined past. In particular, they attribute a lack of valuation of U.S. citizenship to Mexican and other (racial-ethnic minority) migrants. The experiences and affects of the Mexican migrants interviewed offer a different story regarding the valuation of citizenship and respect for the United States. Despite their experiences with multiple forms of exclusion, they are grateful for their eventual inclusion as U.S. citizens and the opportunities they have found in that space.

CHAPTER 3

The Janus Face of Citizenship

THE SIDE OF EXCLUSION

Discussions of juridical citizenship tend to examine inclusionary or exclusionary dimensions of citizenship without taking into account its dual nature.[1] A noteworthy exception to this is James Holston's (2008) detailed examination of the entanglement of citizenship, inequality, and democracy in Brazil, though his focus is not on the simultaneous factors examined here.[2] The processes of inclusion and exclusion are central to fostering the high valuation of, and privileging associated with, U.S. citizenship. Those who can claim U.S. citizenship can assert their privileged position; those who perceive that they lack the full measures of citizenship (i.e., "second-class citizens") can demand absent privileges; and those who are not included/represented desire inclusion/representation.[3]

Work is central to capitalist economies, both in terms of determining an individual's ability to survive economically and in shaping social identifications (e.g., day laborer, police officer, stay-at-home mom, first responder, soldier, or professor). Work-related activities not only relate to class and status hierarchies in the society (Marx [1843] 1972; Weber 1927) and the division of labor (Durkheim [1893] 1964); they also intersect with gender constructions. As perceptively articulated by Judith Shklar (1991, 63–101), earning—the ability to work, be paid an earned reward, and be perceived as an economic contributor—are critical qualities to the social standing dimension of citizenship. Membership in the circle of citizens and recognition by other citizens as belonging encompass perceptions related to being a taxpayer and a self-supporting economic subject.

While it is common to find discussions that portray citizenship as an adhesive force that binds individuals together as members of a larger social whole (i.e., a nation-state) and furnishes affective ties to it, many of these evade the simultaneous exclusionary tendencies of the process. Benedict Anderson's (2006) superior discussion of the cohesive forces of nationalism, for example, sidesteps the disjunctions and exclusions within nations. Likewise, many discussions regarding the exclusionary effects of citizenship tend to overlook the co-acting forces that foster inclusion for particular groups. For instance, perspectives associated with neoconservatives who stress the role of family and schools in forming the character, virtue, and patriotism of the young citizen as the solution to upholding liberal democratic capitalism tend to be silent about individual interests, diversity within nations, and the inequality that is "a fundamental reality of the modern world-system" (Wallerstein 2003, 650). On the other hand, liberal perspectives that emphasize personal liberties, freedom, and an expansive civil rights agenda tend to ignore the issue of how individualism can foster a common interest and the roles played by the "Other" in creating the "we," "*Volk*," "the people," or *natio*. Chantal Mouffe (1992b, 1993), David Trend (1996), and others have similarly noted the limitations of liberal perspectives. They point out that the dichotomy between liberalism and civic republicanism is too simplistic and suggest the need for liberalism to address the dimension of how to create a common good. Although their point is important, the aim here is to contextualize citizenship by tracing its exclusionary elements as a means to better understanding the discourses and practices of citizenship in the United States.

What follows is my effort to contribute to the contemporary analysis of the fundamental concept of citizenship. The objective is to outline the broader context within which the contemporary notions of citizenship are situated, and that informs the juridical, sociopolitical, and everyday use of it. Individuals interested in acquiring citizenship, such as the Mexican émigrés I interviewed, are aware of the inclusionary and exclusionary effects of juridical citizenship. For example, the individuals I spoke with were aware that informally authorized children can and do attend local public schools (i.e., the inclusiveness of schooling); that all males between eighteen and twenty-five years of age, even if they are informally authorized, must register with the Selective Service System (i.e., the inclusiveness of the military with reference to males, but excluding females); that all individuals, including informally authorized persons, pay the same taxes paid by citizens and file an income tax return with the Internal Revenue Service (i.e., the inclusiveness of government taxes); and that noncitizens can be prohibited from voting in state and national elections, serving on juries, or applying for federal employment (i.e., exclusion by the government based on citizenship).[4] In other words, their lived experiences in the United States have simultaneously encompassed both inclusion and exclusion.

Prior to being granted citizenship they were members of, but not included (i.e., not represented) in the United States (Badiou 2004). After gaining U.S. citizenship, they recognized their juridical inclusion. Though they also recognized that segments of the broader community, including Mexican Americans/Hispanics/Latinos, continued to see them as "Mexican immigrants" or "*Mexicanos.*"

HISTORICAL CONTEXT AND FORMS OF EXCLUSION

Juridical citizenship is a category that entails both exclusion and inclusion. Historically the concept of citizen has been based on the evolving dichotomy of citizen-alien. This dichotomization and oppositional determination remain and are inscribed in the Immigration and Nationality Act (INA) of the United States: a citizen is a person who is not an "alien," and an "alien" is a person who is not a "citizen." Under the juridical construction, millions of individuals who migrated here from many parts of the world and for many reasons (most voluntarily, others involuntarily) were granted citizenship and thus acquired the position of "member and represented." Such individuals, sometimes labeled "Americans by choice" (Gavit [1922] 1971), such as Jean de Crèvecoeur ([1782] 1963), have brought with them "their national genius" and benefited from opportunities found here—the "great American asylum." The motto of all migrants, particularly poor migrants, is "Ubi panis ibi patria" (Where I earn my bread, that's my nation) (de Crèvecoeur [1782] 1963, 63). For such individuals, their experience is one of inclusion. Others, however, report opposite experiences.[5]

EXCLUSION FROM ENTRY

Although most of the discussions on the exclusion of noncitizens from work-related activities focus on the forms of these exclusions (e.g., the common exclusion of noncitizens from law enforcement), prior to that point other exclusions have already taken place. Exclusions from entry are crucial in defining the specific noncitizen status of persons. Laws that define legal exclusions and inclusions affect individuals who enter without formal authorizations from the state. However, there are noncitizens who initially are legally permitted to enter the United States (e.g., with tourist or student visas) but become subject to removal when they overstay their visas and/or work in jobs that are not authorized by their visas. The initial exclusions and inclusions at entry have a significant impact on a person's access to certain forms of employment. As will be evident from the following examples, significant variations exist in our migration laws, and so the category of noncitizen, even for those who enter without formal authorization, encompasses multiple juridical categories that imply differences in authorization to work.

In most cases, exclusion from entry also means exclusion from U.S. citizenship. Those not allowed to enter have few opportunities to become U.S. citizens. However, there are four notable exceptions: (1) the registry provision in the INA can be used to apply for permanent residency by individuals who have established a long-term residence (since January 1, 1972), even though they entered without formal authorization;[6] (2) the implementation of legalization programs such as those implemented under the Immigration Reform and Control Act (1986) that allowed informally authorized persons to petition for temporary, later permanent residency, and eventually U.S. citizenship; (3) the special exception provided for Cuban nationals who manage to enter without authorization; and (4) U.S. citizenship granted in vivo or posthumously to informally authorized persons who performed military work.

From the colonial period to the present, individuals wishing to enter the territory have been excluded on several grounds. The list of conditions over time has expanded, though a small number have been eliminated. Past exclusions (some of which continue to exist) were based on religion, gender, race/ethnicity, class ("liable to become a public charge"), morality ("good moral character"), sexuality, pregnancy, political beliefs and activities, nationality, crimes committed, health status, and others. Each of these has its own history in terms of what motivated the particular exclusion, its implementation, and, if eliminated, a particular rationale for its removal.

Over time, the United States has had a number of policies aimed at regulating migration (i.e., primarily entry) and migrants (i.e., the status and privileges of persons once in the territory). Contrary to the common perception that the regulation of migration and migrants has always been a federal responsibility, states and the federal government historically shared the regulation of migration. Over time, however, there has been a gradual transfer of regulation from state governments to the federal government. From the founding of the colonies to 1790, the colonies and later the newly minted states regulated both migration and migrants. In 1790 the U.S. Congress adopted the first federal act regarding naturalization. It aimed to establish a uniform system for naturalization, though, as already discussed, it was not until 1990 that naturalization became a sole federal authority, and it was not until 1882 that Congress established a comprehensive migration statute.

However, the 1882 act left the actual implementation to states. It was not until 1891 that the U.S. Congress set in place a comprehensive federal law administered through federal agencies. Two important issues should be noted about the aforementioned. One, prior to 1891 the colonies and later the states had a substantial role in determining who was allowed to enter the territory and who was excluded from it, as well as in governing the lives of migrants. Many of the policies formulated by states, such as denying entry to those who might become a public charge, became part of the federal statutes. The second point that is commonly overlooked is that the 1891 act did not prohibit states from regulating the lives of migrants within their territories. States and local governments have implemented a broad set of regulations that limit the ability of noncitizen migrants, particularly informally authorized migrants, to earn a livelihood.

In 2011 the INA contained ten broad categories of grounds for exclusion—or, more correctly, based on the terminology passed in 1996, grounds for "inadmissibility." The details of the grounds for exclusion/inadmissibility (Section 212, INA; 8 U.S.C. 1182) cover about fifteen pages and so will not be repeated here. The exclusions encompass ten broad categories based on multiple criteria. They are (1) health (e.g., communicable diseases, HIV, mental disorders); (2) morality/criminal acts (e.g., crimes involving moral turpitude, drug offenses, money laundering); (3) security/politics (e.g., association with a terrorist organization, member of a totalitarian party); (4) class/income (e.g., likely at any time to become a public charge); (5) work/labor (e.g., possessing the right type of labor certification); (6) entering or remaining without formal authorization; (7) lacking necessary documents; (8) ineligible for citizenship (e.g., draft evaders, departure from the U.S. to avoid military training or war work); (9) previous removal/deportation; and (10) miscellaneous morality/political grounds (e.g., practicing polygamy, unlawful voters, former U.S. citizens who renounced their citizenship to avoid taxation). One or more than one of these can be invoked by the State Department or the Customs and Border Protection (CBP) division of the Department of Homeland Security (DHS) to deny entry.

These categories of exclusion represent de jure statements in the discourse of exclusion. What actually happens at land borders, airports, and ports can be different from these. Migration and human rights advocacy groups, such as the American Friends Service Committee and the American Civil Liberties Union, have documented cases of customs and other officials who have used their discretionary power to prevent individuals from entering who were admissible.

Of the many stories I have been told or with which I have been involved, I will cite two. The first is the case of an individual who possessed a green card (i.e., was a lawful permanent resident) and was entitled to enter the United States after a brief trip outside the country. His letter of complaint summarizing the events that transpired was assigned to me when I was a policy analyst at the Governor's Office in Texas. According to the letter and subsequent phone conversations I had with him, he had traveled to Nuevo Laredo for a short visit and when he tried to reenter the United States, the migration official took his green card, tore it up in front of him, and impolitely told him that it was not his card and to go back to Mexico. Thus, he was excluded from entry under the officer's discretionary powers. After I communicated with the INS regional office and they later verified that the person had been issued a green card, the INS regional official apologized to me for the error and noted that the border officer would be reprimanded and that they would issue a new green card to the gentleman. In this case, de jure admissibility did not automatically translate into de facto admissibility.

The second incident occurred to a friend born and raised in a Texas border city who grew up with Spanish as his primary language until he entered public school. He traveled to the Mexican city adjacent to where he lived and upon returning was asked the standard question regarding citizenship/ nationality. My friend was engrossed in the conversation he was having with his friend in Spanish, and so when the official asked him the usual question, my friend responded "*soy Americano*" (which from the context and everyday use of the word along the Mexico–United States border would have been taken as "American"—that is, U.S. citizen—by all local residents, including the official who resided in the same border city), rather than the expected "American citizen" or "U.S. citizen." The response in Spanish was grounds for exclusion. Switching to English by that point was futile; the violation had already occurred. My friend had to call home and have someone locate his birth certificate and then bring it to him so that he could prove that he was a U.S. citizen. His friend, who simply replied, "I'm a U.S. citizen" was recognized as admissible; no proof was needed. Consequently, to understand the practices of exclusion/admissibility at entry, one must examine the laws as well as the discretionary power of officials who implement them.

The policing of the land borders, particularly the Mexico-U.S. boundary, ports, and airports, is the most visible form of exclusion from entry. Since a significant literature already discusses this topic in detail, I will here summarize the various efforts to "regain control of the border," the phrase used by President Reagan, later adopted by Presidents Clinton and George W. Bush but less common in the language of Obama administration officials. It should be observed that the term "border" for Clinton and Bush, and for many federal policy makers, was and continues to be largely understood as the Mexico-U.S. boundary, not the northern border or the multiple other land and ocean borders that bound the territory, including its possessions.

The Mexico-U.S. boundary area has been transformed over the past fifteen years by what some refer to as its "militarization." Accompanying the substantial build-up in the number of border patrol agents (which currently exceeds 20,200), a substantial budget increase led to the incorporation of technology that included electronic ground sensors, night-vision equipment, taller and more sophisticated fences, "cyclopes" (portable, elevated guard booths), flood lights, laptop commuters, helicopters, and, more recently, radio-controlled drones with cameras. The period has also seen the emergence of a discourse about the Mexico-U.S. border as a "war zone" (Chávez 2001), and more recently into a discourse about the threat of Latinos (Chávez 2008).

An important strategy within the militarization of the Mexico-U.S. border is the preemptive enforcement efforts that began in 1993. The new policy was implemented to prevent entry rather than apprehending persons after entry. This policy placed a significant number of agents at a short distance apart from each other so they could see each other and visually monitor the border. To date, four major efforts have been implemented: Operation Blockade/Hold-the-Line (1993, El Paso), Operation Gatekeeper (1994, San Diego), Operation Rio Grande (1997, Rio Grande Valley), and Operation Safeguard (1999, Arizona). The net effect of the efforts, particularly in the aftermath of Operation Gatekeeper, was to shift migration flows from Tijuana–San Diego to the Sonora desert leading into Arizona; which has resulted in a high number of migrant deaths; some estimate that the total number may exceed 5,000. The desired goal of halting (or significantly reducing) unauthorized entry remains an aspiration.

Exclusion from Naturalization

From the first naturalization statute in 1790 to the present, U.S. naturalization law is exclusive. It excluded on the basis of race/ethnicity, gender, class (property ownership), nativity, political beliefs, and other arbitrary criteria. The inclusion of various categories of persons has been gradual. The following is a list of the categories of exclusion and eligibility for naturalization and citizenship from 1790 to 1952.[7]

1790   Free white male persons eligible (1 Stat. 103, Chapter III).

1798   Nationals of countries with which the United States is at war (i.e., enemy aliens) excluded (repealed 1802).

1848   Treaty of Guadalupe Hidalgo granted citizenship to Mexicans who continued to reside in the annexed territory (Mexico-U.S. War).[8]

1857   *Dred Scott* Supreme Court Decision excludes African-born and African Americans from citizenship (60 U.S. 393).

1868   Citizenship extended to most persons born in the United States regardless of migration status of parents (Fourteenth Amendment).

1870   Persons of African nativity eligible to naturalize (1870
        Naturalization Act, 16 Stat. 254).

1882   Chinese and persons from the Asiatic Barred Zone excluded
        from naturalization over the next forty years.

1887   Dawes Act grants citizenship to Native Americans who give up
        their tribal affiliation.

1897   *In re Rodríguez* allowed eligible Mexican émigrés to naturalize in
        the San Antonio area.

1901   Citizenship granted to Native Americans living in Indian
        Territory (Oklahoma).

1906   Anarchists and polygamists excluded from naturalization.

1912   Military deserters and migrants who left the United States to
        avoid basic training or the draft excluded from naturalization.

1917   Jones Act grants collective citizenship to Puerto Ricans.

1922   Women, regardless of marital status or citizenship status of
        husband, independently eligible (Cable Act, 42 Stat. 1021).

1924   Noncitizen, U.S.-born American Indians granted citizenship
        (Indian Citizenship Act, 43 Stat. 253).

1943   Chinese granted eligibility for naturalization.

1946   Filipinos allowed to become citizens.

1950   Communists or those who teach that the U.S. government
        should be overthrown are excluded from citizenship.

1952   Naturalization extended to all racial/ethnic groups and
        nationalities (eliminated 1790 "free white person" provision;
        McCarran-Walter Act, 66 Stat. 163).

It is only since 1952 that the United States adopted a more inclusive policy regarding the categories of persons who can petition and possibly be granted U.S. citizenship. I say possibly because the June 1952 Immigration Act established a broader basis for the granting of U.S. citizenship, but it did not eliminate all of the restrictions related to qualifications for naturalization.

Although qualifying requirements have varied over time, I will enumerate only the current restrictions. There are three general requirements to petition for U.S. citizenship: the individual must be eighteen years of age to apply directly; the person must hold the status of lawful permanent resident

(LPR) for five years, three years if married to a U.S. citizen, or less time if performing war work; and the person must possess an understanding of the English language, U.S. history, and form of government (the latter are waived for persons in the military).[9] In addition, there are ten categories of exclusions from the granting of citizenship. They are the following: (1) being absent from the United States (limits the time that an LPR can reside outside the United States), (2) enunciating U.S. citizenship (a noncitizen verbally or in writing claiming to be a U.S. citizen), (3) registering to vote when ineligible, (4) voting when ineligible, (5) failing to file an income tax return or owing money to the federal government, (6) having been declared legally incompetent or confined to a mental institution, (7) having questionable political affiliation (being associated or supportive of communism or supporting the overthrow of the U.S. government), (8) deserting from the military, (9) being relieved from military work because of alien status, and (10) possessing questionable morality (lacking "good moral character") (INA, Sections 313 to 316; U.S. CIS 2004).

As mentioned, this list represents de jure statements that do not necessarily indicate how they may be interpreted within the discretionary authority of migration officials, or how individuals may inadvertently trespass against one of the ten citizenship commandments. Of the many examples shared with me by migrants, advocates, and attorneys, here are two.

The first example relates to the civic knowledge requirement and the second to the registering-to-vote provision. An older Mexican migrant female, Sra. Campo, with a long residence in the United States who had taken English-as- a-second-language and citizenship classes (including one that I taught) had diligently prepared for an interview at the San Antonio CIS office. She held off submitting her application until she thought she was ready. It was evident in her class participation that she took the class seriously, both in her active participation, her questions, and completion of suggested practice exercises. She also had a strong respect and appreciation for the nation that facilitated a degree of economic opportunity and improvement in her life, and her children's life. She expressed that she had a long-term desire to become a U.S. citizen; she wanted to more fully participate and vote.

The long-awaited day of her interview finally came and she was ready: she had become sufficiently fluent in English and had studied religiously, reviewing the 100 questions over and over. She wanted to become a U.S. citizen—a citizen of the country she loved, where she was a respectful, tax-paying, law-abiding resident. Yet she did not pass the oral interview, and she felt a certain *verguenza* (shame) about having failed.

She failed because the CIS official chose to test her civics and government knowledge by asking her to name the branches of the military. She did not know these because they are not part of the 100 test questions.[10] The CIS official, within his discretionary powers, chose to ask a question that he should not have and thus the applicant failed. Although citizenship applicants have the right to immediately ask for another examiner or supervisor and question the first decision, she, like most applicants, did not know this, and so she accepted the enunciated verdict: "study more and come back at a later time." She did that. She went home and later enrolled in another citizenship class. Her case illustrates how an eligible applicant, despite her best efforts to comply with all the requirements, can fail the final interview; and how CIS officials can manipulate their discretionary power. I speculate that if she had asked for a review of the interview by a supervisor, and if the supervisor would have asked an additional question from the 100 questions, she probably would have passed and moved a step closer to achieving her desire to be a U.S. citizen.

The second example deals with registering to vote and is based on accounts provided by advocates and attorneys. It is reported that some citizenship applicants make the inadvertent error of signing a voter registration card. What is important here is not the act of signing, but the context. It appears that young active citizens involved in voter registration drives in Latino communities are so assertive and effective in registering voters that they forget to ask important basic questions such as, "Are you a U.S. citizen?" before pressuring the person to sign a card. Instead, they ask, "Are you a resident of this county?" The result of this practice of citizenship and promotion of democracy is that in some cases permanent residents are convinced they should register to vote. In principle they agree with the importance of voting, and so they sign the card. Some permanent residents who have passed their CIS interviews and are waiting to take their naturalization oath have been known to get ahead of themselves. Knowing that they soon will be citizens, they want to be ready to vote and so sign a voter registration form.

What some citizenship promoters and migrants fail to take into account is that when individuals sign voter registration cards, they are attesting to being U.S. citizens (a felony), even if they leave blank the space that indicates they are such. When these citizenship applicants honestly report that they have registered to vote, it eliminates their chances of being granted U.S. citizenship and makes them subject to removal because they have committed a felony. If they choose to indicate that they did not register to vote and the fact later emerges that they did, they can be accused of providing false and misleading information on their citizenship application, which is grounds for denial and removal as well. Improper training of volunteers for voter registration drives can have serious consequences for migrants pursuing a path to citizenship.

EXCLUSION FROM PRACTICES OF CITIZENSHIP

The United States has never had universal suffrage. There is an extensive literature on the development of suffrage in general (including the elimination of the poll tax); the woman's suffrage movement; the 1965 Voting Rights Act; the 1993 National Voter Registration Act; and the recent reform in the aftermath of the 2000 presidential election, the 2002 Help America Vote Act.[11]

Prior to discussing the disenfranchisement of noncitizens, it is useful to outline the forms of voting exclusions imposed on citizens. Cortland Bishop's (1893) summary of the history of elections in the colonial period is an excellent overview of the range of exclusions that the multiple colonies employed to exclude the political participation of colonial residents. These exclusions covered race/ethnicity, religion, gender, class, politics (e.g., persons naturalized in another colony), morality, and other categories. Some were eventually eliminated, others were added, such as literacy and poll taxes, and others continue, albeit in more subtle ways.

An example of the expansion of suffrage is the passage of the Nineteenth Amendment (1920) that allowed women to vote. Currently, minorities and poor and/or working class people are excluded in indirect ways such as the disenfranchisement of felons, which tends to have a disproportionate impact on low-income African Americans, though it also affects low-income Latinos.[12] Currently, thirteen states temporarily disenfranchise

U.S. citizens convicted of a felony, while some states disenfranchise U.S. citizens for life, including persons who already have completed their sentences and supervision under probation or parole. Only two states do not disenfranchise citizens who have been convicted of a felony. It is estimated that close to 5 million persons are disenfranchised and that one-third of these are African Americans. The American Civil Liberties Unions and researchers involved in analyzing this issue suggest that the purging of voter lists by states—such as was done shortly before the 2000 presidential election in Florida and repeated in other states in the 2008 election, which resulted in many African American voters erroneously being excluded—is a modern technique to accomplish what in the past was done through literacy, poll taxes, and other means. It also has been asserted that the disenfranchisement of U.S. citizen felons, the single largest group being African American and likely to vote for Democratic candidates, has resulted in several electoral contests in southern states won by Republicans.

In addition to disenfranchisement, U.S. citizen felons are excluded from an activity deemed important to citizenship: jury service (Kalt 2004). After the seventy-two-year struggle that led to the passage of the Nineteenth Amendment, which granted the vote to women, many states did not automatically extend jury service to women, for which women fought for many years after 1920 (Ritter 2000). Mexican Americans, in spite of their possession of birthright citizenship, also contested their exclusion from juries. It was not until the Supreme Court ruling of *Pete Hernández v. Texas* (1954) that U.S. citizens of Mexican descent were de jure allowed to participate in that important practice of citizenship (Sheridan 1999). However, U.S. citizens of Mexican descent considered unable to speak sufficient English or to possess limited literacy continue to be de facto excluded from jury duty in many counties across the country, though the exact number is unknown. In the case of New Mexico, for example, it was not until January 2000 that the state's supreme court ruled that the state could not exclude non–English-speaking U.S. citizens from jury duty.[13]

These two examples highlight the limitations of the discourse lamenting the contemporary status of citizenship and democracy, particularly those discussions that express a concern with "vanishing" or "disappearing" voters—or, as Robert Putnam (1995, 2000) often asserts, Americans are now "bowling alone." They overlook the fact that democratically instituted practices adopted by states contribute to the weakening of democracy and citizenship through exclusions of felons, non–English-speaking U.S. citizens, women, and others, produce lone bowlers. Moreover, the examples also foreground the intrinsic problem in arguments about the devaluing of citizenship by academics and journalists who lay the onus of the weakening of U.S. democracy on feminists, migrants, minorities, and the courts in expanding the principles of equality and due process. They do not take into account state and federal government actions to exclude U.S. citizens from carrying out practices of good citizenship.

EXCLUSION FROM VOTING

Noncitizen voting in the United States has had an ambivalent history.[14] Leon Aylsworth offers a succinct history of noncitizen voting up to 1926, a history that is not often noted:

> For the first time in over a hundred years, a national election was held in 1928 in which no alien in any state had the right to cast a vote for a candidate for any office—national, state, or local. Because of a reversal of opinion by the state supreme court, alien suffrage in Arkansas became illegal in 1926, and the last vestige of this political anomaly passed from our election system. . . . During the nineteenth century, the laws and constitutions of at least twenty-two states and territories granted aliens the right to vote. This tendency reached its greatest extent about 1875. . . . The movement to withdraw the right began with Illinois in 1848. (1931, 114)

Historian Donald Smith, writing about the 1860 election in the Northwest territories (i.e., Midwest), also notes the enfranchisement of foreign-born persons in the Midwest, and the use of the vote to induce migrants to settle in states with small populations. In some cases, noncitizen migrants were enfranchised within as few as four months after entering the territory and declaring their intent to become citizens (Smith 1932, 93). Whether they eventually naturalized or not was not the important thing. Elected officials, railroad companies, and land speculators were more interested in selling and occupying the available land; thus their declaration of their intention to petition for citizenship in an unspecified time in the future was sufficient to give them the vote. Raskin also observes that Congress at times promoted "alien suffrage," such as when it authorized the Northwest Ordinance of 1787, and when it authorized such persons to vote in the constitutional conventions of Ohio, Indiana, Michigan, and Illinois. The U.S. Supreme Court also took similar actions authorizing noncitizen participation (Raskin 1993a, 1423).

In Texas the change was made by statute in 1921, not in the Constitution. Prior to that year noncitizens as residents of a county could vote in both primaries and local elections. In 1921, however, voters in Texas decided to exclude noncitizens from voting in the primaries; the vote was 57,622 to 53,910, a 51.7 percent victory. The fact that the change was made in statute and not in the Constitution means that constitutionally Texas legislators could modify the relevant statute, or that municipalities and advocates could pressure legislators to make the necessary changes that would reestablish noncitizen suffrage at the local level. In contrast, the state of Arizona never allowed noncitizens to vote.

The case of Texas illustrates the interpretive nature of the voting exclusion in many states: noncitizens are explicitly excluded from voting in federal and state elections—that is, the primaries. As a consequence, noncitizens are typically excluded from voting in local elections by interpretation of what constitutes a state election.

Aylsworth's and Smith's accounts, as well as those of Ron Hayduk (2006), Jamin Raskin (1993a), Stanley Renshon (2009), and Gerald Rosberg (1977), point out the limitation of the contemporary hegemonic narrative that argues voting is and always has been a privilege of U.S. citizenship. Mark Krikorian, at the Center for Immigration Studies, for example, asserts that "voting is like a sacrament of America's civil religion, part of what makes you an American, and extending the vote to noncitizens eliminates one of the few remaining unique characteristics of being an American citizen" (2004). However, as the previous examples illustrate, Krikorian and others ignore history when they make such statements.

In the late 1960s, the issue of noncitizen voting in local elections began to receive some attention by scholars as well as municipalities. In 1968 New York City was the first large city to allow noncitizens to vote in local school board elections. Mayor Bloomberg disbanded the local school boards and thus also eliminated the suffrage that noncitizens possessed in that city. Though it should be noted that even when suffrage existed in New York

City, local political interest made it difficult for noncitizens to actually vote. For example, it was difficult for noncitizens to actually locate the right registration form, and almost no effort was made to inform eligible persons of their rights.[15]

In 1992 the Illinois legislature, in its effort to reform the Chicago School Board, disbanded the board and in its place created local school campus boards. The legislature authorized parents with children in the respective school to vote for members of the campus board, as well as run for a position on the board; it thus allowed informally authorized parent/guardians to vote. That same year, Takoma Park in Maryland amended its charter to allow all residents to vote in municipal elections. There are now five smaller municipalities in Maryland that also grant suffrage to noncitizens.

San Francisco also considered adopting noncitizen suffrage through Proposition F in 2004. Proposition F would have modified the city charter to allow residents eighteen years and older with a child in the school district to vote in school board elections. On November 2, 2004, the voters decided. The opponents won: 51.39 percent of voters opposed the measure, 48.61 percent supported it. In November 2010, San Francisco and Portland, Maine, included measures in their ballots that would expand noncitizen suffrage. In the former the provision would have allowed adult parents of public school children to vote in school board elections; in the latter it would have allowed legal immigrants to vote in city elections. In San Francisco, 54 percent of the voters rejected the measure, and in Portland 52 percent. A significant element in the results is not that the measures lost, but the proportion of supporters.

Exclusion from Livelihoods

Throughout most of the economic-political history of the United States, persons categorized as noncitizens have been excluded from multiple economic activities. The process simultaneously creates two outcomes. One, it reinforces the inclusiveness of juridical citizenship for those who possess it; those who can claim it gain access to livelihood activities. It also diminishes the competition from noncitizens wishing to participate in the desired activity. Economists call this process monopolistic practice or, more precisely, a special-privilege monopoly.[16] In addition, it reinforces the exclusiveness of citizenship for those who do not possess it. An ultimate effect is the creation of a kind of economic-political monopoly. Bryan S. Turner astutely observed that, sociologically, citizenship is a "method of distribution of resources" (1993a, xi), and thus it foregrounds two central factors of citizenship: creation of solidarity and conflict (1993b, 8).

Juridical citizenship, through its relationship to exclusions from entry, exclusions form naturalization, and exclusions from certain practices of citizenship, is transformed into a kind of monopoly created within the context of the power relations in the United States. In other words, the privileges we associate with juridical citizenship do not emerge in a vacuum, they are constituted through inclusions and exclusions for those protected by the special-privilege monopoly of citizenship. The examination of the patterns and practices of noncitizen exclusion from a wide range of livelihood activities, it is suggested, allows us to explore some of the processes involved in constituting the often taken for granted privileges associated with U.S. citizenship.

Currently noncitizens are excluded at the federal, state, and local level from various livelihood activities. At the federal level a few additions were made, largely in reaction to the September 11, 2001 events. Although states have over the past thirty years reduced the number of excluded occupations, many still exist (Plascencia, Freeman, and Setzler 2003). Limited scholarly attention has been given to trends in local restrictions that exclude noncitizens, such as "lawn-sprinkler installer" or "pesticide applicator." Francis Kalnay's *The New American* (1941) remains the last extensive work on the topic. While many things have changed in local licensure and certification, specific cases are only sporadically mentioned in the print media. Consequently, we have a fairly complete knowledge of federal restrictions, a partial knowledge of state restrictions, and very limited knowledge of local restrictions (Plascencia 2001; Plascencia, Freeman, and Setzler 2003).

I first note that historically noncitizens were excluded from what can be labeled ordinary to expected activities. An example of the former would be the case reported by the historian Abraham Hoffman. According to Hoffman, "In 1923 Pennsylvania passed a law demanding full citizenship for owners of dogs" (1974, 18). Since Hoffman does not say any more about the statute or rationale for its passage, one can only speculate what may have hounded Pennsylvania legislators to approve the law. This particular case also serves to illustrate that "the growth of [occupational] licensing in America has been a haphazard, uncoordinated, and chaotic process" (Shimberg, Esser, and Kruger 1973, 1). Shimber, Esser, and Kruger and others have pointed out that at times legislators sponsor a bill regarding an economic activity or license simply to please an individual or group. The Pennsylvania exclusion of noncitizens from owning dogs may have had a similar origin: perhaps its aim was to please a single constituent bothered by a noncitizen who bred dogs and may have been seen as a competitor, or simply a noncitizen neighbor who owned a noisy dog.

Another more familiar example of noncitizen exclusion is found in article 2, section 1, item 5 of the U.S. Constitution: "No person except a natural born Citizen, or a Citizen of the United States, at the time of the adoption of this Constitution, shall be eligible to the Office of the President." This exclusion is unique because the position of president is the only federal category that requires the occupant to be a "natural born Citizen." Neither senators, members of the House of Representatives, nor Supreme Court Justices must possess this birthright criterion. Moreover, while senators and representatives must be citizens of the United States, Supreme Court justices are not required by the Constitution to be U.S. citizens. This is a somewhat odd distinction given that the Supreme Court is one of the three branches of government. The presidential natural-born citizen provision, however, may change in the near future.[17]

In addition to the aforementioned exclusions, a multitude of other noncitizen exclusions exist that many take for granted. Some of these exclusions explicitly address noncitizens (e.g., the American Anthropological Association's Minority Dissertation Fellowship is limited to U.S. citizens, bail bondsmen in Texas), while others ostensibly address a different issue, such as language (mandating English for renters) or public safety (requiring a Social Security number to obtain a driver's license), yet are targeted at excluding certain categories of migrants.

Persons have been excluded from what economists label "property"— "the right to the future benefit of economic goods"—sometimes also labeled "property rights," because lack of juridical U.S. citizenship. Property rights encompass the ability to benefit from title to land (or its inheritance and disposition), the operation of a business, one's knowledge and skills, membership in a labor union, and an occupational license or certificate. Stated more succinctly, the ability to survive economically based on one's access to certain resources, including selling one's labor power. As noted, noncitizens are excluded from federal, state, and local property rights.

Federal Exclusions

Although many persons in the United States assume that most federal restrictions have existed for a long time, perhaps dating back to the founding of the nation, this is not the case. The principal action that prohibits noncitizens from federal employment is Executive Order 11935 (1976) enacted by President Gerald Ford. Thus, noncitizens have been barred from most federal jobs for less than forty years. The one notable exclusion, enacted in reaction to September 11, is the position of airport screener.

There exists, however, a notable irony in the scheme of federal exclusions: an exemption is granted to the military—military work is federally paid work but is not considered federal employment; it also is not considered work but service. Noncitizens are welcomed into military work; they cannot, however, be promoted to the rank of officer. Even informally authorized individuals are theoretically excluded (despite the fact that all males are required to register with the Selective Service System upon turning eighteen), an unknown number are currently on active duty (Plascencia, n.d. b. The combination of these two elements—excluding noncitizens as airport screeners and including noncitizens in the military—creates odd juxtapositions.

The one juxtaposition that comes to mind is a scene at the Austin airport in 2002. I took my daughter to the airport two hours before her flight, as required at the time, and saw a young, presumably Latino male standing in a military-style pose with an automatic rifle a few feet from a woman inspecting suitcases. As I witnessed the setting, it seemed ironic that the person with the weapon guarding the inspection area could have been a noncitizen, yet the weaponless person rummaging through luggage had to be a U.S. citizen. Who is performing the real national security work?

President Ford's exclusion of noncitizens from federal employment is not absolute. In 2000 and 2010, the Bureau of the Census was authorized to hire noncitizens as temporary census workers for the respective Decennial

Census. The temporary waiver allowed the inclusion of a significant number of noncitizens as federal employees. Subcontracting arrangements also facilitate the inclusion of noncitizens in federally funded work, at least until migration officials discover the person. Two recent examples are the discovery of an informally authorized person working on the White House grounds for a special events company, and the discovery of a crew of informally authorized persons repairing the USS *John F. Kennedy* at the Mayport Naval Station.

State Exclusions

States have been the principal actors in excluding noncitizens from what Supreme Court Justice Charles Evans Hughes labeled "the ordinary means of earning a livelihood" (1915).[18] The reason for this is the authority granted to the states under the juridical power relations between states and the federal government. Under article 1, section 8 of the U.S. Constitution (i.e., the commerce clause), the federal government retains the power to control international and interstate commerce, which has been interpreted as encompassing immigration, and states, under the Tenth Amendment (1791), can decide on matters not delegated to the federal government nor prohibited by it. Thus, states can govern resources, including occupational licenses, within their territories.

The types of exclusions and chronology of implementation carried out by states do not appear to follow a clear logic. Although a complete profile for a single state does not exist, the case of *Nyquist v. Mauclet* (1977) provides an informative list from 1871 to 1976 for New York. The attorneys for the plaintiffs compiled the information on noncitizen exclusion for licensed occupations; the data are summarized in table 3.1.

The table illustrates Shimberg, Esser and Kruger's (1973) suggestion that noncitizen livelihood restrictions, such as those in New York, appear to be a "haphazard, uncoordinated, and chaotic process." There were no wholesale introductions during World War I, the Great Depression, World War II, or the early part of the Cold War, although all of these periods were marked by phantasmatic fears and fantasies about foreign-born persons—aliens, enemy aliens, and disloyal aliens. Rather, it appears that New York legislators acted in a piecemeal fashion; for example, there were only three

TABLE 3.1

NEW YORK OCCUPATIONS REQUIRING CITIZENSHIP, 1871–1976

Year	Occupation/profession
1871	Attorney
1883	Pawnbroker
1885	Grand jury stenographer
1892	Plumbing inspector
1894	Laborer on public employment projects
1896	Liquor trafficker
1896	Certified public accountant
1899	Blind adult vendor of goods and newspapers
1909	Private investigator
1911	Certified shorthand reporter
1913	Ship masters, pilots and engineers
1914	Bank directors and trustees
1915	Architects
1917	State police officers
1918	Teachers
1920	Surveyors
1922	Operator of billiard and pocket pool halls
1923	Physician
1924	Pharmacist
1926	Real estate broker
1927	State trooper
1929	Embalmer
1931	Engineer
1933	Dentist
1938	Forest service guide
1938	Nurses
1939	Competitive classes in civil service

(*continued*)

TABLE 3.1

NEW YORK OCCUPATIONS REQUIRING CITIZENSHIP, 1871–1976 (*continued*)

Year	Occupation/profession
1940	Racing track pari-mutuel employee
1944	Funeral director
1956	Veterinarian
1956	Psychologist
1957	Dental hygienist
1958	Employee of private institution acquired by the state
1960	Landscape architect
1963	Chiropractor
1967	Masseurs and masseuses
1971	Physical therapist
1976	Animal health technician

Sources: Compiled from *Nyquist v. Mauclet* (1977), brief for Appellee Rabinovitch, 19–22; *Foley v. Connelie* (1978); and *Ambach v. Norwick* (1979). This table appears in Freeman et al. (2002).

sets of occupations enacted in the same year, there were significant gaps of time between some of the exclusions, and some restrictions seemed to affect a small number of persons (e.g., grand jury stenographer, blind adult vendor of goods and newspapers), while others encompassed a fairly large number of persons (e.g., teachers). In short, it does seem to be a "haphazard, uncoordinated, and chaotic process." The result is that for nearly a century the state of New York enacted legislation to exclude noncitizens from "the ordinary means of earning a livelihood." Moreover, since the attorneys focused their legal brief on occupations and professions, their list did not include other citizen-based restrictions, such as employment in local public works, civil service employment, or ownership of real property.

An important source of noncitizen exclusions implemented by states and local governments are the cases heard by the U.S. Supreme Court. Table 3.2 summarizes the principal property-rights cases (excluding

TABLE 3.2

PROPERTY-RIGHTS CASES HEARD BY THE U.S. SUPREME COURT, 1886–1984

Property right and case	Case summary

Use of public resources

Patsone v. Pennsylvania (1914)	**Issue:** Pennsylvania statute prohibiting noncitizens from owning a shotgun or rifle to kill wild game. **Decision:** State has the right to protect its natural resources, and natural resources are not protected under the treaty with Italy.
Takahashi v. Fish Commission (1948)	**Issue:** California statute denying commercial fishing license to persons "ineligible to citizenship" (i.e., Japanese). **Decision:** Supreme Court held statute violated the equal protection clause of the Fourteenth Amendment. A state has control over its natural resources; however, its control must respect the constitutional rights of persons.

Receiving a public benefit

Graham v. Richardson (1971)	**Issue:** Arizona statute requiring fifteen-year residency to be eligible for a combined federal and state funded program and Pennsylvania statute requiring citizenship for state-funded general assistance program. **Decision:** Both statutes held to violate equal protection guarantees and to encroach upon federal authority over immigration. "Alienage" classification is inherently suspect.
Nyquist v. Mauclet (1977)	**Issue:** New York statute excluding noncitizens from financial assistance in public universities. **Decision:** Statue violates equal protection clause of Fourteenth Amendment.
Plyler v. Doe (1982)	**Issue:** Texas statute allowing local school districts to exclude informally authorized children from public schools or to charge tuition for such students. **Decision:** Statute violates the equal protection of informally authorized children.

Public employment

Heim v. McCall (1915)	**Issue:** New York statute requiring citizenship and granting preference to citizens in local public works projects. **Decision:** Statute did not violate the Fourteenth Amendment or the treaty with Italy.

(*continued*)

TABLE 3.2

PROPERTY-RIGHTS CASES HEARD BY THE U.S. SUPREME COURT, 1886–1984
(*continued*)

Property right and case	Case summary
Crane v. New York (1915)	**Issue** and **Decision:** same as in *Heim v. McCall* (1915).
Sugarman v. Dougall (1973)	**Issue:** New York City civil service requirement that some categories be filled by U.S. citizens. **Decision:** Statute violates equal protection guarantee of the Fourteenth Amendment.

Private employment

Yick Wo v. Hopkins (1886)	**Issue:** San Francisco ordinance limiting the operation of laundries by Chinese. **Decision:** Immigrants are "persons," as used in the Constitution, and thus afforded the protection of the Fourteenth Amendment. Local ordinance, while neutral on the surface, was held to have discriminatory intent and as such violated the equal protection clause.
Truax v. Raich (1915)	**Issue:** Arizona statute requiring all employers of five or more employees to have 80 percent of workers be qualified electors or native-born citizens. **Decision:** In violation of the Fourteenth Amendment.
Asakura v. Seattle (1924)	**Issue:** Seattle ordinance requiring operators of pawnshops to be U.S. citizens. **Decision:** In violation of the Constitution and the treaty with Japan.
Clarke v. Deckenbach (1927)	**Issue:** Cincinnati ordinance requiring operators of pool and billiard rooms to be citizens. **Decision:** Valid since it is part of a state's police power to regulate "evil" places.

Professions and occupations

In re Griffith (1973)	**Issue:** Connecticut statute requiring citizenship of attorneys. **Decision:** Violates the Fourteenth Amendment.
Re Examining Board v. Flores de Otero (1976)	**Issue:** Puerto Rican statute requiring citizenship for licensure in common occupations. **Decision:** Violates the Fourteenth Amendment.
Foley v. Connelie (1978)	**Issue:** New York statute requiring citizenship for state troopers. **Decision:** Valid since it is related to the exercise of a state's police powers.

(*continued*)

TABLE 3.2

PROPERTY-RIGHTS CASES HEARD BY THE U.S. SUPREME COURT, 1886–1984
(*continued*)

Property right and case	Case summary
Ambach v. Norwick (1979)	**Issue:** New York statute requiring citizenship for public school teachers. **Decision:** Given their powers to regulate their "political community," states may justifiably require that public school teachers be citizens because of the inherently political dimension of public education.
Cabell v. Chávez-Salido (1982)	**Issue:** California statute requiring citizenship for probation officers. **Decision:** The right to impose citizenship-based requirements on positions related to the exercise of a state's police powers extends to include any "peace officer" whose primary function is the enforcement of law.
Bernal v. Fainter (1984)	**Issue:** Texas statute requiring citizenship for notary publics. **Decision:** Citizenship-based limitations violate the Fourteenth Amendment in appointments that are essentially clerical rather than political.

ownership of real property) heard by the Supreme Court from 1886 to 1984 related to the exclusion of noncitizens (in the post-1984 period, the Court has not explicitly addressed similar cases). The cases are divided into five property-rights resources: (1) use of public resources, (2) receiving a public benefit, (3) public employment, (4) private employment, and (5) professions and occupations.

As is shown in the case summaries, noncitizens successfully challenged municipalities and state governments in some cases and were not successful in others. The data in the table also illustrate the presence of nonspecific race/ethnic criterion, in so far as noncitizens of multiple nationalities are excluded (e.g., excluding noncitizens from New York City's civil service), while others explicitly exclude a specific racial/ethnic group, using the euphemism "ineligible to citizenship" to mean "Japanese," or excluding informally authorized children from Texas' public schools, which aimed to exclude Mexican-origin children. The data in the table also highlight the range of actions that municipalities and states took to grant special privileges (a method of distribution suggested by Turner [1993a]) to citizens by excluding noncitizens—including the privilege to possess a commercial fishing license, access publicly funded schooling, operate a laundry business, and receive a professional license to practice medicine or law.

At times, states underestimated the intelligence of the justices of the Supreme Court. In *Bernal v. Fainter* (1984), the attorneys representing the state of Texas argued that a notary public was a kind of officer of the court and that such persons performed actions on important legal documents (i.e., notarization). According to them, this type of legal function involved matters that "go to the heart of representative government." Thus, they concluded, the functions of notary publics should be reserved for U.S. citizens.

On an 8–1 vote, the Court rejected the state's argument (the lone dissenter was Judge Rehnquist). Judge Marshal wrote the Court's opinion and pointed out the following: Texas does not require a test or knowledge or proficiency on any activity carried by a notary public. The only state requirement is age, and thus anybody who reaches the specified age can become a notary public. The functions of a notary public are essentially clerical, and the state official granting the authority (i.e., the secretary of state) is not required to be a U.S. citizen.

This case illustrates that at times states defended their exclusion of noncitizens with a discourse about why it was important for citizens to perform the activity in question, and it was often grounded on either some sense of protecting the right of American citizens to perform the activity (i.e., economic protectionism from the competition of aliens), or a more general notion about protecting the public, which was ultimately a public safety concern regarding the danger that an alien worker might pose (the presumption being that resident noncitizens are not part of the public). Under this logic, local and state governments took action to exclude noncitizens from ordinary livelihoods such as collecting garbage, selling liquor, cutting hair, driving taxis, selling soda pops, and working at a pari-mutuel race track. This logic appears to be grounded in a distribution of resources for those possessing U.S. citizenship, as well as some imaginary fantasies about the potential danger posed by aliens. It also simultaneously has the effect of excluding noncitizens from the ordinary means of earning a livelihood.

Exclusion from Owning Land

The ownership and inheritance of real property, particularly agricultural land, has been prohibited for noncitizens. The best-known example is the implementation of alien land laws.[19] In the early 1900s, starting in California in 1913, states implemented land laws to protect citizens from the perceived unfair competition posed by Chinese and Japanese farmers, such as Chin Lung (also known as the "Potato King"), who represented one of the most successful entrepreneurs in the Sacramento–San Joaquin Delta. He began as a tenant farmer on 200 acres and later owned thousands of acres in California and Oregon, apparently posing an economic threat to white farmers.[20] Between 1913 and 1943, at least eleven states implemented similar anti-Asian land laws. Most of these exclusions relied on federal exclusionary language—"aliens ineligible for citizenship"—so states did not have to explicitly deny Chinese, Japanese, or Asians, including South Asians.

Since the 1940s, two additional campaigns to exclude noncitizens from ownership or inheritance surfaced. According to Mark Shapiro (1993, 222–223), during the Cold War several states passed legislation to limit inheritance, and in the 1970s state legislators, alarmed about foreign investment, enacted legislation to limit the amount of land and the location of the land considered for purchase. Based on his analysis, Shapiro concludes that by the early 1990s "almost half of the states have laws that, to varying degrees, restrict the rights of aliens to own real property. These laws range from complete prohibitions to simple reporting requirements. . . . six states still restrict resident aliens to varying degrees. The most prohibitive restrictions involve the acquisition of agricultural land" (1993, 223).

Citizenship and property rights also intersected the sociopolitical position of women. Coverture rules and citizenship status affected a woman's dower rights and thus her ability to acquire and inherit land. According to Polly Price (2000, 62–63), naturalization would allow a married woman to take on a right of dower, yet a noncitizen married woman, even if married to a natural-born citizen, would be excluded from dower rights in the nineteenth century.

The survival of anti-Asian land laws recently stimulated a debate on the merits of such exclusions. In 2003 Florida legislators were apprised of the 1926 provision that restricts ownership, inheritance, and disposition of real property on the part of "foreigners who are not eligible to become citizens of the United States." In response, a state senator (Democrat) drafted a resolution to remove the provision; however, a Republican senator amended the resolution to exclude "illegal aliens" from owning land. The addition of such a provision, it was recognized, would likely impact certain migrant communities in Florida, including Cuban, Haitian, Jamaican, and Nicaraguan. At the end of the debate the original resolution was withdrawn and the matter left as it was. Longstanding efforts to restrict noncitizens from owning, inheriting, and disposing of property remain. The property rights of citizens are thus protected through the exclusion of noncitizens from those rights.

Exclusion from Labor Unions

The final example of an exclusion of noncitizens from the ordinary means of earning a livelihood is the past exclusion from labor unions. Over the past thirty years, labor unions have become less exclusive of women, African Americans, Latinos, and noncitizens. Within the last eleven years, the AFL-CIO has made a substantial shift in their position on migrants and migration. Some of their most important recent victories, such as the janitors strike in the Los Angeles area, principally involved Latino migrants, including informally authorized migrants. Notably, however, certain unions within the AFL-CIO, such as the Service Employees International Union and United Electrical Workers historically accepted noncitizens, including informally authorized within their ranks. This recent stance, however, was not fully embraced in the World War II period. Clyde Summers's (1946) detailed examination of the constitutions and bylaws of 185 major international unions shows that 32 international unions explicitly excluded noncitizens from their ranks. The list included major unions such as the Teamsters, Carpenters and Joiners, Boilermakers, Hodcarriers, Musicians, and others. The combined membership of the 32 unions was close to 3 million at the time. Consequently, the union level wages of U.S. citizens belonging to one of the unions were protected while simultaneously excluding noncitizens from earning such wages.

In summary, this chapter has sought to contextualize citizenship in the United States through an examination of the ongoing political actions of the federal, state, and local government and the labor unions to privilege U.S. citizens and augment the valuation of citizenship. This move of inclusiveness transforms citizenship into a kind of special-privilege monopoly and resource distribution mechanism. However, like all monopolies, the privilege bestowed on one entity comes at a cost to another entity. In the case at hand, the privilege and inclusiveness granted to citizens is inseparable from the disadvantages imposed on noncitizens—part of the power relations within which both citizens and noncitizens are embedded.

The subjectivization of both noncitizens and citizens is grounded within the dynamic created by the inclusion/exclusion process. Citizens take for granted their juridical citizenship and the privileges it allows without necessarily recognizing how they are forged. In other words, they misrecognize the social relations in the fundamental concept of citizen. Moreover, there seems to be a tacit acceptance of the difference that separates them from noncitizens. Citizens are involved in requesting, promoting, and legislating the exclusion of noncitizens. The natural-born citizens naturalize their citizenship.

Noncitizens recognize the difference and privilege of citizenship and struggle to overcome the difference—not unlike the process described by Hegel and elaborated by Alexander Kojève regarding the *herr-knecht* (master-servant/master-slave) relationship. Noncitizens have repeatedly used the juridical system to contest their exclusion from the ordinary means of earning a livelihood. Moreover, it seems that the very process of exclusion increases their valuation and desire to be represented. As the Iraq War has shown, a significant number of noncitizens volunteer to carry out one of the most highly valued activities of U.S. citizenship: to enlist in the military and accept the duty to kill and possibly die for the United States.

In order to understand the exclusion of noncitizens from the ordinary means of earning a livelihood, one must also take into account other exclusions that precede and coexist with these. The exclusions on entry, naturalization, and certain practices of citizenship, such as voting, inscribe and reinscribe the political status of noncitizen. These exclusions are not absolute: the state and individuals (before being constructed as noncitizens) find ways to exempt, waive, or bypass them.

CHAPTER 4

The Making of Citizens

PROMOTING AND SCHOOLING

The path to citizenship is diverse and reflects a combination of individual and external efforts that promote the acquisition of citizenship and assist migrants in the process, including direct local actions encouraging permanent residents to apply for citizenship and citizenship classes for those who need additional assistance. Although these components are an important bridge to citizenship, scholars have allocated scant attention to them.

Among the participants in the citizenship classes I taught, all individuals held jobs, some more than one. Although they had family responsibilities, they attended a weekday evening or Saturday morning citizenship class and listened to cassettes or watched videos that I provided on the 100 Citizenship Questions. They also studied the Spanish-English printed version of the questions. Most of the adults took the citizenship class more than once, some several times.

Citizenship advocacy groups, or corporate and government sponsors, sometimes create irony and conflicts within the promotion of citizenship. Local conflicts tend to reduce the effectiveness of promotional campaigns, as well reduce the number of eligible persons ultimately assisted in obtaining U.S. citizenship. The overall process encompassing these efforts, particularly citizenship classes, is similar to the K–12 schooling process. Both are concerned with the biopolitical project of incubating good citizens and producing governable subjects loyal to the United States. This process of governmentality is generated in the interaction between the demands of the state, the mediation of local organizations and individuals, the subjects' pursuit of their own goals, and the promise that citizenship will fulfill some of their needs and desires.[1]

Dominant discourses become most productive when they make sense to and meet the needs of the individuals involved, which lends efficacy to the creation of subjectivities (subject-making). Those participating in citizenship classes desire citizenship, want to be good citizens, and want their children to be good citizens. Contrary to the assumptions and arguments of English-only advocates, they are aware of the importance of English to employment, job mobility, and everyday life in the United States. Most would like to be more proficient in English and want their children to be proficient English speakers as well.

Moreover, their migration to the United States and improvements in their individual and familial economic well-being, despite some experiences of prejudice and discrimination, creates a sense of appreciation and respect for the United States—a foundation for building fidelity toward the country. As one hardworking migrant said to me, "Donde gano el pan, esa es mi patria" (where I earn my bread, that's my nation). In "What Is an American?" Jean St. John de Crèvecoeur (1782, 63), a naturalized U.S. citizen at the time, wrote that the motto of all migrants, particularly poor migrants was "ubi panis ibi patria." Poor migrants anchor their allegiance in the nation-state that offers them economic opportunity—a pragmatic nationalism that starts with a simple appreciation of access to jobs and a livelihood.

Adult citizenship classes, as guided by the federal 100 Citizenship Questions, commonly referred to as simply the 100 Questions (*las cien preguntas*), represent an elementary interpretation of U.S. history and civics, replete with simple facts, great male heroes, and a rational and efficient government. Thus, adults in citizenship classes and children in elementary school are both subjected to, and subjects of, a parallel discourse about the state and a parallel aim to foster the proper fidelities toward its institutions and its leaders.

Contextualizing IRCA and Naturalization

Between 1972 and 1986, an acrimonious debate on several immigration issues was waged. Although the intensity waxed and waned, a national concern with the size of the informally authorized population and its possible negative consequences on U.S.-born workers and the economy, as well as its utilization of public assistance programs, persisted during that period. Two solutions to these issues were proposed and debated. The one advocated by those wishing to reduce migration and the alleged negative impact of migrants was to implement sanctions against employers who hired persons not authorized to work. This proposal was based on the premise that by reducing the economic incentive for migration—that is, jobs—migrants, particularly informally authorized migrants, would leave and other aspiring migrants would lose interest in coming to the United States. Secondarily, it was argued that employer sanctions needed to be supplemented with greater border enforcement, particularly on the nation's southern border. The border strategy would prevent further entry—a way, as President Reagan said, to "regain control of the border."

Those generally supportive of migrants opposed the implementation of employer sanctions without a simultaneous effort to formalize the residency status of those already here. Their solution was to grant legalization (also referred to as amnesty) to the many residents who had entered without the necessary documentation or had overstayed their visas and become integrated within local communities. The premise of the second solution was that the nation needed to recognize the roots that many informally authorized migrants had established in the United States, as well as their economic contribution to the nation's economy. After all, it was suggested, many had been here over a decade without detection, most had U.S.-born children, many owned homes, and most were law-abiding taxpayers, and so it would be inhumane to uproot so many families and their U.S.-citizen children.

The 1982 U.S. Supreme Court decision in *Plyler v. Doe* ordering public schools (K–12) to enroll all children, irrespective of their migration status, played a role in the debate. In broad terms, the Court acknowledged and gave a degree of protection to persons whom the first group claimed had no right to be here and posed a financial cost to local communities. The second group supported the decision and used it to buttress their argument for seeking a similar protection for the parents and non-school-age family members. The debate since 2001 on what became known as the DREAM Act has been about the juridical status and higher education of the youth who benefited from the *Plyler* decision.

After fourteen years of debate on the two pivotal provisions, Congress passed the Immigration Reform and Control Act (IRCA) in November 1986, and President Reagan signed it. The compromise that emerged included provisions for penalizing employers who knowingly hire persons not authorized to work, and granting legalization to persons who could prove that they had resided in the United States since 1982, as well as to those who could provide evidence that they had worked in the harvesting of perishable crops for a specified number of workdays. It also augmented resources for border (i.e., the Mexico-U.S. border) control.

Over 3 million persons came forward and applied for the opportunity to remain in the country and to work without fearing deportation by the Immigration and Naturalization Service (INS). The total number of legalization applicants included about 1.8 million able to document their residency in the United States since January 1982 and about 1.2 million who furnished evidence of having worked in the nation's agricultural fields. Of the initial group of applicants, about 2.7 million were granted temporary residency and later permanent residency. The 2.7 million figure, though it is the official number cited by CIS and the Office of Immigration Statistics (both in the Department of Homeland Security), is not the final figure due to two class-action suits regarding the original processing of legalization applications. An additional 60,000 to 400,000 persons may still be granted legalization due to legal challenges.[2]

Texas, California, New York, Florida, and Illinois accounted for 85 percent of the population that applied for legalization. After California, Texas had the largest number of legalization applicants (almost 15 percent of the total for the nation, or 440,712). With the second largest number of legalization applicants, Texas received the second largest amount of funds available through the State Legalization Impact Assistance Grants (SLIAG) program. SLIAG was created by Congress to reimburse states and local governments for the impact that the legalization program would have on educational, public health, and social services utilized by eligible legalization applicants. Funds were available from about 1988 to 1991.

The importance of the SLIAG program is that it funded the initial set of English/civics (also sometimes referred to as amnesty) classes that persons applying on the basis of time had to take in order to show proficiency in civics and English when applying for permanent residency. Some of the current entities providing citizenship classes, such as school districts, community colleges, and community-based organizations, entered the adult migrant schooling enterprise in response to the generous funds made available by SLIAG. Some of the citizenship promoters and advocacy organizations discussed in this book also participated in assisting eligible applicants to apply for legalization. Thus, the IRCA-related events are part of the background to subsequent citizenship efforts.

Although the pre-IRCA debate on employer sanctions versus legalization sounds quite dated, and chronologically it is, politically it has contemporary reverberations. In the late 1990s and early 2000s, several advocacy groups and some members of Congress renewed the call for a new legalization program. The events of September 11, 2001, however, reduced the immediacy of their concern. Now with some distance from those events, the issue has reemerged. However, the pivotal provisions are now enforcement, a guest worker program, and legalization. On May 12, 2005, Senators John McCain (R-AZ) and Ted Kennedy (D-MA) introduced their proposal, Secure America and Orderly Immigration Act, which includes such provisions. Shortly after the McCain-Kennedy bill was introduced, a second migration proposal was filed that excluded legalization but included a guest worker provision. In September 2010, Senators Leahy (D-VT) and Robert Menendez (D-NJ) introduced the Comprehensive Immigration Reform Act of 2010, which includes enforcement components, a temporary worker provision, and a legalization measure. Other bills introduced in 2011 focus principally on enforcement. In the current debates, both proponents and opponents rely on the debates leading to, and experience with, the IRCA legalization programs. From 2005 to 2011, the question of whether there should be a "path to citizenship" (i.e., an IRCA-like legalization program) in a comprehensive immigration reform has been a contentious issue for members of Congress.

The people who applied and were granted legalization were classified as temporary residents (a new immigrant category created by IRCA) and given a red card. Such individuals then had to apply within eighteen months for permanent residency (a green card). Individuals who applied on the basis of time (i.e., the January 1982 threshold) as part of the application for permanent residency had to show evidence of meeting the English/civics requirement; those who applied on the basis of agricultural work did not.

One of the ways that residency aspirants could meet the English/civics requirement, and the one close to half chose (U.S. INS 1990), was to enroll in authorized English/civics classes and obtain a course of study certificate, generally based on meeting the number of required hours of instruction.

School districts, community colleges, and other entities saw the opportunity afforded by the SLIAG funds and began providing English/civics classes to the new temporary residents. Most of the persons who enrolled in the citizenship classes I taught had participated in such classes. The important points are that the student desiring citizenship had to again prove their knowledge of English and civics (i.e., U.S. history and government structure) as part of the citizenship application process, and a segment of students still struggled to become more proficient in English more than five years later.

Persons granted permanent residency had to wait five years (or three years if married to a U.S. citizen) to apply for naturalization. Of the 2.7 million persons granted permanent residency under the legalization provisions of IRCA, 36 percent (957,000) had been granted U.S. citizenship by 2003. Sixty-eight percent of these (650,760) were born in Mexico. A significant number of those who obtained permanent residency through the legalization programs became eligible to apply for naturalization in 1994. By 2009, the most recent year reported, 53 percent of all those who applied on the basis of time had naturalized, while only 34 percent of those who applied on the basis of agricultural work had done so (Baker 2010). These two elements, the number of persons eligible in 1994 due to IRCA and the proportion from Mexico, played an important role in creating the pool of potential applicants in Arizona, California, and Texas.

NATURALIZATIONS: 1908 TO 2010

Although a considerable amount has been written about naturalization, here I focus on the number of persons granted U.S. citizenship. Between 1943 and 1944, more than 300,000 persons were granted U.S. citizenship, and in 1944 the number exceeded 400,000. The contrast is quite marked when compared to the early 1950s, when less than 100,000 persons were naturalized. The 1990s and 2005–2010 represent major shifts from preceding decades. Table 4.1 summarizes the pattern for those naturalized in

TABLE 4.1

PERSONS NATURALIZED IN ARIZONA, CALIFORNIA, TEXAS, AND
THE UNITED STATES, 1990–2010

Year	Arizona	California	Texas	U.S.	Percentage from Mexico	Number from Mexico
1990	2,152	61,736	24,529	267,586	40.8	109,065
1991	2,090	125,661	16,266	307,394	7.4	22,878
1992	3,037	52,411	17,631	239,664	5.4	12,873
1993	2,548	68,100	26,403	313,590	7.5	23,615
1994	3,894	118,567	25,148	429,123	10.8	46,169
1995	4,059	171,285	32,209	485,720	16.8	81,655
1996	6,838	378,014	57,970	1,040,991	24.5	254,988
1997	3,767	187,432	39,172	596,010	23.9	142,569
1998	4,105	154,793	30,862	461,169	24.4	112,442
1999	8,737	284,071	58,849	837,418	24.8	207,750
2000	10,755	300,662	66,800	886,026	21.4	189,705
2001	8,239	202,668	43,287	606,259	16.9	102,736
2002	6,064	149,213	42,767	572,646	13.3	76,310
2003	7,218	135,599	28,638	462,435	12.1	55,946
2004	6,500	145,593	35,417	537,151	11.9	63,840
2005	6,785	170,489	38,553	604,280	12.8	77,089
2006	9,707	152,836	37,835	702,589	12.0	83,979
2007	12,091	181,684	53,032	660,477	18.5	122,258
2008	24,055	297,909	82,129	1,046,539	22.2	231,815
2009	12,377	179,754	54,024	743,715	15.0	111,630
2010	10,340	129,354	49,699	619,913	10.8	67,062

Sources: U.S. Department of Justice 1998, 2000; U.S. Department of Homeland
Security 2011, tables 20, 21, 22, supplemental table 1.

Arizona, California, Texas, and the U.S. as a whole, plus the share of the U.S. total from Mexico.

Table 4.1 highlights the important trend that began in 1993, markedly increased in 1994, and led to the unprecedented number of over 1 million new U.S. citizens in 1996 and 2008. The number of people who became U.S. citizens in the intervening years exceeded the previous historical peak in 1944. Although declines after 2008 are significant, in both 2009 and 2010 over 600,000 migrants were granted citizenship. A total of 2.2 million migrants from Mexico became U.S. citizens from 1990 to 2010.

Scholars and journalists have hypothesized several explanations for the surge in interest among permanent residents to seek U.S. citizenship, which led to the 1996 and 2008 peaks and continued interest. Frequently cited reasons are the following: (1) the mandatory green card replacement program initiated in 1992 by INS; (2) the antimigrant rhetoric initiated in California in 1993 that led to the passage of Proposition 187 in November 1994 and the subsequent antimigrant discourse that surfaced throughout the nation; (3) the completion of five years of residency in 1994 by persons who received their permanent residency based on legalization under IRCA; (4) the antipermanent resident debate in 1995–1996 that led to the passage of the 1996 Personal Responsibility and Work Reconciliation Act (PRWORA); and (5) the passage of the 1996 Illegal Immigration and Immigrant Responsibility Act (IIIRA).

Less commented upon is an important irony among the factors that stimulated the efforts to acquire U.S. citizenship. California's Governor Pete Wilson and Proposition 187 seemed to have accomplished more in a short period of time than all the years, dollars, and energy that multiple organizations, such as the National Association of Latino Elected and Appointed Officials and many other local groups, have devoted to citizenship promotion campaigns.[3] The 1993–1994 debates and passage of Proposition 187 led a large number of permanent residents in California to take steps to acquire citizenship. In fact, in 1996 alone, 278,014 migrants were granted citizenship in California; the importance of this can be appreciated in light of the fact that the nation's single-year peak was 441,979 in 1944. The 1996 figure in this one state represent 63 percent of the national total in 1944.

The irony is that the efficacy of a positive message regarding the importance of citizenship—its many benefits, including the right to vote, to become a full member of society, and access to federal jobs—was less than that of negative messages and actions. Researchers have not yet fully examined why permanent residents responded the way they did, given that Proposition 187 was explicitly targeted at informally authorized persons and not at permanent residents. It also is evident that in the aftermath of Arizona's Proposition 200 (November 2004), there has been a continuing interest in attaining citizenship. As shown in table 4.1, from 2005 to 2010 a greater number of individuals have obtained citizenship in each year than in 2004.[4]

An important policy debate in the mid-1990s was the issue of the distribution of public resources and the determination of whether citizens and noncitizens were equally deserving of such resources. The ending of welfare as we know it, through President Clinton's enactment of the 1996 PRWORA marked a major policy shift. While the focus of the migrant debate up to the late 1980s had focused on the health and human services costs of informally authorized persons, PRWORA shifted the debate by eliminating most federally funded benefits for five years for permanent residents (excluding Cubans).

Although overlooked by policy and migration experts, PRWORA not only eliminated permanent residents from the deserving column, it simultaneously elevated the value of U.S. citizenship. This illustrates what Giorgio Agamben suggests with the concept of double movement (2000, 29–34), a simultaneous biopolitical exclusion and inclusion. Lawful permanent residents (LPRs) were the subjects of a dual violence of exclusion. The nation-state had granted LPRs the privilege to enter and indefinitely reside in the United States and receive equal protection under the Constitution, yet PRWORA disavowed that protection by asserting a heightened distinction. Secondly, at least in terms of public assistance benefits, LPRs were placed in equal position to illegal/undocumented migrants, as both were excluded by the distribution of resources function of citizenship. The exclusion simultaneously reinforced an inclusion. We as citizens had our citizenship valorized through the exclusion of the alien, or more correctly, using Weber's observation, the metic (semicitizen)—those persons occupying the midpoint between alien (outsider) and citizen. Our privileged political position as deserving persons was reinscribed within the fundamental concept of citizenship.

IIRIRA, labeled by one Mexican American migration attorney as the Mexican Exclusion Act, also has an important connection to citizenship. It allows the revocation and removal of permanent residents if they have been convicted of specified crimes, even if they have served prison time for the offense and it took place decades before. In fostering the cancellation of permanent residency for those convicted of certain crimes, IIRIRA has had two important effects. First, it modifies the common understanding of "permanent." Individuals who believe that their possession of permanent residency means that they are here to stay now have to reassess what "permanent" means. Secondly, it indirectly valorizes birthright citizenship. While permanent residency can be cancelled, and procedures exist to cancel naturalization (denaturalization), birthright citizenship remains a largely protected status.

The continued high number of citizenship applications in the post-1996 period, while partially stimulated by the earlier noted five factors, has some distinct motivators. The primary factor has been the post September 11, 2001, enforcement actions taken by the Justice Department, particularly the FBI, with the support of state and local law enforcement entities. One target has been foreign-looking persons, principally of Arab descent, but also Muslims in general. The passage of the U.S.A. Patriot Act has reduced the privacy and other civil liberties of individuals and has been the FBI's key tool to investigate migrants and detain persons suspected of supporting terrorist groups. A secondary factor has been tighter border and airport control measures that complicate matters for noncitizens reentering the United States. The possession of U.S. citizenship, while not guaranteeing protection against additional scrutiny, at least can potentially reduce the level of scrutiny. Consequently, some individuals have recognized the clear advantage of possessing U.S. citizenship and have opted to more quickly acquire it.

In summary, the IRCA legalization efforts, the implementation of SLIAG-funded English/Civics classes, the antimigrant rhetoric, and the increasing valorization of U.S. citizenship have been part of the context within which citizenship promotion and citizenship classes have operated in the past. The annual growth of permanent residents, based on new arrivals and those already residing in the United States, of about 1 million for the past few years means that the pool of eligible new citizens is substantial. Consequently, current promotion and assistance efforts have the potential to assist a significant number of migrants who wish to obtain citizenship.

Promoting Citizenship

The promotion of citizenship is not a singular or consistent activity. It encompasses a broad range of activities, from informal encouragement among coworkers, friends, or relatives to large-scale organized efforts.

Through my involvement with several groups engaged in migration issues in Austin and Phoenix, I was able to attend several local events aimed at encouraging eligible permanent residents to apply for citizenship. My discussion of conflicts within these efforts to promote and assist citizenship aspirants are not aimed at fostering a distinction between good and bad efforts. Rather, it has to do more with the recognition of the multiple power relations that organizations and individuals, including researchers trying to examine events taking place, are embedded in. All of the individuals involved in the activities described here are trying to do good and make a positive difference in the lives of migrants interested in citizenship. However, they and the researcher bring their own perspectives and experiences to bear and in doing so become engaged in negotiating and shaping actions and in defining what "citizenship" is.[5]

Austin Citizenship Day Fair

While attending a meeting of a local organization, Adelante, a staff person (Elsa Caso) announced an upcoming citizenship workshop. Adelante is an organization involved in social justice advocacy and some direct services to migrants, including legal assistance. It was announced that Justice in Austin (JA) had contacted Adelante, some other local organizations that provide legal assistance to migrants, and some attorneys to cosponsor a citizenship fair to assist migrants wanting to petition for U.S. citizenship, and that Adelante was going to participate in the event.

JA is an organization that is both respected and cautiously approached by other organizations. It is involved in a number of social justice issues and can claim several successful efforts. About three years prior, JA made the decision to add the issue of immigration to its list of advocacy concerns, an issue that they defined as important and that they could bring their experience and expertise to bear on. Moreover, the attention to the promotion of the acquisition of citizenship dovetailed well with their broader interest in promoting electoral participation. Linking both issues—increasing the number of citizens and increasing electoral participation—was a positive strategic decision.

Some local organizations that are more focused on migration issues are cautious about JA because they feel that although it is an overall effective and broadly respected organization, once it adds an issue to its plate, it seems to claim ownership over the issue, and, in addition, some feel that it seems to be relatively fixed on how it goes about addressing local issues.

In small and medium size cities such as Austin, it is common to find a significant degree of overlap in the boards of directors of similarly oriented advocacy and service providers. The case of Adelante and JA reflected this pattern. Consequently, collaboration among organizations is at times partly driven by the overlap in leadership. The collaboration announced by Caso was not made with much enthusiasm.

In a private conversation after the meeting, Caso reiterated that she clearly saw the importance of helping eligible persons complete their application for citizenship and decided that it was a worthwhile event in which to participate. Yet she had her reservations about actually participating as a cosponsor with JA. The overlap of a key individual in both organizations made the invitation by the JA staff person difficult for her to turn down. So she reluctantly made arrangements with Adelante staff to prepare for the upcoming citizenship fair.

Scheduled from 9 a.m. to 2 p.m. on a Saturday at the hall of a local church (St. Augustine), the fair began with an orientation meeting with potential applicants. They conducted initial screening interviews and then held a second meeting the following month, where the actual N-400 applications would be completed, including photographs. After talking to some of the attendees, I surmised that they were not advised to bring necessary documentation, money orders, etc.

JA staff, from what I later learned from Caso, said they would take charge of the recruitment of attendees and would use their network to generate the crowd. The impression was that the other organizations did not need to publicize the event. Caso suggested that the message was more like, "Don't invite your people, since we are inviting from our network." Thus, the cosponsors did not publicize the event.

On a pleasant fall day in Austin, I arrived at the fair early, a cup of coffee in hand and ready to lend a hand. Inside St. Augustine Church some of the staff from the participating organizations were busy setting up about 100–125 chairs in the middle of the hall. A few single adults and some families were waiting at the sides of the room. Gradually more staff and volunteers arrived. At the front of the room was a podium draped with a Justice in Austin banner. At about 9:30 the moderator, a young Euro-American woman with JA, announced in Spanish that the meeting was ready to start and asked everyone to take a seat; she then repeated the message in English.

She welcomed the audience and introduced the individuals from the organizations cohosting the event (four in addition to JA) and two private migration attorneys. Thirty-five people were in the audience, including volunteers, staff from the participating organizations, and me. I estimated that about ten were staff or volunteers. Most attendees were Latinos, likely of Mexican origin (one couple was probably from Eastern Europe, but they left early).

The moderator had us break up into four to five groups around tables at the sides of the room. A Latino volunteer with JA facilitated my group of about seven adults and one child. He asked us to introduce ourselves and then, without much introduction as to the purpose of the small group, he launched into his first question: "¿Por qué es importante ciudadaña?" (*ciudadaña* is not a word; it should have been *ciudadanía*). He expected the individuals to explain why citizenship is important; instead, several participants looked at each other for clues as to what exactly was being asked. In keeping with the politeness that is often exhibited by working-class Latinos, no one corrected him. However, after a period of silence, one man asked, "Why is it important to become a U.S. citizen?" The facilitator responded yes. After another pause, an older woman spoke up: "Hay mas oportunidad estar [*sic*] aquí" (There are more opportunities here). The facilitator then asked whether voting and sponsoring family members were part of becoming a U.S. citizen. Several individuals said yes. The moderator then explained that he was taking notes and would like someone from the group to report what the group had come up with.

The facilitator came back to his question and waited for others to add their comments. A man added "lo mismo" (the same). A younger woman seemingly more fluent in English added "justice, freedom, vote, do anything they want, exercise your civil rights." Some of the other comments were "celebrarlo, es muy importante" (it is very important to celebrate it); "votar" (to vote); "ayudar a otras personas" (assist other persons); "mas oportunidad, derechos de libertad" (more opportunities, civil liberties).

The brainstorming was interrupted by an older woman trying to make sense of what was going on. She bravely asked, "¿Y qué ayuda van a tener hoy?" (And what assistance is going to be provided today?). This was an important question given that neither the sponsors nor the facilitator had specified the objective of the day's workshop. The question had the effect of terminating the brainstorming and moved the discussion to a description of what was planned.

It was then noted by the facilitator that the focus of the day was to initiate screening interviews for those who were interested in applying for citizenship, that the organizations that were cosponsoring the event and the private attorneys were going to carry out the interviews, and that in the following month those eligible to apply (and, though it was not stated, those who had the money to pay for the application) would return and receive assistance with their application. By the time the facilitator had finished describing the plan for the fair (about forty-five minutes after the group had started), the small groups were called to end their discussions and reconvene as a whole group. Representatives from each of the small groups reported their list of items to the whole group. Most of the items were similar to the ones noted in the group in which I participated.

For the remainder of the day, a representative from each of the organizations spoke briefly on a topic related to applying for citizenship, such as the importance of being current with IRS tax payments, being current on child support payments, and being truthful about any interaction with law enforcement entities. While the presentations were being made, I estimated that about five to eight people left, including the Eastern European couple. My guess is that the presentations were probably too long and too numerous. The eighteen to twenty individuals still present were directed to one of the rooms set aside for the interviews. A couple of the staff, including one person affiliated with JA, commented that it was too bad so few people showed up.

The second phase of the fair was scheduled a month later and was also held at St. Augustine Church. The cosponsoring organizations and one of the private attorneys at the first meeting returned. Elsa Caso, staff from the other three organizations, and the private attorney made several comments regarding their disappointment with what was scheduled for the day: only about seven to ten persons actually came to complete the application. The number of staff and volunteers, ten to twelve, was greater than the number of citizenship applicants. Part of the disappointment was not only with having to get up early on a Saturday morning, but in order to start at 9 a.m., staff had to arrive about thirty minutes before and make several trips from their cars to the hall to bring in laptop computers, wireless connectors, printers, a camera, forms, and related materials. Caso wryly noted, "the seven to ten individuals could have simply gone to the office to complete their application." Instead, she had gone through all this.

The results of the Austin Citizenship Day Fair underscores some of the issues and conflicts that can surface in local efforts to assist migrants, and which ultimately limit the number of people assisted in petitioning for citizenship. One issue is the common problem of power relations among local organizations, which generally manifest themselves in questions of turf. Justice in Austin does not have the expertise, nor does it provide direct assistance on citizenship, yet because of the organization's general importance in the community and broad involvement, and the politics of overlapping leadership among organizations, it obtained the agreement of direct service providers to cosponsor the event and provide citizenship assistance to individuals. JA's role, which they could take credit for, was to coordinate and convene an event to assist migrants in applying for citizenship.

Another issue was the limited publicity given to the event. JA's insistence on recruiting individuals from within its network ultimately resulted in a small audience attending. Since it was really JA's event, the organization did not want others to extend invitations. In early 2004, in contrast, an event hosted at another church to inform migrants (particularly informally authorized persons) about President Bush's guest worker announcement drew an overflow crowd of 300–500. This event, however, was publicized through radio announcements, newspapers, and fliers. All of the same organizations (with the exception of one), and one of the same migration attorneys, at the citizenship fair participated at this event. Justice in Austin did not.

The third issue is the unequal power relations between the participating organizations and its intended audience. Attendees at times have to tolerate the agendas and processes that organizations feel are appropriate (e.g., small group brainstorming), even when they do not seem to make sense. I am not suggesting that such activities are not valuable. Certainly efforts aimed at creating dialogue, reflection, and a process to reach consensus have merit. However, such exercises need to be mediated with the agendas and interest of the people being asked to participate. The woman who interrupted the process to ask "¿Y qué ayuda van a tener hoy?" not only illustrates that migrants seeking assistance can assert themselves and interrupt other agendas, but also points to the practical priorities that individuals may have. I do not take her comment to imply that she was saying that citizenship is not important and that it is not worth talking about, even if in an abstract form, but that her immediate concern was with how she was going to get closer to obtaining it. It was a practical, pragmatic concern.

My participation in three citizenship application sessions in Phoenix allowed me to experience two different approaches to assisting applicants. Two of these were organized by the same entity and were exceedingly well-organized events. The organization had a list of who would attend, documents each applicant should bring, and the exact amounts of money orders needed. The volunteer assistants, including myself, attended a training workshop on the completion of the N-400. Although I already helped to complete several applications, the training session was nonetheless useful, as there are ongoing changes in the form and rules. On the actual day of the event, we completed close to 100 applications and the event ended about noon. I assisted with about five applications, each ten pages in length and requiring a significant amount of detail, including all dates of departures and arrivals to and from the United States. Sometimes complex questions would arise, and I would have to speak with the attorney on hand.

A second event that I participated in was quite different from the others. With a crowd of close to 150 people to complete their N-400s, no communication had taken place between the organization and the citizenship aspirants. Individuals were there to apply but had not brought the necessary documents. Consequently, I started several N-400s but only completed about two. Despite the disorganization of the event, the organizers had no interest in collaborating with other organizations. They saw their political positions as different, making such an effort undoable. From my interaction with the first organization, it is my sense that the feeling is mutual.

The dynamics at the two cities were different, but at both places the distinctions and power relations among organizations impeded their ability to assist migrants pursuing citizenship.

Houston Citizenship Promotion

I originally did not plan to include Houston as part of the research for this book. However, after reading an article that appeared in a Houston newspaper regarding a unique collaboration there that involved CIS, organized labor, several Latino community-based organizations, and churches, which had resulted in citizenship assistance to several hundred migrants, I decided to inquire about the effort. The article mentioned the names of some individuals, some of whom I had already met. In August of 2004, I contacted the individuals I knew and asked their help in identifying some of the key people involved in the effort.

The Houston Citizenship Collaboration is unique in several ways, particularly for Houston. Prior to the current Citizenship and Immigration Services leadership, Houston had a long history of conflicts between local migrant advocacy groups and past INS directors. Shortly after the appointment of a Mexican American as district director of INS in 2003, the new director began to meet with local groups. One of his interests was to build partnerships with local groups. After several meetings, some local advocates agreed to initiate a series of workshops to assist migrants applying for citizenship. This arrangement included an organized labor group, several Latino community-based organizations, a Pakistani business-oriented group, local governments, and others.

The first citizenship workshop was held on August 2003, and it was an impressive effort. Simultaneously held in three Houston locations, the workshop's success was attributed to the experience of a Latino organization that was accredited to perform migration assistance. Those interested in applying were scheduled by appointment, and at each site the local organizations provided direct assistance with applications, photographs, etc.,

and CIS staff reviewed and accepted the applications. Three hundred applications were processed in one day. I should also point out that one of the
local organizations involved high school youth, some of whom were informally authorized—thus noncitizen youth were performing an important
civic act by assisting permanent residents applying for citizenship.

Given the success of the first workshop, a second workshop was scheduled for March 2004. It was similarly organized, and 500 applications were
processed. It appears that word of the first workshop's success had spread.
However, there was one important change. CIS turned its attention more
toward the business community. A local Latino business group and the
Pakistani business group took a more prominent role in the implementation of the second workshop. However, because of their lack of expertise
and accreditation in the processing of migration-related applications, these
groups needed the assistance of the organizations that had participated
previously. The latter organizations, however, began to reassess their
involvement.

A third workshop was scheduled for September 2005. However, I had
relocated to the Phoenix area and was not able to attend. My sense is that
the initial Latino advocacy partners may not have been as engaged at the
September workshop as they were at the first one, or even the second.

The workshop partners seem to have misunderstood the diversity of
interests within the local Latino community. The Latino migrant advocacy
groups' interests do not completely overlap with those of the Latino business community. The Latino (and Pakistani) business groups appear to be
interested in goals such as expanding the entrepreneurial pool and assisting
current business owners and their families' in petitioning to obtain citizenship. Latino advocacy groups are more focused on assisting larger groups of
struggling individuals with limited means.

In addition, the Latino business community does not have expertise in
migration law and practices, particularly in handling complex cases. Thus,
if migrants turn to the business community for direct assistance, they in
turn must request the assistance of advocates. The net result is that advocates do not have a high incentive to participate. There are several reasons
for this: One, they are not brought in as full partners; instead, they are
placed in a secondary role (to assist the business community in carrying out
the event). Two, their expertise and skills are not being fully recognized.

Three, they are not likely to want to be seen as assistants to business leaders, particularly those with seemingly poor labor practices.

Another element, though indirectly related, was the change in leadership in one of the key organizations providing citizenship assistance. Having become dependent on this leader for his expertise and for generating the funds needed to continue their activities, the organization's ability to provide services was uncertain at the time of the fair.

Workload also presented a problem for Houston community organizations. Two finally decided not to participate in future workshops at all. One had received additional projects and responsibilities from its headquarters, and the other was already stretched to its limits with multiple program services—although it still assists individuals through its offices.

While conducting interviews I realized a dimension I had not thought about before: the important role of noncitizens, including informally authorized, in the promotion of citizenship. Of the six community organizers interviewed in Houston, four were not U.S.-born, and two of the four were permanent residents. One of the four not born in the United States became a U.S. citizen after he was drafted during the American/Vietnam War. While in the military he learned that as a permanent resident he could ask for citizenship, so he did. As he recalled, "I'm already here, might as well be part of decision making, vote, and all that." The second of the four came as young child and later applied and was granted U.S. citizenship. The other two, not yet U.S. citizens, were both at one time informally authorized (i.e., undocumented). One estimated that in the organization where he works he has helped thousands apply for citizenship. It is noteworthy that some noncitizens are passionate about promoting U.S. citizenship and allocate much of their energies toward helping others obtain it.

In summary, the Austin Citizenship Day Fair and the Houston Citizenship Collaboration Workshops illustrate that local efforts to promote citizenship are not singular or consistent activities. They are embedded within power relations among organizations and interests. Individuals seeking assistance in obtaining citizenship have to navigate within those relations. The Houston case in particular, though it also applies to some individuals and organizations in Austin and Phoenix, points to the generally overlooked role that noncitizens have in promoting U.S. citizenship. Yet, as mentioned, journalists and academics overlook the passion and interest Latinos, including noncitizens, have toward U.S. citizenship. The many Latino noncitizens, including undocumented migrants and citizen volunteers in Houston, for example, who helped others acquire citizenship are not devaluing U.S. citizenship. Through their efforts they are promoting it and valorizing it.

Schooling Adult Permanent Residents

Citizenship classes are sites where multiple interests (and policies) are negotiated.[6] For adult migrants, the classes represent a site that can allow them to augment their knowledge of U.S. history and government material, which they may be asked about during their interview with a CIS examiner. It is also a place where they can improve their English to pass the verbal and written portions of their interview. For volunteer teachers, the classes provide a means for making a difference and contributing to the community. For sponsoring organizations, the classes support their goal of helping those in need. For school districts and community colleges, citizenship classes help to fulfill their mission of offering adult educational opportunities. In essence, all of these individuals and organizations are fostering fidelities toward the state and producing good citizens.

Class Settings

Contemporary settings for adult citizenship classes in general may not be the most modern and accommodating, yet they are an improvement over the common settings for the former SLIAG-funded English/civics classes, which were typically held in elementary schools and required adults of various heights and weights to sit in tiny, uncomfortable chairs. Adults applying for legalization on the basis of time had to take those classes and tolerate the settings, an issue I will return to later.

Contemporary settings for citizenship classes range significantly in age and comfort. The most modern site that I have visited is the Margarita Huantes site in San Antonio. It is a fairly new facility, has carpeted floors, new tables, adult-size chairs, blackboards, clean restrooms, and many more amenities. The two Austin sites where I taught classes do not match the Huantes center, but they are not as bad as other locations in Texas. At one of the Austin sites (San Miguel), one of the classrooms was actually a small waiting area for a health clinic. It had about twelve chairs along two walls and a play center for children at one end—no blackboard and no desks. Students wrote on their laps. I stood or walked in the small space between two rows. At the same site, one of the other classrooms was at the back of the building and was used for storage. At the Esperanza, the classrooms had window-unit air conditioners whose blowers competed with the voice of the teachers—but they had tables for writing, at least.

Volunteer instructors sometimes had to supply their own chalk, photocopies, and other supplies. I got used to carrying chalk, extra pens and pencils, and some writing paper. I also always carried my small U.S. flag made in China, which I purchased at a dollar store. I carried it because classrooms did not always have a flag that could be used in discussing flag-related topics in the 100 Questions.

For those readers who have worked in community-based not-for-profit organizations, the above probably sounds familiar. Small community-based organizations operate with small budgets and struggle to make organizational ends meet. Both of the organizations I worked with did not charge for citizenship classes and relied on volunteer instructors. Based on my interview with Esperanza's director, informal conversations with San Miguel's education coordinator, and my own observations, Latino bilingual instructors are sought but not often found. Consequently, the general pattern is to have a Euro-American instructor (frequently a female) and all Latino students in the citizenship classes. My presence as a bilingual Latino male was not the norm. In my visits to multiple English/civics, ESL, and citizenship classes in Texas, the rare Latino instructor was generally female.

Working-class Latinos who have limited formal education generally attend citizenship classes. Individuals with higher levels of formal schooling are not as likely to attend citizenship classes—although they may enroll in ESL classes if they feel the need to improve their English. The actual range in level of education of all the students who enrolled in the classes I taught ranged from zero (no formal education) to between six and eight years of schooling. Many had between one and three years of formal schooling. Educational level plays a dominant role in students' classroom experiences and ability to pass the CIS interview. Although advocates and CIS personnel commonly note that English is the biggest hurdle that citizenship applicants have in passing their citizenship interview, I think what is being indexed by the term "English" is ultimately educational level.

Although up to now I have made reference to "citizenship classes," this is somewhat of a misnomer. Citizenship classes are actually citizenship/ESL classes. A substantial part of the class is devoted to teaching English. This is why I think that the majority of students who take a citizenship class end up taking it more than once. It is not that they do not understand the question of how many states are in the Union; rather, it is that they have to answer it in English and then write the full answer, which requires an understanding of English homonyms (there, their), singular-plural markers (is, are), why "states are there" becomes "there are . . . states," etc. Consequently, it is not the content that is the issue that students struggle with, it is the intersection of their limited formal education, the need to become proficient in a language, and the need to learn content material.

Class Interactions

The most impressive aspect of citizenship/ESL classes is the determination of the students to learn the content. Despite their work, family responsibilities, and, for some, long commutes, these students try to keep up with the class, learn the 100 Questions, and learn enough English to write basic sentences. A friend of mine who used to coordinate classes in Austin would at times comment on the distances some students traveled to attend class. Apparently, one man from Waco drove two hours to Austin once a week. Others came from surrounding communities.

Although no one drove such long distances to attend citizenship classes that I taught, I did have a regular evening student, an older woman, who lived in Cedar Park, about thirty miles from the class site. Another woman drove from the southern part of Travis County to attend classes on Saturday mornings. She even came to class when Austin had a hard freeze and many roads were closed. We found a note on the door that classes were canceled because of the weather, so we sat outside for a while and talked. Nobody else showed up. Given the danger, she should not have driven. But the citizenship class was important to her. To me, her actions valorized U.S. citizenship.

As a researcher, I found that some of the most interesting observations made by the class participants were made before and after class. I sensed that most of the participants felt more comfortable talking about their individual experiences, problems, and changes in their life (e.g., an older man told me that a week before he had married the woman he was dating) on a one-to-one basis instead of in class. I thus sought to maximize available time before and after class, yet I was conscious that the students had worked all day, were tired, and might have long drives home. Sometimes during class someone would elaborate on an experience or observation in their life. For example, one day when we were reading a section of the Bill of Rights regarding search and seizure, an older man described the mistreatment and improper search of his daughter's car by local police. In reading the section, he came to realize that the police officers had overstepped their authority that day. The ensuing discussion raised insightful questions regarding the link between the students' permanent residency status and whether the Bill of Rights and the Constitution applies fully to them or only to citizens by birth. A multitude of law journal articles and books have been written about the same question, and multiple interpretations have been offered.

At another time, in the context of talking about education, a woman proceeded to relate the difficulties she had as a young girl trying to attend the nearest rural school in Mexico. Because of demands at home, she finally stopped attending altogether, which she regretted. She said that she sought to impress on her own children the importance of educational opportunities in the United States. She felt that her sacrifice motivated her to promote the value of education for her children. Her emotional account made it evident that while she may not have been placing the full blame on the Mexican state for its limited educational system, she did acknowledge that "México tiene problemas, siempre ha tenido" (Mexico has problems, it always has had problems).

Although generally there are no tuition costs for citizenship classes, there are opportunity costs incurred by forgoing the potential gains of doing some income activity instead. In the case of lower-income workers, attending citizenship classes can be significant. A 1990 survey of persons attending English/civics classes reported that many reduced their number of work hours, lost overtime pay, or even had to quit a job.

On several occasions, men would come to class in a work uniform or dirty work boots and would apologize for being late. It appeared to me that they were embarrassed about having to come to class in a work uniform, but they had no time to change clothes. Some students commented that they could generally reduce their work hours on the evenings they had class, but they were not always successful. Women with young children sometimes brought them to class when a relative or neighbor could not babysit and they were not able to find someone else to do so (presumably by paying or exchanging services). Thus, attending citizenship classes had costs for most students.

What Is to Be Learned?

The 100 Citizenship Questions constitute the core of citizenship classes. They cover topics related to the flag, holidays, structure of government, notable figures in history, colonies, and names of selected current leaders. The following are some of the questions: What do the stripes on the flag mean? In what year was the Constitution written? What is the Fourth of July? Who elects the president of the United States? How many representatives are there in Congress? Who becomes president of the United States if the president and vice president die? Who said, "Give me liberty or give me death?" Who was Martin Luther King Jr.? Which president freed the slaves? What is the basic belief of the Declaration of Independence? Can you name the thirteen original colonies? Can you name the two senators from your state?

After reflecting on my primary education and the primary education of my two children, I noticed that there was a close parallel between historical narratives in elementary education and the 100 Questions, which present a narrative about unproblematic facts, naturalized events, great male heroes (all Euro-Americans, with the exception Rev. Martin Luther King Jr.), and an efficient and rational government. President Lincoln freed the slaves, but nothing is said about slavery ever existing or that some of the other great male heroes in the 100 Questions (Jefferson, Washington) were slave owners. Lincoln did not end slavery; he freed slaves. The wording implies more of a noble act than the erasure of an evil or the political calculations made in eventually supporting the termination of slavery. The answer to the question of "Who was Martin Luther King Jr.?" is "An African American leader who provided inspiration to many people seeking equality for African Americans and others." The answer to "What is the basic belief of the

Declaration of Independence?" is "All men are created equal." But if we are all created equal, why would there be a need to inspire people to seek equality? Lastly, the content of the questions suggest that there are three social groupings in the United States: Indians, African Americans, and a third group that is never named (what linguists label an unmarked category) but must include the groups and individuals listed in other questions: Pilgrims, George Washington, Thomas Jefferson, Patrick Henry, chief justice of the Supreme Court, current president, and current vice president.

As noted earlier, for some adults taking these classes the elementary representations of U.S. history and figures are physically reinforced by the elementary school chairs in the classrooms used for some of the English/civics classes in the post-IRCA period. Drawing on Lauren Berlant's insight, both practices contribute toward creating an "infantile citizenship" (1993). Infantile citizenship encompasses efforts aimed at producing political identities that emphasize idealistic, utopian, uncritical views of the nation-state; a process similar to efforts aimed at creating the subjectivities of what constitutes a "good citizen." A complex and conflictive history is made to fit childlike representations, and the adult bodies are made to fit child-size seats. Forcing migrant adults to sit in child-size seats in elementary schools can be interpreted as a biopolitical practice that symbolically converts adults into children.

The 100 Questions and citizenship textbook materials related to the organization of the U.S. government contain an explicit and implicit message. The explicit message describes the three branches of government (the executive, the legislative, and the judicial), the main functions of each branch (e.g., the legislative branch makes the laws), and some facts regarding the composition of each (e.g., there are nine Supreme Court judges, and each is appointed for life). What is not explicitly asserted, but is implied, is that the U.S. governmental structure is an efficient and rational format, and because of the dominant political and economic position of the United States in the world, its structure is to be emulated by other nations. In short, the U.S. structure is a sort of world standard. And, by implication, migrants seeking citizenship should embrace the United States and its form of government as an already perfected system. The only exception to this within the 100 Questions are the two items related to whether the Constitution can be amended and how many amendments have been adopted. This, of course, can be interpreted as either a process of correcting previous errors, or a self-correcting process to make things better.

Discussions and comments by citizenship class participants on the U.S. governmental structure were generally positive, but not because of the economic and political position of the United States in the world. Instead, they were associated with more basic elements: greater equality and liberties, limited corruption, and better state benefits, such as school meals, assistance for poor people, and Social Security benefits for retired workers. Students appeared to associate the distributive functions of the state with its structural arrangements. Thus, the positive assessment of the U.S. governmental structure was tied to their direct everyday experiences.

The positive evaluation of the U.S. governmental structure, however, was not complete. Certain elements were often questioned. One element that surprised many of the class participants was the fact that U.S. voters do not directly elect the president. They found it hard to believe that even though individuals voted for one of the candidates for president, the electoral college actually selected the president and that voters did not vote for the members of this entity. They did not regard this arrangement as a rational element in a democracy—after all, in Mexico and other Latin American nations the voters directly elect the president. A second element that frequently elicited facial expressions of surprise and some questions was the lifetime appointment of Supreme Court justices. The appointment of government officials for life seemed to suggest to some participants the possibility of political patronage and lack of accountability. A lifetime appointment to a government post struck some participants as someone not likely to do very much or to be responsive to the people since they cannot be fired or voted out.

A Class Semester, a Class Session

Generally a citizenship class covered a six- to eight-week period and involved an initial group of ten to twelve students. Most classes comprised an equal number of women and men. The initial enrollment of ten to twelve would over the semester be reduced to about eight students. Younger males (mid-twenties to mid-thirties) generally did not finish a semester and were frequently absent. Judging from the informal conversations before and after class, it seems the reason was often related to employment, particularly for those who worked in construction, painting, and manufacturing, which demanded long hours. Even though some were willing to forgo the over-time pay for one night, their supervisors did not always allow them to leave earlier on the evening of the class. Commutes were also a common issue for those working in construction and painting. If the job site was close to town, they were able to go home, take a shower, grab something quick to eat, and rush to class. Otherwise, it was difficult or impossible to attend class.

In the case of women, childcare responsibilities seemed most likely to impede class attendance. Some felt comfortable bringing small children to class, while others would miss class if they could not find child care. All of the children who attended were school age and invariably participated in class. The content of the 100 Questions was familiar to them. They might not know that William Rehnquist was the chief justice of the Supreme Court at the time, but they certainly knew about the Pilgrims, the flag, Lincoln, Washington, etc. The elementary construction of the 100 Questions made sense to them and paralleled their elementary understanding of U.S. history.

Absences made teaching the class difficult. Those who missed a lecture/discussion would then be at a loss when in the following session we referred to terms or questions from that material. This meant that each session had to repeat a certain amount of material but still allow new material to be covered. Depending on a number of factors, such as their status of their application, understanding of the 100 Questions, English proficiency, and availability of another class, some students would enroll in subsequent citizenship/ESL classes. At San Miguel, because of its larger size and budget, citizenship classes were generally offered every semester (with about a two-week break in between semesters). At Esperanza, class offerings depended on the availability of a volunteer instructor or a staff person willing to work extra hours.

When I first contacted San Miguel and spoke with the educational coordinator (a bilingual Latina), she was happy to have received the call and welcomed my interest in volunteering to teach one of the citizenship classes. I told her I was a graduate student writing a dissertation on citizenship. At the time, they were planning on offering three to four citizenship classes. A few days before the start of classes, she briefed me on the material some of the previous instructors had used and gave me a copy of the citizenship curriculum outline. I was also handed an English version of the 100 Questions.

The outline was in English and was organized around a partially chronological sequence: (1) Basic Orientation (e.g., general information about citizenship, the flag, and the national anthem); (2) Colonization and Independence (e.g., Pilgrims, *Mayflower*, independence); (3) The Constitution; (4) Further Historical Highlights (Lincoln, World War II); (5 and 6) Government Structure; (7) Catch-up, Review, Drill, and Cheerleading for Exam; and (8) Presentation on Legal Process.

As I thought about the course and reflected on the outline, it seemed that it assumed too much. It assumed a certain level of literacy, English proficiency, and background knowledge. Irrespective of my doubts, I developed some materials in English regarding the initial topics in the curriculum. On the first day of class, there were ten students enrolled, with two others added later. After the students introduced themselves, I distributed a one-page in-class assignment regarding the flag (i.e., stripes, colors, stars). After noticing the time it took to complete the assignment, and some of the difficulties students were having, I decided to do something different for the next session.

I started the second session of the course with a Spanish version of the 100 Questions, which I was able to obtain from a national organization. My logic was that if students could first overcome apprehensions about the content of the questions and learn the content, then we could transition to the English version. From the response of the students, it seemed that they were more comfortable with what the 100 Questions were asking, and so when we transitioned to the English version of the questions, they already knew what was being asked. Now they had to concentrate on listening to the question and responding in English—a response they already knew in Spanish. Through this approach, the focus on the second part of the course became the English language, not the content of the questions.

In order to multiply the opportunities for students to hear and see material related to the class, I made copies of a free video that covered the 100 Questions and gave them to interested students. I also made audiocassettes by recording my reading of each of the 100 Questions, followed by a short pause, and then my reading of the answer. Some of the students I interviewed still had their videos and cassettes.

When I informed the coordinator of what I was planning to do in the class, she seemed uncomfortable; but then she thought that perhaps the suggestion might actually help students, particularly those with limited English proficiency. She then indicated that I should go ahead with the experiment and let her know how it went. Starting the class in Spanish also facilitated the students' comfort in expressing what they did not understand. They could ask questions in Spanish and talk about what they were having problems with. This was also useful after we switched to English.

In each class session, generally two hours, some time was allocated to English vocabulary (part of it drawn from the 100 Questions), a question-and-answer period, dictation (generally short sentences based on the content of the 100 Questions or everyday life, such as, "I have two children, a son and a daughter"), reading short passages from different documents or texts, and taking sample bubble-type tests. I sought to familiarize the students with all of the possible formats they could encounter in the interview with a CIS examiner.

The elements and tasks within the class are driven by the citizenship interview at CIS. At the interview, the CIS examiners take different approaches to their task. Some interviewers actually begin the interview when the person enters their office; the CIS interviewer, without using any hand or arm motions, verbally instructs applicants to sit at a specific chair. If the applicants do not sit at all, or sit in the wrong chair, then the interviewer counts that against the person. The San Antonio CIS office uses the bubble-type test for the history and government portion of the interview; thus, individuals have to be comfortable reading a test question and filling in the bubble for the correct response. Even if test takers have filled out the bubble test correctly, the CIS interviewer uses one of the 100 Questions as a test of the person's English proficiency. An important part of the test, and one that students tend to be most fearful of, is the dictation portion. CIS interviewers ask applicants to write phrases that are dictated to them. Interviewers can apply their discretion in accepting or rejecting spelling errors.

Like many other types of classes, in the initial session most individuals tend to limit what they say. However, once they get used to each other, the interaction can be relaxed and jovial. At times there is some teasing back and forth, though it always tends to be respectful. For example, some of the students who have not missed classes will query students who missed a class upon their return. A sort of where have you been type of ribbing.

In some semesters, the organization hosts an end-of-semester get-together for classes. The last class I taught at Esperanza had such an event. It was a potluck meal that lasted about an hour, and the students expressed their appreciation for my time and asked about the next citizenship class. I informed them that that particular class was my last citizenship class in Austin.

⨎

CHAPTER 5

Bearing True Faith and Allegiance

ENTERING THE CIRCLE OF CITIZENSHIP

For the individuals interviewed in this study, the discourses of citizenship in the United States were productive in creating the subjectivity of citizen because elements in the discourse made sense to them. They recognized the value and privileges associated with citizenship, wanted to be good citizens, and wanted their children to be good citizens, too. They became involved in constructing themselves as citizens—*hacerme ciudadano* (make myself a citizen/become a citizen)—reflecting the role of the self in subject-making. Moreover, the productivity of the discourse was facilitated by the fact that becoming a citizen held out the promise of meeting their needs; specifically, their desire to belong (to be a full member in the political community), and to be recognized (to be accepted as a human being, not just a dominated category). However, disenchantment with unmet expectations and desires related to citizenship is also a possibility.

Consequently, the biopolitical project of constituting citizens and governable subjects with desired fidelities toward the United States is not a singular hegemonic or ideological process. It is more than the interaction of the state and the immediate needs of individuals, as articulated insightfully by Aihwa Ong (1995, 1996); it also involves the long-term desires of individuals. The process of governmentality is generated through interactions between the demands of the state (e.g., knowledge of the English language, U.S. history, and civics; payment of fees; being photographed and

fingerprinted; being examined by CIS; and taking the oath), the mediation
of local organizations (e.g., citizenship promotion, assistance with the
N-400 form, and ESL and citizenship classes), and the individuals' own
pursuit of their own needs and desires (e.g., sponsoring relatives, wanting
to vote, and desiring inclusion and recognition). The proposed theoretical
formulation adds to an understanding of how power achieves its productivity and the link between productivity and the process of subjection.

Petition and Examination

An element generally not commonly noted by researchers or the media is
the taken-for-granted spatial dimension of the application process. Much
of the research and media coverage of persons petitioning for citizenship
takes place in large cities such as Chicago, Houston, Los Angeles, Miami,
New York, or Phoenix; however, many applicants in rural areas must
make long commutes to CIS offices, particularly in states such as Texas.
For example, Waco and Austin residents must travel to the San Antonio
CIS office, 102 and 80 miles away, respectively. The jurisdiction of the
Dallas/Irving office (between Dallas and Fort Worth) covers the entire
northern region of Texas, including the entire Panhandle and the northeast
sections of the state, plus portions of Oklahoma. Consequently, individuals
in Dalhart, north of Amarillo, must drive eight to ten hours to reach the
Dallas/Irving CIS office.

The problem of wide geographic coverage is compounded by the socioeconomic status of many of the migrants applying for citizenship. Older
vehicles and lack of public transportation can make it hard for applicants to
travel long distances. Such issues are not considered by most researchers or
critics, who simply assume that it is a matter of dropping by the migration
office to pick up or file necessary paperwork.

The telephone answering system at CIS offices is another problem. It
consists of a long menu of prerecorded options, none of which leads to the
possibility of talking to a CIS employee, even when pressing *O* for an operator at each prompt (a procedure I have tested). The CIS public information policy stands in contrast to most other federal entities: the White
House, the Department of Defense, the Department of Homeland Security,
and the FBI. Moreover, it is a paradoxical setup: individuals who do not

need the direct citizenship application assistance of the agency can gain access to telephone numbers of individuals in the agency; yet those who need the assistance get prerecorded messages. In addition, individuals who may not have reliable sources of information often visit their nearest CIS office in person, which is costly and time consuming. To the agency's credit, most forms can now be downloaded from the organization's main website, though this assumes a certain knowledge about computers and access to an Internet service provider.

To petition for naturalization, individuals must either obtain the N-400 form and complete it by themselves or seek the assistance of an attorney, a notary public, or a local agency. Although some individuals do choose to complete the form by themselves, none of the persons interviewed chose this option, which assumes a certain level of formal schooling, familiarity with legal forms, and the ability to correctly interpret seemingly innocuous questions, such as, "Have you ever claimed to be a U.S. citizen?" This query, by the way, must be answered in the negative. To answer it in the positive can automatically lead to complete and permanent disqualification from U.S. citizenship. It is a federal offense for noncitizens to claim that they are U.S. citizens.

The N-400 form is ten pages, six of which are instructions. In addition to the biographical questions one would expect to find in such forms, there are several confessional questions. The form also assumes that the average person maintains a detailed log of their comings and goings. Applicants, for example, are asked to report the exact number of days spent outside the United States in the past five years; the exact number of trips twenty-four hours or longer, including the date of departure and return for each trip; information on current and previous spouses, including the date of marriage, divorce, and how the marriage ended; previous marriages of current spouses; and all affiliations to organizations and groups in and out of the United States. Such questions are in addition to the many regarding arrests and detentions, drinking, gambling, child support, alimony, military registration, and tax filings with the IRS.

In 2004 the cost for obtaining assistance for simple or average cases ranged from about $125 (Catholic Charities in Texas) to about $1,200–$1,6000 for an attorney. Notary publics were about $125. Individuals requiring more assistance due to mitigating factors, such as a DWI charge, could expect to hire attorneys handling such cases (cases not handled by migrant assistance organizations) and to pay higher fees depending on the complexity of the case.

The above fees are separate from the application fees paid to CIS. (The bulk of the budget for naturalization activities is generated from the fees charged.) In the late 1990s INS began a series of fee increases for the required fingerprint verification by the FBI and the actual application. In 1999 the application fee more than doubled, from $95 to $225 per person. It increased to $310 in 2002, and to $390 in April 2004. In 2011 the application and the biometric record was $680. Even though researchers have not explored the question of whether the increase in fees has reduced the number of people who can apply, from my conversations with migrant assistance services providers, it is their opinion that the increases have had this effect. A person filing their application must be able to put aside a minimum of about $900 to cover the cost of fingerprints, photographs, a medical exam, application assistance, certified mail fees, and CIS application fees. However, if the person seeks the assistance of an attorney, the minimum amount is likely to be around $2,000. Although $900 may not seem like much to some, for persons I interviewed that amount represents about two weeks' wages.

Eligible migrants living in Austin file their application with the San Antonio CIS office. In 2004 the agency was scheduling interviews three to six months after the receipt of the application. After CIS verifies the information in the N-400 and the FBI responds to the fingerprint background check, CIS then sends a letter to the petitioner indicating a date and time for an interview, the portion that is the most stressful part of the application process. Those who have completed the process used the words "fear" and "nerves" to describe it and recalled worrying about forgetting civic and historical facts, not understanding the examiner's questions, not answering in proper English, and misspelling words in the written section of the interview.

The worries of citizenship aspirants reflect an important element in the interview process: the naturalization examiner's discretion. Their worry is merited. The examiners' discretion is well known and criticized by migrant advocates. It is difficult to address, however, because it can be both positive and negative. The leniency of an examiner can lead to the approval of a person who seemed ready but was perhaps too nervous at the time of the interview to do well; or the examiner may empathize with an applicant and ask one of the simpler questions (e.g., Who is the current president of the United States?). Simultaneously, hard-nosed examiners can reject applicants who should have passed. The story of Lyaman and Ilyana Savy demonstrates the extent of discretion of INS/CIS examiners. These young women are identical twins who migrated from Azerbaijan at the same time and under the same conditions. Both women submitted their applications at the same time and with the same supporting documents, and both were sufficiently proficient in English and knew the civics and history material. Ilyana's application was approved and she was granted citizenship in 1998; Lyaman's was not approved. Two years later, after their mother initiated a letter-writing campaign and publicized Lyaman's case, the second daughter's application was approved. The examiner who reviewed Ilyana's file found everything in order; however, the adjudicator who reviewed Lyaman's application did not accept some of her documents (the same ones in Ilyana's file).[1]

The experience of Sra. Campo (introduced in chapter 3), who diligently studied and prepared herself for her interview and yet did not pass the interview because of a question regarding U.S. military branches, was noted previously. Her case illustrates how an eligible applicant, despite her best efforts to comply with all the requirements, can fail the final interview. It also shows how CIS officials can manipulate their discretionary power and neglect the rights of applicants. Campos's interview experience, however, is not the same as those who have been granted citizenship. They mostly found their interviews to be fair and even easy. The latter were pleasantly surprised about how "*facil*" (easy) the interview turned out to be. At my own citizenship interview, the adjudicator invoked his discretion not to ask me any questions, surmising that since I was in college and had attended U.S. schools since the fourth grade, he did not need to ask.

Instituting Citizenship, Consecrating Citizens

The oath-taking ceremony marks the final stage in the naturalization process. The focus here is on the oath-taking ceremonies that I observed or participated in, as well as the views of other individuals who have taken the oath. Part of the productivity of the ceremonies in creating the subjectivity of citizen lies in the fact that it overlaps with other well-known practices (e.g., graduations and weddings). All of these practices create overlapping discourses about fidelity and allegiance. In addition, naturalization ceremonies not only institute a distinction between citizen and noncitizen, but more fundamentally a distinction between citizen and the category of "illegal alien" of "undocumented" migrants.[2] In the case of migrants formerly informally authorized—Pierre Bourdieu's notion (1977) of instituting may not be as complete as the concept implies—they may retain their perceived alienness after becoming citizens.

The phrases "oath-taking ceremonies" or "naturalization ceremonies" (including my own uses up to now) are both misleading and correct. They are misleading because for many U.S.-born citizens who have never attended a ceremony, the phrases may suggest the presence of a significant collectivity of individuals, multiple displays of the U.S. flag, a judge in a robe, and other elements that can be associated with a ceremony. A citizenship ceremony, however, can be quite unceremonious—although some can have all these elements and more.

Historically, due to variations in federal policy and political priorities of different administrations, naturalization requirements and ceremonies have varied significantly since Congress adopted the first naturalization statute in 1790. Prior to the creation the Bureau of Immigration and Naturalization in 1906—the federal entity responsible for the implementation of naturalization regulations—local, state, and federal courts had a large role in granting citizenship.[3] Formally, citizenship was largely a legal matter. After applicants filed their intention to seek citizenship (the "first papers") and presumably had met the requirement of the law in terms of length of residency, good moral character, and other requirements, they could file a petition in a local, state, or federal court and be placed on its docket. On the day of the scheduled hearing, the presiding judge would review the applicant's petition, possibly ask the person's witnesses about the veracity of the application, and if the judge did not have any doubts would approve the petition, administer the oath, and congratulate the new American by choice.[4] Moreover, the actual oath was much narrower and simpler than today's, as it was simply a statement about supporting the Constitution.

The aforementioned description summarizes the general process. It does not include the multiple problems related to it or the political contexts within which it operated.[5] Some of the more noteworthy problems noted by Gavit ([1922] 1971), President Roosevelt's Commission on Naturalization, and others are the following: (1) some of the sitting judges had a limited knowledge of federal migration law, as such knowledge was not required; (2) the statements on the petitions were not necessarily verified, and it was left up to the judge hearing the case to surmise if the information appeared to be correct; (3) some of the judges granted citizenship as a political aid to the Democratic or Republican Party, particularly in presidential election years. Accounts of George Washington Plunkitt's Tammany Hall and the building of the Democratic Party in New York City, or the similar practices deployed by the Republican Party in Philadelphia are examples of the active and successful promotion of American citizenship, albeit in violation of the law.

Thus, the acquisition of citizenship between 1790 and 1905 encompasses a wide variety of experiences and practices across the more than 5,000 courts (federal and state) that were involved. While the majority of individuals most likely were granted citizenship following the established laws, others acquired it because of the absence of judicial and administrative accountability in the naturalization process or the political manipulation of those processes. The extensive problems with the records for this period (e.g., records spread across thousands of courts, lost and absent records, selling of files as old paper, incomplete forms, incorrectly completed forms, and forged naturalization certificates) make it difficult for researchers then and now to ascertain what proportion of persons should not have been granted citizenship.

In March 1905 President Theodore Roosevelt appointed a commission to examine the naturalization process "and to suggest appropriate measures to avoid the notorious abuse resulting from the improvident of unlawful granting of citizenship"—what some labeled a "chaotic condition" in terms of records, "vast naturalization frauds" in the process, or naturalization as a "farce" (Gavit [1922] 1971). The report of the commission noted the great variance, including fraud, which existed in the entire process, and made several important recommendations: standardized forms; the creation of a Bureau of Naturalization to oversee the process; and knowledge of the

English language. The commission reiterated the importance of standardizing the oath and listed what it should contain, but it did not recommend
a specific text.

Congress adopted most of the commissions recommendations and codified them into the 1906 Naturalization Act. However, even after the act was
implemented, since the statute still authorized state and local courts to be
involved (reducing the number of courts involved to a total of 2,244 by
1908), problems remained in the relationship between the Bureau of
Immigration and Naturalization and the courts: neither one could overrule
the other. In addition, at times some courts would en masse clear pending
cases by putting them through the mill. Representing a national organization
involved in promoting citizenship, Harold Fields (1935, 266) reports that one
court cleared 2,500 applications in one day; another court heard 10,000 citizenship applications in one month. After citing many of the problems in
naturalization between 1906 and 1935, Fields expressed his concerns about
how naturalization practices were "disruptive of the spirit of true American
citizenship" and argued for a greater role for the Bureau in the granting of
citizenship. The 1940 Immigration Act granted such a role to the bureau.

The preceding description highlights the limitations of contemporary
accounts regarding an idealized past about individuals who obtained citizenship then, such as the critics discussed previously and others (e.g.,
William Bennett, Patrick Buchanan, and Samuel P. Huntington), as well as
some of the members of Congress involved in the debate regarding the oath.
Their laments about the devaluing of citizenship or the need to ensure that
those taking the oath now and in the future value the sanctity of the oath, as
did the migrants of the past, are based on overidealized, enchanted views of
that past. In their argument, the citizenship applicants of the past are portrayed as individuals who worked hard to learn English and the civics and
history of the United States, truthfully completed the required application,
met all the conditions of citizenship, solemnly took the oath at a patriotic
naturalization ceremony, and abjured all previous allegiances. Yet it ignores
the multiple historical accounts, including a presidential State of the Union
message that indicated extensive fraud and abuse in granting citizenship in
the past.

John Fonte, senior fellow at the Hudson Institute (one of the individuals
invited to testify at the House hearing on the oath), for example, in a

short essay in 2000 about the current assimilation problem argues the following:

> During our earlier immigration wave one century back, we had self-confident elites in politics, education, business, religion, and civic associations who insisted the new immigrants Americanize. . . . In 1915, Democrat Woodrow Wilson and Republican Theodore Roosevelt explicitly and forcefully called for the "Americanization" of new immigrants. . . . Back then, the federal government promoted Americanism. . . . Back then the Oath of Citizenship, in which newly naturalized Americans promised to renounce all prior allegiances, was taken seriously. (Baron and Fonte 2000)

Mr. Fonte's reference to "back then" is to "circa 1900," the same period President Theodore Roosevelt characterized in his 1905 State of the Union message as having seen "notorious abuse resulting from the improvident of unlawful granting of citizenship." Fonte overlooks what took place back then.

Such narratives take current idealized practices and project them into the past. The past thus becomes the place where these practices existed and the point of reference for assessing current practices. Because they are an idealized, enchanted set of practices, current experiences are interpreted as falling short of those that existed in the past. Drawing on Susan Stewart (1984, 23), I suggest that laments about the devaluing of citizenship and the past sanctity of the oath are fantasies and utopias about an ideological past that never existed. It is a longing for an ideologically perceived past based on reactions to the significant proportion of Asian and Latino citizenship petitioners in the present—many of whom are thought of as unassimilable and as harboring fidelities to their countries of origin, possibly even after taking the oath.

Between the passage of the 1940 Immigration Act and the 1990s, the naturalization process became a more standardized and regularized process. The federal agency responsible for naturalization (variously named and located within different federal agencies) assumed a direct role in governing the application process, evaluating petitioners, recommending or rejecting the petition for naturalization, and determining how ceremonious the oath-taking would be. Problems such as lost records continued to exist during this period, but overall (from the perspective of policymakers and the state) it was an improvement over the pre-1940s problems—applicants filed the same forms and faced the same basic set of regulations, and judges relied on the recommendation of the federal agency prior to administering the oath.

Over the past thirty years, oath-taking ceremonies have remained variable. Two significant changes have been the emergence of large-scale ceremonies in the mid-1990s and the naturalization of persons outside the United States. Not much will be said about the latter other than the fact that on October 1, 2004, CIS Director Eduardo Aguirre supervised the first overseas naturalization ceremony at Bagram Air Force Base near Kabul, Afghanistan, for seventeen noncitizens in the military. Since then, CIS staff members have traveled to Iraq, Germany, Japan, and South Korea to perform naturalization ceremonies. Prior to the Bagram Air Force Base ceremony, noncitizens were naturalized on U.S. territory or onboard U.S. ships at U.S. naval ports.

In the mid-1990s, largely stimulated by President Clinton's Citizenship USA initiative (1995–1996), several large-scale naturalization ceremonies were held around the nation, generally in the states with significant migrant populations and electors (e.g., California, Florida, New York, Texas). In June 1996, a total of 10,000 citizenship aspirants were sworn in at one event in Los Angeles as part of several planned mass ceremonies in southern California. About 38,000 were scheduled to take the oath in that month alone. A group of 7,000 petitioners took the oath in June 2000 at the Broward County Convention Center (one of the contested counties in the 2000 presidential election).[6]

Although INS and elected officials in Los Angeles and Broward County would most likely assert that the timing of the ceremonies was simply random, the fact that in both instances those who were naturalized would be eligible to register and vote in the 1996 and 2000 presidential elections, respectively, raises doubt about their randomness. Moreover, the events in Miami in July 2004 also reinforce skepticism about the nonpolitical nature of contemporary ceremonies. At that event, where about 200 petitioners took the oath, CIS officials directed persons to stop at a table where they could register to vote if they wished. The two volunteers staffing the table handed the new citizens the registration forms with the party affiliation already checked off: Republican. After local complaints by Democratic Party representatives, CIS officials indicated that they did not authorize the table, nor did they know why only the Republican Party was there to participate. Similar to the 1996 and 2000 events, those at the 2004 Miami ceremony could register and vote in the presidential election taking place that same year. News accounts such as these suggest that even though we normally perceive citizenship ceremonies as simply about the granting of citizenship and taking the oath, they remain embedded in agendas of political parties and interests beyond the individuals taking the oath, and that federal migration officials are not necessarily neutral parties, though by law they are mandated to be nonpartisan.

Turning in My Green Card

Luckily for me, my hearing was scheduled for early afternoon, and it was a beautiful early summer day. I was a full-time student at San Diego State University, and I had gotten off work about 7 a.m. from my full-time, third-shift job as a computer operator. My roommate and a second friend (both full-time college students) had agreed to witness my oath-taking ceremony, as required by law. I decided to wear a dress shirt, dress slacks, and a sport coat. We took two cars because my roommate had some errands to run after the ceremony.

We arrived at the federal building about twenty minutes early and were told to wait until the clerk of the district court, William W. Luddy, called me. I already had reviewed the book I was using to study (which I brought to the event anyway), and so I was comfortable with its contents: the first president, how many colonies, colors of the flag, etc. I already had learned the facts several times, including in Mrs. Skahill's fourth grade class, junior high, high school, and a two-semester U.S. history course in college (colonial period to 1865, 1865 to the present). I, of course, knew the Pledge of Allegiance, which I had repeated, according to my estimate, about 1,500 times since the fourth grade. I did, however, have to take some notes on things such as the total number of representatives.

Luddy finally called me and instructed me to follow him. Once inside the office, with a partition between us, he asked me for my green card, which I handed to him. He then took a few seconds to review my citizenship application, compared the number on my card with the one in the application and the Certificate of Naturalization. Then it was time to examine me. He said something to the effect of, "Oh, you're in college," and then proceeded to direct me to sign over my picture on the certificate. The interviewer apparently made the decision that since I was in college, and because of my attendance in U.S. schools, I knew the civics and history of the United States. He therefore decided not to ask me any questions. Moreover, since we communicated in English, he determined that I possessed the requirement initiated by the 1906 Naturalization Act: "knowledge of English." He then called my two witnesses into the room. He asked them how long they had known me, something about my moral character, and some minor questions. Afterwards, he asked me to raise my hand and repeat the oath after him. Although I had not studied it, I repeated what he said. I then became a naturalized citizen—although my Alien Registration Number (A12-628-001) remains on my Certificate of Naturalization—and the court official congratulated me.

Peter Brimelow's and Georgie Anne Geyer's critique of current citizenship and naturalization practices is based on their generalizations about interviews and ceremonies such as mine. An editor with the *National Review* and *Forbes* magazine, Brimelow noted that his INS interview went quickly. He was granted U.S. citizenship in 1994 after living in the United States for close to 25 years (he migrated from Britain). In a short article in the *National Review*, Brimelow noted the following:

> Citizenship has become in effect, merely a license to collect welfare. . . . I realized what was going on when I was sitting in an INS waiting room, trying to calculate how long it would be before I was called for my naturalization interview. I saw with surprise that the huddled masses were actually shuffling along very quickly. Incredibly, it even seemed likely that I would be through in less time than we had been officially advised. This was a unique experience in my interactions with government. I was about to get a welfare license much faster than I could get a New York State driver's license. (Brimelow 1995, 26–27)

During his interview, Brimelow was asked only one question: What country did the U.S. break away from? In his article he suggests that he thought about or may have jokingly said Mexico. Brimelow points out that in the late 1800s and early 1900s the naturalization system "protected" the United States by denying citizenship to radicals and strictly ensuring that petitioners met conditions such as attachment to the principles of the Constitution. He added that "to learn those principles, working men and women went to night schools . . . attending courses lasting seven months on average, with classes held daily" (26–27), yet he does not cite sources. Brimelow notes that at his oath-taking ceremony there were about 150 people, "including perhaps 20 whites." Based on his own experience with the interview and oath-taking ceremony, Brimelow concludes that there has been a "collapse of the naturalization system," suggesting that in the past the system worked fine, but is now granting citizenship to individuals who do not merit it (presumably "nonwhites").

Since *Americans No More* (1996) was published, Geyer has repeated in many articles the same points regarding citizenship that she raised in her book. In a 2002 article, for example, she laments the "internal unraveling that is occurring within the American fabric," and how the U.S. has changed from a "transformational society . . . imposing our principles on others within America . . . [to where] we now grant cultural and political concessions to others" (2002, 58). The only "others" noted in her article are "Spanish speakers" and "Mexicans." Papa's account is used to represent what existed in the past, an idealization that ignores many real problems.

Both Brimelow and Geyer construct a critique of current naturalization processes and current petitioners (nonwhites, Spanish-speakers, and Mexicans) based on a limited understanding of both the history of natural-ization and the current diversity of interviews and ceremonies. In other words, their arguments combine fantasies and utopias about the past and a narrow understanding of the present. Ultimately, their critique seems to be about changes to past gender and racial/ethnic hierarchies; they appear to be concerned with contemporary diversity in the United States and the pos-sibility that unassimilable nonwhites may be receiving U.S. citizenship.

You Will Have to Wait Outside

I was in El Paso, Texas, in 1997, about the middle of the summer, as part of a project with the Public Policy Institute at the University of Texas at Austin, for which we conducted interviews with persons enrolled in

ESL/citizenship classes regarding their interest in petitioning for citizenship (Freeman et al. 1997). I visited the El Paso INS offices and talked to officials regarding the citizenship application process. The INS official in El Paso told me that they were going to have an oath-taking ceremony and invited me to attend.

When I arrived, I noticed a sign on the door directing the attendees to wait outside. Given the temperatures in El Paso in the summertime (especially in the late afternoon), I wondered why they would not let the people simply wait inside where it was air-conditioned. A clerk told me that they needed to first clear the building of all the other people there on regular business matters (i.e., those not attending the ceremony). Although the clerk seemed clear on the logic, I still wondered why they could not simply ask those attending the oath-taking ceremony to wait on one side of the sufficiently large waiting area.

I, on the other hand, could wait inside if I wanted to since I was an invited guest of the district director. I elected to wait outside, which gave me the chance to talk to the soon-to-be citizens and their family members and friends. The entrance to the building had no shade to speak of. Moreover, most of the people were wearing their Sunday best: women in stockings, dresses, and heels; men in dress shirts, ties, and coats; young boys in white long-sleeve shirts, uncomfortable shoes, and crooked clip-on ties.

The patience of parents was tested by the inevitable "I need to go to the bathroom" and "I'm thirsty." Across the street was a small grocery store where they could buy soft drinks or bottled water. However, finding a bathroom was a challenge. Parents with boys walked to the back of the building, but those with girls had to drive to a nearby fast-food restaurant.

At 5:45 p.m. an INS official opened the door and directed the individuals to sit in the chairs that had been set up in the waiting area of the office. Those taking the oath were asked to sit in the front rows; family and friends (and one guest) could sit in the rows behind. About twenty-five people sat in the front rows and about thirty sat in the back. Most of the twenty-five individuals appeared to be of Mexican descent. About four individuals were Asians, and another person appeared to be South Asian.

Although the director of the INS (a Mexican American male) was in the office, the deputy director (also a Mexican American male) hosted the event. He welcomed the attendees and offered some short comments about the importance of citizenship. He then instructed the petitioners to stand and repeat the oath after him. He read the oath from a sheet of paper (presumably to make sure he said it correctly). The petitioners repeated the oath as it was being read, and then they were told that they were now U.S. citizens. The deputy director congratulated them and proceeded to give some instructions regarding the Certificate of Naturalization.

He then invited the family and friends at the back of the room to congratulate the new citizens and take photographs, if they wanted, of the moment when he was going to hand out the certificates. Most of the family members had brought cameras and took at least one photograph of the happy, smiling person receiving a certificate. In forty minutes, the ceremony was over. Their new status had been conferred.

Based on informal conversations with some of the Mexican petitioners while waiting outside, most seemed excited. They had taken citizenship and ESL classes and had struggled to learn the material, with the English language being the most difficult hurdle to overcome. (The INS officials, ESL/citizenship class teachers, and the adult education program coordinator in the local school district I interviewed during this study also agreed that learning the English language most impeded the acquisition of citizenship.) Some had not passed the INS interview the first time they were examined and so were quite happy; however, most had no special plans for the evening. All in all, it was a relatively low-profile event: no flags, no DAR, no voter registration, no videos of the president, no speeches by invited guests, no judge, no color guard.

At the time, and afterwards, I found it interesting that it was the deputy director who hosted the event and administered the oath, rather than the director, who was in the building—especially in light of the fact that the event took only about 40 minutes. If U.S. citizenship is as important as most INS (and now CIS) officials, congressmen, elected officials, and others claim it is, then it would seem that the director would have time to administer the oath and be the one to welcome a group of individuals into U.S. citizenship.

IN THE SHADOW OF THE HEMISPHERE

The San Antonio citizenship ceremony stands in clear contrast to the other two. To start with, it was an event for about 300 petitioners, held in the large rotunda of the Texas Folk Life Museum, with multiple built-in projection screens and sound system. On the day of the event, the center area was filled with folding chairs in neat rows. Family members and friends would be required to stand in the areas surrounding the seats, on the edges of the rotunda.

Petitioners were expected to wear formal attire and arrive two hours before the event. Most of the women wore formal dresses or pantsuits. Most of the men wore suits or dress slacks with a dress shirt, sport coat, and tie. A few male military personnel wore dress uniforms.

The beginning of the event appeared a little chaotic. The CIS staff seemed to have had an idea of how they wanted the process to flow—where people should enter, where they should wait prior to entering the rotunda, how they should sit, how they should line up to receive their certificate, how they should return to their seats, and how they should line up if they wanted to take a photograph with the judge. The petitioners and their guests did not have this information, so some ended up standing in areas where they were not supposed to be. Gradually the CIS staff guided the petitioners to a room off to the side where they were shown a film and given instructions.

At the beginning of the ceremony, a CIS representative welcomed the petitioners and their family and friends. The petitioners were asked to stand while a small color guard entered the rotunda and solemnly walked down the center aisle between the chairs toward the stage. The guards were dressed in military uniforms and had serious expressions on their faces. The soldier in the middle carried the U.S. flag, another carried the Texas flag, and the others carried marching rifles. When they reached the stage, they turned to face the audience, placed the flags on either side of the stage, and then stood at attention in front of the stage.

The audience was then asked to stand and recite the Pledge of Allegiance to the flag. The presiding judge and CIS official began the recitation and the audience followed, with their right hands over their hearts. The CIS representative introduced the presiding federal judge and some of the special guests, including a member of the Daughters of the American Revolution and a representative of the Bexar County Republican Party. (No representative from the Democratic Party was introduced.)

On multiple video screens around the room, President Bush expressed his congratulations to the petitioners and welcomed them as new citizens, as new Americans. He recognized their struggle to obtain citizenship and their contribution to date to the United States. Another video aired after the president's prerecorded message. It showed multiple scenes with the U.S. flag; historical sites of the American Revolution and the Civil War; Mount Rushmore; Washington, D.C., monuments; clips of President Kennedy, President Johnson, and Rev. Martin Luther King Jr.; and images of a school building in the Edgewood School District (in the West side of San Antonio, a predominantly Mexican-origin section of the city). The audio track of the video played segments of the national anthem and other patriotic scores.

A letter from President Bush, given to all of the participants as part of the ceremony, was addressed to "Dear Fellow Americans" and reiterated some of the points in the video. Following are key passages:

> I am pleased to congratulate you on becoming a United States citizen. You are now a part of a great and blessed Nation. . . . Americans are united across the generations by grand and enduring ideals. The grandest of these ideals is an unfolding promise that everyone belongs, that everyone deserves a chance. . . . Our country has never been united by blood or birth or soil. We are bound by principles that move us beyond our backgrounds, lift us above our interest, and teach us what it means to be a citizen. Every citizen must uphold these principles. And every new citizen, by embracing these ideals, makes our country more, not less American. . . As you begin to participate fully in our democracy, remember that what you do is as important as anything government does. . . . When this spirit of citizenship is missing, no government program can replace it. . . . Welcome to the joy, responsibility, and freedom of American citizenship. God bless you, and God bless America.[7]

The language in this letter is very similar to a six-panel brochure produced by the Office of Citizenship, which is distributed to publicize the office and its promotion of citizenship. The letter was given to the petitioners in a white envelope by the judge in lieu of the Certificate of Naturalization. This process is similar to the procedure in college graduations wherein a blank sheet of paper is given to the graduate in lieu of the actual diploma; the diploma is later mailed to the graduate. The certificate was mailed to the new citizens after the event.

Before turning the floor over to the judge, the CIS official noted the number of nations represented at the ceremony and acknowledged that persons from Mexico were the single largest group. He also asked the four people who had volunteered to speak for two to three minutes to walk up to the front of the room. All four would become citizens that day. I was unable to learn how the volunteers were selected, but they had prepared speeches for the occasion. Each spoke about what U.S. citizenship meant for them. Each of the speakers had a good command of English, and they all spoke with emotion in their voices. The key ideas expressed by the speakers were a love for the United States and the opportunities it has provided to them; a recognition of the values, principles, and rights found here; thankfulness for what the United States has been able to offer them in terms of their ability to start businesses, or the work that they have found here; and respect and love for the flag and other symbols.

The CIS official then turned the floor to the federal judge sitting on an elevated stage. The judge welcomed the petitioners and their family members and friends. He spoke about the value and importance of citizenship and that on this day they were going to become full U.S. citizens. Prior to reading the oath, the judge reiterated its importance and signified that they were pledging their allegiance to the United States. He then asked the petitioners to stand and repeat the oath. Afterward, he noted that the petitioners were now U.S. citizens, and he congratulated them. He also indicated that those who wanted to take a picture with him could do so after the ceremony and that he would stay for that.

Each person was then called to receive their certificate from the judge. Slowly the line progressed as persons stood up, walked to the side of the room, lined up on the side, walked toward the front of the room, received a white enveloped from the judge, shook his hand, and then walked back to their seats. The process resembled a graduation ceremony, with individuals sitting in folding chairs in a specified order, being called one by one to walk to the front of the stage, accepting a symbolic certificate with the left hand, shaking the giver's hand with the right hand, exiting on the opposite site, and returning to the assigned seat. The judge adjourned the ceremony and indicated that the color guard should proceed with their exit march. Then the ceremony ended about four hours after it had started. Some of the petitioners took up the judge's offer for pictures. Some lingered to chat with family and friends or to look at the exhibits on Texas cultures. Others left quickly.

I had the opportunity to attend three naturalization ceremonies in Arizona. One took place at the Phoenix Public Library, a second at the South Mountain Community College, and a third at the Chandler Multicultural Festival. The events at the public library and in Chandler were smaller events presided by CIS and a federal judge who administered the citizenship oath. They were larger in size than the one in El Paso, but they were not as elaborate as the one in San Antonio. On the other hand, the South Mountain event, which took place on the Fourth of July (2009) in a multipurpose gymnasium and involved a color guard and many medium-size U.S. flags, resembled the one in San Antonio.

Taken together, the three principal ceremonies show the variability of formality in being granted U.S. citizenship—in terms of size, duration, basic format, and patriotic elements. At the San Antonio ceremony, I felt as if I were standing in Victor Turner's forest of symbols: symbols indexing the nation-state intended to dramatize the divorce from one nation-state and marriage to another nation-state simultaneously taking place. The initiates declared their abjuration of ties to the nations of their birth and publicly vowed their fidelity and allegiance to a new state.

Marrying the State, Graduating from Alienage

Formal naturalization ceremonies have several parallels to a graduation ceremony. Some of the common elements include speeches, seating arrangements, lining up to receive a document, walking onto or in front of a stage, receiving a symbolic document, and shaking the hand of an official. The University of Texas at Austin, which has close to 50,000 students and multiple graduation ceremonies, has a ceremony at night for all graduates that include fireworks, a light show, the school song, and other special effects. However, as observed at a recent graduation at the Tempe campus of Arizona State University, in place of having each graduating student walk on stage to receive a symbolic document, students are asked to stand, the audience and students cheer and clap, and then they sit down.

The lavishness of such ceremonies may contrast with a graduation at small rural high schools, but based on my own experiences attending eight graduations over the years, the core elements of most are quite similar. Moreover, it is not uncommon to find some of the same patriotic elements at naturalization ceremonies and graduations: U.S. flag, the Pledge of Allegiance, and the national anthem. The speeches of keynote speakers at graduations can also reference citizenship.

Graduations, in contrast to naturalization ceremonies, may not involve an oath; however, they do mark allegiance and fidelities (school spirit) in other ways. Individuals graduating the same year are labeled, and may label themselves, as the graduating class of X year of X high school or college/university, and private businesses encourage the purchase of a class ring, which marks fidelity to the institution. Windshield decals, t-shirts, sweatshirts, mugs, jackets, pens, tie clips, and myriad other commodities all represent material expressions of institutional fidelity. Though separate from graduation, but related to college life, fraternities and sororities play a role in creating an institutional allegiance, as well as a specific fidelity to a particular sorority or fraternity. Students who join fraternities and sororities experience months of activities when they are pledges, followed by a ceremony during which they repeat an oath that affirms their fidelity to and institutes them as full-fledged members of the (local and national) group.

College life and graduations are also important elements in the fostering of postgraduation fidelities to the institution, and colleges depend on these. The creation of faithful alumni who will support their alma matter (a kind of motherland/fatherland) through the purchase of football season tickets or substantial financial donations are critical to the institution. Schools commonly have an individual or an office dedicated to alumni affairs that seeks continued support from alumni through direct phone and mail solicitation, the promotion of credit cards that bear the logo of the institution and provide a percentage of the charges made to the institution, and the hosting of special events and activities for alumni. A hierarchy among alumni is created: those who make substantial contributions are granted greater privileges (e.g., buildings named after them, enclosed box seats in the stadium, parking privileges, etc.).

Fidelity also materializes at sporting events. Students, faculty, and alumni don clothing or paraphernalia representing the school colors, or they may even apply paint directly on their face and torso as a means of showing their school spirit. The objective of these markers is to display a distinction between one's school and the opposing school; an opposition also marked spatially by the location of seating (one side is allocating to the home team, and the opposite side to the guest team).

Weddings also have parallels to citizenship ceremonies. For example, in *Americans by Choice* ([1922] 1971), Gavit notes that "naturalization, the legal ceremony . . . is in its significance and essentials very ancient—it goes back to the blood transfusion and other primitive ceremonies. . . . It registers and effectuates two distinct things—a divorce and a marriage, so to say" (69). He later speaks of naturalization as being "consummated" and provides a long quotation by a judge involved in naturalization wherein the judge equates the "declaration of intention to seek citizenship" to a "marriage proposal" and naturalization to marriage. In this quotation, the state is represented as a female and the petitioner as a male, with an implied heteronormativity:

> The young lady who meets a young man and likes him, would be very much out of place if, without any other tie between them, she began to tell him what she wanted him to do, what she wanted him to study, and how she wanted him to study, what she wanted him to drink, and how she wanted him to dress. It would be very immodest and impolite, to say the least. If that young man has made her a proposal of marriage, and she were considering it, these suggestions from her would be entirely proper, and she would be performing her duty to the young man and to herself. This illustrates . . . the proper limits within which our country can guide, advise, and direct aliens who through the declaration of intention have made, as it were, a proposal of marriage. (106)

There are two other key elements that naturalization and weddings have in common: both involve a publicly enunciated oath where fidelity and allegiance are expressed, and both stress the value of fidelity, faithfulness, obedience, loyalty, devotion, protection, duty, respect, and support. In the past, weddings were more explicitly genderized: the man was asked to "cherish" the woman he was marrying, and the woman was asked to "obey" the man she was marrying. Naturalization ceremonies imply that the citizenship aspirant will both cherish and obey the state. One of the traditional Christian versions of wedding vows that has been used in the United States notes the following: "I, [name], give you this ring, wear it with love and joy. I choose you to be my husband/wife: to have and to hold, from this day forward. For better or worse, for richer or poorer; in sickness and in health; to have and to cherish, as long as we both shall live. And hereto, I pledge you my faithfulness to show to you the same kind of love as Christ showed the Church when He died for her, and to love you as a part of myself because of His sight we shall be one."[8]

This wedding vow asserts two important things: One, both parties are abjuring fidelities and allegiances to previous partners. Two, they are expressing a willingness to bear true faith and allegiance to each other. Using the language that I have used, which is taken from the oath, suggest not only the flexibility of the language for both naturalization ceremonies and weddings, but also how both categories of events rely on fostering fidelity among the participants. Moreover, an unstated notion is that the marriage will fulfill a lack in their individual lives; through the wedding they achieve completeness in their lives.[9] Noncitizens seeking citizenship who want to "hacerme ciudadano" (become a U.S. citizen/make myself a citizen) also are expressing a sense of incompleteness (a lack); the acquisition of citizenship also offers a sense of completeness in their lives.

Even though Mexico and the United States may have different notions of citizenship and citizen, the notion of fidelity is present in the practices of graduation and weddings in both countries. Consequently, the descriptions discussed would resonate with individuals who have participated in these ceremonies in Mexico. The trans-state discursivity of fidelity facilitates the incorporation of the notions of fidelity attached to U.S. citizenship by Mexican noncitizens pursuing citizenship.

Mexican civil ceremonies (required of all marriages irrespective of religion) stress the importance of fidelities, protection, duty, obedience, respect, deference, and completeness:

> Marriage is the only moral foundation of the family, to preserve the species and to supplement the imperfections of the individual who is unable alone to reach human perfection . . .
>
> The married partners should be sacred to one another . . .
>
> The man who is the principal source of courage and strength, should and will give the woman protection, nourishment and direction.

He should treat her always as the more delicate and sensitive partner, and generously offer her his strength, especially in her time of need.

The woman, whose principal talents are self-sacrifice, beauty, compassion, keen insight and tenderness should and will, give her husband obedience, pleasure, assistance, consolation and advice. She should treat him always with a delicacy and with the *respect* due to the one who supports and defends her.

Each deserves respect, deference, fidelity, confidence and tenderness.[10]

Notions in the U.S. naturalization ceremonies and the oath find a close parallel to the elements in the Mexican civil ceremony. The state is naturalized; it is assumed to be essential, and the individuals undergoing the ceremony are marrying the state and declaring their fidelity, obedience, support, deference, and defense of it.

In the case of weddings, the core element of fidelity is materialized through wedding rings, which in principle remind the bearers and others of the oath of fidelity, allegiance, and indivisible union that they have undertaken. As already noted, graduations also can incorporate rings as symbolic vehicles to express fidelity. Naturalization ceremonies, in contrast, do not materialize the event with rings, though the handing out of tiny or medium-size flags by the Daughters of the American Revolution at the ceremonies may substitute for rings on the day of the event.

Graduations and weddings show the power of the discourse of citizenship, its power to produce the subjectivity of citizen. Its power does not rest fully on its independent operation, but rather on its overlap with parallel discourses common in the lived experience of individuals. Even persons who have not been direct participants in either a graduation or a wedding are likely to have attended such events as family or friends, and hence have been exposed to such expressions of fidelities.

Moreover, for those who have gone through their own graduations and/or weddings, their attendance at the graduations or weddings of family and friends seems to reinforce their memories and sentiments about their own experiences with those acts. While perhaps a stereotype, I have observed that married couples at weddings sometimes give each other a tender look or squeeze each other's hand when the vows are exchanged.

Presumably what is taking place is the reinforcement of their expression of fidelity toward each other.

In similar ways, the production of the subjectivity of citizen draws upon and reinforces other parallel discourses that incorporate notions of fidelity and foster perceptions of a good graduate (someone who studied hard and submitted all work in partial fulfillment of the requirements for the degree earned), a good couple (a couple that has made a commitment to each other), a good wife/husband (one who is faithful, devoted, loyal, caring), a good mother/father (one who sacrifices, is responsible, provides for family members, is considerate, and controls the behavior of their children, particularly in public), a good daughter/son (one who is responsive to and sacrifices for the needs of her/his parents, particularly ill and elderly parents), a good sister/brother (one who recognizes the ties of blood and is supportive, particularly in times of crises). As Constance Perin has insightfully described, a good neighbor (one who is considerate, particularly in controlling the actions of their children and dogs so as not to disrupt or infringe on the lives and property of neighbors) is a valued neighbor, a good citizen (Perin 1998).

In sum, many of the characteristics and virtues that most of us strive for are part of discourses that draw on the notion of fidelity, the same notion that is central to the production of the subjectivity of citizen, and the self subject-making of citizen. The Mexican migrants I interviewed are also enmeshed in the same discourses of fidelity and strive for the same virtues: being a good wife/husband, a good mother/father, a good daughter/son, and a good citizen. Consequently, the elements in the discourse of citizenship make sense to them and to us, and we desire to have such virtues. Taken together, they validate the commonsense world that is part of our lived experience. They are essential to our lives, and because we perceive them as essential they go "without saying because they come without saying" (Bourdieu 1977, 167).

INTERPRETING NATURALIZATION CEREMONIES

Pierre Bourdieu, in "Rites as Acts of Institution" (1992), building on previous work regarding how educational tests are forms of "social consecration," critiques the work of Arnold van Gennep and Victor Turner. He suggests that instead of seeing initiation rites as rites of passage, some should more properly be labeled "rites of institution." For Bourdieu, a rite of institution "lead[s] towards the consecration or legitimization of an arbitrary boundary, . . . it attempts to misrepresent the arbitrariness and present the boundary as legitimate and natural; . . . it effects a solemn, that is to say a licensed and extraordinary, transgression of the boundaries which constitute the social and ideational order which it is concerned at all costs to protect" (81). Using the well-described example in the anthropological literature of the ritualized circumcision of boys, he suggests that whereas the common interpretation is to say that the ritual marks the transition from boy to man, the rite is instituting a more fundamental distinction: "by treating men and women differently the rite consecrates the difference, it institutes it—and at the same time it institutes man *qua* man, that is to say, circumcised, and woman *qua* woman, that is to say incapable of undergoing this ritual operation" (81). In other words, the consecration institutes a gender hierarchy—a socially created hierarchy—as a legitimate and natural hierarchy.

He also applies the concept to the scholastic exams of the Grand Écoles in France. He suggests that while one can speak about a distinction between students who have taken (and passed) the exams and those who have not, the social consecration separates all students from "those who will under no circumstances undergo [the exam], and thus institute a lasting difference between those whom the rite concerns and those whom it does not concern" (80). What is instituted is a misrepresentation of class hierarchy and dominance as legitimate and natural. Those who have taken the exam and obtain elite positions are interpreted as being naturally deserving of those positions; they presumably have the intelligence that others do not. What is misrecognized is the link between their elite position to begin with and the fact that the taking of the exams is related to the subject position of the takers.

Drawing on the above insights, I would suggest that the citizenship ceremonies mark a distinction between citizen and noncitizen, which valorizes citizenship. However, there is a more fundamental valorization of citizenship in marking the boundary between citizen and illegal alien or undocumented migrant. Those granted citizenship are separated from those defined to be outside the possibility of citizenship, those who can be involuntarily ejected from the body politic at the whim of the state. Through the rite of institution of naturalization, the arbitrariness of the juridical force of law (or the arbitrariness of the formal categories themselves) is misrepresented as being rational, legitimate, and natural actions of the state. A sovereign state is expected to guard its borders. This action is inherent and natural to sovereignty; all sovereignties do it, so it is natural that it be done. The arbitrariness of what constitutes sovereignty, the use of military power to violate the sovereignty of other nations while adhering to the sanctity of the sovereignty of the aggressor, and the contradiction between international agreements that claim to endorse the free movement of people while militarizing borders to prevent such movement are erased by the misrepresentation of the notion of sovereign nation.

The rites of naturalization reinforce the value and privileges of citizenship. They institute the legitimacy of the value and privileges that constitute citizenship. Those who possess citizenship can assert their distinction from those who "have no right to be here," who are placed outside the possibility of citizenship, and who, following Badiou, are present but not represented. Bourdieu's analysis can be said to apply to citizenship petitioners in general. It is applicable to the extent that the core categories are mutually exclusive (e.g., lawful migrant versus informally authorized). However, because of the added complexity that some of the persons granted citizenship were once informally authorized, we have to distinguish between full and partial instituting (a distinction not made by Bourdieu). For those formerly informally authorized, the institution of distinction is only partial. Their lived experiences with immediate family members who may be informally authorized limits the institution of distinction.

Enhancing the Ceremonies

In 2002, as part of the Homeland Security Act, Congress created the Office of Citizenship within the Citizenship and Immigration Services division of the Department of Homeland Security. Although it is not clear what motivated the insertion of the particular provision into the Act, the Office of Citizenship was given the responsibility "for promoting instruction and training on citizenship responsibilities for aliens interested in becoming naturalized citizens of the United States, including the development of educational materials."[11] As explained by a CIS representative at the Houston CIS office, after the passage of the act and then the transfer of INS, Border Patrol and Customs from the Justice Department to the Department of Homeland Security in March 2003, community relations officers were first placed under the Immigration and Customs Enforcement (ICE) division. Shortly after, they were transferred to the Office of Citizenship, where they are now located.

The Office of Citizenship has three goals:

Goal 1: Enhance information and educational opportunities provided to legal immigrants to support their integration and participation in American civic culture. . . .

Goal 2: Promote education and training on citizenship rights, privileges, and responsibilities for immigrants interested in becoming citizens. . . .

Goal 3: Infuse citizenship-related ceremonies and events with greater meaning and stature by: Standardizing and enhancing the meaning of naturalization ceremonies [and] promoting celebration of the meaning of citizenship.[12]

These goals highlight the importance of naturalization ceremonies as a way to augment the meanings of citizenship. Although the public materials on the bureau do not indicate or define specific meanings of citizenship, the meanings could be interpreted as instituting proper fidelities toward the state, its policies, its institutions, and its leaders. Thus, the underlying premise of the third goal is the assumption that contemporary citizenship petitioners lack a set of unspecified meanings about citizenship and/or that the ceremonies are somehow falling short of conveying the meanings that they should be conveying. Though unstated, these assumptions appear to be founded on a notion that in the past the ceremonies conveyed the right meanings to participants, and that perhaps the unassimilability of contemporary citizenship aspirants requires a stronger patriotic message, something that was not needed in the past because of the assimilability of past petitioners (presumably because the melting-pot process was working in the past).

Of the three ceremonies described above, the third ceremony probably meets or comes closest to the vision of enhanced or infused ceremonies. The CIS representative at the Houston CIS office indicated that in Houston and other districts the term "enhanced," to date, has meant including local

athletes and entertainers who are naturalized citizens as speakers at naturalization ceremonies. He added that the term "enhance" may soon be interpreted as a more explicit attempt to infuse patriotism and nationalism into
the ceremonies (such as including a video message by the president, the
color guard, guest speakers, a patriotic video, etc.). His concern is that
patriotism cannot be imposed. One cannot forced another to be patriotic;
it is something that develops in the individual.

In my study, those I interviewed who had experienced a naturalization
ceremony had fond memories of their naturalization ceremony; however,
their love, loyalty, and respect for the United States did not emerge at the
ceremony, it was already in place prior to the ceremony. During one interview, a woman in her mid-fifties proudly showed me her framed Certificate
of Naturalization, which she hung on the wall. She also showed me pictures
of her and the judge presiding at the ceremony. The event was held in San
Antonio, and her description was similar to the San Antonio ceremony
described earlier. Her oath-taking ceremony was special for her, and she
emotionally described the event to me: "Muy hermosa la ceremonia, bella;
nunca se me va a olvidar. . . . Ni donde naci en mi país, he sentido eso"
(It was a beautiful ceremony, really beautiful; I'll never forget it. . . . What
I felt there, I have never felt before, not even where I was born, my country).

This woman migrated to the United States when she was twenty-four
and entered the country without formal authorization. Under the time provision, she was able to take advantage of the IRCA legalization program.
Because she has lived in the United States longer than she ever lived in
Mexico, this country is her point of reference. It is where she worked hard,
met her husband here, married, bought a house, gave birth, raised her two
children, and is now grandmother to her second-generation U.S.-born
grandchildren. The United States is the nation that provided her, her
children, and now her grandchildren multiple opportunities. She is grateful
for what she has been able to accomplish here. Although she has heard
from coworkers and friends of the *racismo* (racism) that exists here, she
does not understand it, since "no me ha pasado nada mal [a mi]; estoy
muy agradecida de este país" (nothing bad has happened to me; I'm very
grateful to this nation).

She took ESL and citizenship classes and studied the 100 Questions in her
spare time. She valued U.S. citizenship and expressed fidelities toward the

United States prior to her naturalization ceremony. The ceremony marked the final stage in her acquisition of citizenship; it was not the place where she formulated respect and appreciation for the opportunities she found in the United States. She liked the elaborate ceremony, but she already loved the United States—"estoy enamorada de este país" (I'm in love with this country). Nevertheless, she still loves her country of birth, too, referring to it as "mi país" (my country). In fact, her husband took her to Mexico to celebrate her becoming a U.S. citizen.

In summary, this interviewee already loved and respected the United States and understood the value of citizenship prior to her naturalization ceremony. Thus the concern with the need to infuse it with the right patriotic elements is a misplaced concern. Her husband's treat of taking her for a short vacation to Mexico was not intended to reinforce Mexicaness, but rather to celebrate her achievement of becoming a U.S. citizen. Also, the proximity of Austin to Mexico (about a four-hour drive) made it an economical choice.

Enhanced ceremonies do not erase the sentiments people have about their place of birth and the fidelities fostered there. Although contemporary critics appear to be on a mission to erase such memories and sentiments, John Gavit had a more insightful view, noting that it is "futile to stamp out childhood memories . . . we cannot beat love of country into any worthwhile person with a club—or a law" ([1922] 1971, 38, 41). Gavit questions the underlying assumption in such efforts. Recognizing the value of individuals having allegiance to "blood" and "locality," he sees their absence as negative. The fact that people can develop long-lasting fidelities to their place of birth means that similar fidelities can be fostered toward one's adopted country. It is more of a problem to have immigrants who can readily drop past allegiances and pick up new ones. Interestingly, it is this type of individual that some congressmen seem to want to elevate as the model for citizenship petitioners.

CHAPTER 6

❧

Desire, Sacrifice, and Disenchantment

The immigrants I interviewed desired citizenship for many reasons, many of which are parallel to what has been reported in the naturalization literature. For example, a survey of persons in citizenship/ESL classes in Austin, El Paso, Houston, and San Antonio reported that 292 out of 526 Latino participants (of which almost 90 percent were of Mexican origin) had immediate plans to apply for citizenship. The others planned to apply once they were more proficient in English, civics, and history. Table 6.1 presents their reasons for wanting to petition for citizenship.

The three most common responses provided by the migrants interviewed were wanting to sponsor a family member, to be a full member of U.S. society, and to vote. The narrow range of statements about why they were pursuing or had pursued citizenship does not reflect the multiple statements they made regarding what they felt about the United States. Some of the comments reflected the gender of the individual. Most of the women at different times invoked the notion of love, such as "estoy enamorada de este país" (I'm in love with this country). Men tended to use notions of respect and appreciation to explain how they felt about the United States and why they were pursuing citizenship (or had pursued it).

When I asked about why they loved or respected the United States, the responses were commonly framed in terms of *oportunidades*—opportunities in terms of jobs, to get ahead, to survive economically, to find

TABLE 6.1

REASONS FOR WANTING TO NATURALIZE ($N = 292$)

	Percent
I want to vote	86.0
I plan to live in the United States for the rest of my life	83.9
I love the United States	73.6
I want better opportunities for my children	72.9
I want to get a better job in the United States	62.3
I want to help my relatives come to the United States	43.8
I am afraid I will lose government services	27.4
I am dissatisfied with my government back home	24.3
The media promotion of citizenship encouraged me	23.6
I cannot return to my home country because of its politics	7.9

Note: Percentages exceed 100 since respondents could select more than one answer.
Source: Freeman et al. 2002, 1018.

stability, and, particularly, their children's education. In one case, all three of an interviewee's children had finished high school, and two had graduated from college. Although it is not explicitly reflected in the responses to why they desired citizenship, the reasons were often linked to positive feelings about the United States and the realization that their lives, and those of their immediate family, were rooted here. They and their families had become integrated into the nation's social fabric. Over time, a set of fidelities was created toward the United States and its institutions. Those who made themselves U.S. citizens formalized those fidelities.

Their loyalty to the United States, however, does not erase their allegiance toward Mexico or their memories of their parents' household, extended family, and the local community in which they formed their initial sense of self. These sentiments reflect the same kind of attachments that historians of European migration to the United States have described in Irish, Italian, Jewish, Polish, and other migrant communities. Affects and sentiments about the Old Country are vividly remembered and can even be found among their U.S.-born children, who may not have ever visited their parents' place of birth. Thousands of Irish Americans in Boston, Chicago, and New York proudly celebrate and participate in St. Patrick's Day celebrations, despite being fourth- or fifth-generation U.S.-born descendants who have never traveled to Ireland.

The conceptual distinction between nation and state is cogently articulated in a statement by Ramon, a day laborer in Heather Courtney's documentary *Los Trabajadores/The Workers* (2001). In one scene Ramon, cooking in his apartment, says to the videographer: "¡Yo lo amo a mi país! [*pause*] Al gobierno no. [*pause*] ¡Al gobierno lo detesto!" (I love my country, not the government. I detest the government!) An informally authorized worker from Tabasco, he expresses his strong affection for his country and his strong dislike of the Mexican state.[1] In his astute observation, Ramon reminds us that expressions such as "I love Mexico" must not be interpreted as representing a dislike or secondary affection toward the United States. A naturalized U.S. citizen can have two loves: a love for the United States nation-state and a love for the Mexican nation. These are not incompatible or mutually exclusive.

A parallel perception was mentioned to me over the course of the interviews I conducted. Persons pursuing citizenship, as well as those who had been granted citizenship, would invoke the notion of "mi país" (my country) in reference to Mexico, yet the positive feelings they expressed were generally about the geographic community where they grew up, not about the government. These national fidelities are separate from their fidelities toward the United States and their respect for U.S. citizenship. One reason for this is the conceptual space between nationality/nationalism and citizenship. It is part of the transition and transformation from Mexican nationality to U.S. citizenship. In Mexico the historical emphasis has been on nationality/nationalism, while in the United States there has been a historical merging of citizenship and nationality, and citizenship is the dominant category.

Some critics of dual nationality are critical of the presence of such a status in the United States because of the concern that dual fidelities may exist. It is not a new concern: the internment of Japanese individuals, and to a lesser extent Germans and Italians, including U.S. citizens, during World War II reflected such a concern. In the case of Mexican migrants who desire and obtain U.S. citizenship, the continuation of older fidelities toward a locality, a home, do not affect the possession or strength of fidelities toward the United States, its Constitution, or its institutions. The object of the fidelities is different.

The people I interviewed expressed wanting to be a full member of this society and wanting to vote. They wanted to belong and to be recognized as a U.S. citizen. Wanting to vote seemed to be an expression of not simply an ability to carry out an electoral task, but of having a *voz* (voice), specifically in reference to the election of the president and members of Congress. Those who mentioned voting spoke about federal offices; nobody mentioned state or local elections in conjunction with wanting to vote.

In summary, the desire for citizenship was expressed in a narrow set of reasons, but these reasons were part of a broader set of notions about fidelities to the United States, and about feelings related to belonging and recognition. The recognition of affective aspects as part of the context of rational, juridical notions such as citizenship has received limited attention in the academic literature. Most writings about citizenship invoke the political-juridical language of the concept but overlook the language of affects and emotion that intersects it. Yet the very language of politico-juridical citizenship relies on the presence of affects: fidelity, faithfulness, loyalty, obligation, patriotism, duty, and responsibility. Benedict Anderson's (2006) classic argument about nationalism is more than about the existence of an imagined community. He articulates the importance of cultural foundations to nationalism and the saliency of affects in fostering and sustaining nationalism.

The Good and the Bad Citizen

There has been much discussion about the topic of what schools should do to inculcate good citizens and the characteristics that some authors associate with good citizenship. The notion of good citizen is frequently invoked in discussions of naturalization and migrants; however, users generally do not specify how they define the phrase. There is a certain taken-for-granted aspect about its use. The existing social science literature on naturalization does not discuss what migrants themselves define as a "good citizen." The present research posed this question to those who are in the process of petitioning for citizenship, as well as those who have been granted citizenship.

The political scientists Orit Ichilov and Nisan Nave (1981), building on previous research, interviewed Israeli adolescents regarding their perceptions of "the good citizen." According to Ichilov and Nave, the top three responses provided by Israeli youth in the early 1980s were the following: obeying the laws of the state (74.8 percent), being loyal to the state (53.9 percent), and performing duties to the state (43.7 percent) (368). In their analysis they note that like U.S. adolescents, they define the good citizen primarily in political terms, but in contrast to U.S. youth, Israeli youth stress obedience and loyalty, rather than participation (374). The reason for noting the results from Israel is that Mexican migrants interviewed provided a similar view: a good citizen is one who obeys the laws.

The answers provided by those interviewed were narrow though informative. All stressed adherence and obedience to laws as the most important element of being a good citizen. The only noncitizens who added another element were two not-yet citizens interviewed in Houston who are active in the promotion of citizenship. They added involvement and participation in local issues as markers of good citizenship (both are from Central America).

The Mexican migrants interviewed, both those petitioning and those who have been granted citizenship, did not hesitate in answering the question. Obedience to laws is what they associate with being a good citizen. Moreover, when I asked them about what is important to inculcate in one's children (*inculcar en los hijos de uno*), a parallel response was given: raise them to obey all laws, to respect the law. Therefore, they seek to be good citizens by obeying and respecting the laws of the United States. They want their children to obey the laws also and thus to be good citizens, too.

Enchantment, Disenchantment, and Citizenship

The acquisition of U.S. citizenship, like the endings in many U.S. large-budget films, is frequently represented as a happy ending in the academic, juridical, and migrant advocacy literature. In my review of the literature on naturalization and the acquisition of U.S. citizenship, its acquisition is generally characterized as the final point in an arduous process, as something obtained after much sacrifice. Migration attorneys, migrant advocates, and individuals pursuing citizenship can easily recall the many difficulties on the path to U.S. citizenship. The two dominant tropes are sacrifice and dream.

The one partial exception to the above is the work of researchers, principally political scientists, concerned with the electoral participation of naturalized citizens after they obtain citizenship. Such research is not concerned with their satisfaction or well-being after being granted that juridical status. Instead, the focus is on specific actions taken by individuals after they have reached the goal of citizenship. The principal concern in this literature is the comparison between naturalized citizens and U.S.-born citizens, or citizen and noncitizen regarding electoral participation or political participation more broadly.[2] Within such analyses, there is an implied assumption that the newly naturalized citizens are better off than before. In general this is correct, particularly in reference to the acquisition of suffrage and the possibility of federal employment. In specific cases, however, the assumption may not be correct.

Promotional booklets and textbooks on U.S. citizenship generally focus on listing its many benefits. For example, the widely distributed *New Americans Guide* booklet, published in English and Spanish, and produced by the Fannie May Foundation and the National Immigration Forum, lists the "Benefits of Citizenship" ("The right to vote," "Greater freedom to travel," "Sponsor a relative," and "Other opportunities as a citizen").[3] Even though the exact benefits may vary, the tendency in citizenship promotional materials is to list voting, sponsoring relatives, and federal employment. Some materials add protection from removal.

Although the actual benefits of citizenship may be thought of as the same in recent times, their representation varies by administration. In 2007, under the Bush administration, the Citizenship and Immigration Services produced an impressive packet, *Civics and Citizenship Toolkit: A Collection of Educational Resources for Immigrants*, which included several multicolor, glossy-paper booklets, a DVD, and a CD related to naturalization. It was made available, free of charge, to libraries, organizations, and individuals involved in naturalization activities, and it was sold to the public through the U.S. Government Printing Office.[4] Included in the tool kit is a booklet titled *Welcome to the United States: A Guide for New Immigrants.* Page 90 lists the benefits of citizenship.

In April 2011 the Obama administration issued a revised version of the booklet, changing the title to *A Guide to Naturalization*. Page 3 lists the benefits of citizenship. In addition to the benefits' placement in the booklet, two noticeable differences in the two lists are the number of items listed (eleven in 2007, seven in 2011) and the order of key items. In the 2007 booklet, the first item is "Showing your patriotism. Becoming a citizen is a way to demonstrate your commitment to your new country." This item is seventh on the list in the 2011 version. And in the 2011 booklet, voting is the first item, while in the 2007 document it is second. These changes show that the answer to "What are the benefits of citizenship?" is contestable and influenced by political perspective.

Although there may be explicit and implicit messages in citizenship guides and textbooks about rights and responsibilities, or what new citizens should do, such as become active electors, the acquisition of citizenship remains the goal, the sought-after dream. Such documents do not discuss any possible disadvantages in acquiring citizenship.

The *New Americans Guide* also has a section titled "How to Become a Homeowner," thereby juxtaposing two dreams: citizenship and home ownership. The two dreams are linked in the guide's preface: "One of the obstacles many immigrants face in realizing their dreams is a lack of information. This guide will provide information on the process of becoming a citizen and becoming a homeowner" (Fannie May 1996, 5). The section on home ownership is introduced as follows: "If you're like most people in America, owning your own home is a major part of the American dream. If homeownership is your dream too, it *can* become a reality" (19). Acquiring citizenship and a house are desired ends. They allow the fulfillment of a lack, presumably offer satisfaction to the individual, and allow migrants to be "like most people in America." Thus, both ends are presented as dreams to hope for, as positive fulfillments. None of possible disadvantages to either dream are mentioned. For example, some of the possible problems of home ownership include a housing market collapse, a dramatic drop in the home's value, mold, and major structural problems. Likewise, as I will discuss shortly, citizenship may also entail some unforeseen problems, or at least disenchantments, for new citizens.

Media coverage of naturalization ceremonies is frequently couched in terms of citizenship being a desire and a dream. A 2003 *People Weekly* story about a Fourth of July naturalization ceremony opens with the following: "American Dreams: For most of us, Independence Day means fireworks, barbecues and baseball. But for these newly minted citizens—many of whom struggled for years to get to this country—this July 4th means so much more." The title of a 2004 *US Newswire* report about a naturalization ceremony in Maryland is "U.S. Citizenship and Immigration Services to Welcome 32 New Citizens: Ceremony Highlights the American Dream in Action." Press releases by CIS also are often framed as the achievement of a dream: "104 Year-old Immigrant Fulfills His Dream of Becoming a U.S. Citizen." Frequently, even if the title of the article does not invoke the dream trope, the text of the article does.

Eduardo Aguirre Jr., former director of the U.S. Citizenship and Immigration Services (CIS), offered a succinct statement of what presumably is achieved with the acquisition of U.S. citizenship. In the cover letter of the agency's ten-year strategic plan, he suggests the following: "The opportunity for social equality, for economic independence, for a bright future; these are the beacons that have attracted people throughout history and from every part of the world to become Americans" (CIS 2005). Aguirre's statement could be applied more broadly and include all migrants, or at least formally authorized migrants, to the United States, not simply those who obtain citizenship. However, given his position at CIS, the content of the report, and previous speeches he has made, I would suggest that his primary reference is citizenship. For example, in his March 11, 2005, speech at the naturalization ceremony held at the George Bush Presidential Library, he referenced sacrifice several times and then added, "As new citizens, from today on, you will be able to fully pursue your version of the American Dream . . . relish in your success, as you have earned it . . . we have no second-class U.S. citizens! Native born or naturalized, as Americans, we shoulder the same rights and responsibilities."[5] The assertion of the absence of differences between U.S.-born and naturalized citizens suggest that Aguirre perceives citizenship as an equalizing process that provides the opportunity of social equality. He also makes a distinction between those capable of petitioning for citizenship and those with almost no hope of doing so. Citizenship, it is suggested, leads to three things: social equality, economic independence, and a bright future. Such themes are commonly implied in governmental and nongovernmental citizenship promotion materials and activities.

Aguirre's narrative valorizes U.S. citizenship, noting the equalizing dimensions of citizenship and underscoring the privileges associated with it. Such discourses on citizenship also generate a degree of enchantment. They highlight the benefits and resources available through citizenship, and the role of citizenship as a "method of distribution of resources" (Turner 1993a, xi). Thus U.S. citizenship's potential to provide access to desired resources is central to its enchanted quality. The process of enchantment is common to most of our lives and can be located in multiple aspects; marriage, for example, when viewed through divorce rates for first marriages (generally around 50 percent), can also be thought of as an enchanted social institution.

The acquisition of citizenship is perceived as a sort of gateway or threshold that an individual crosses (similar to the well-developed theme in anthropology stimulated by the work of Arnold van Gennep, Audrey Richards, Victor Turner, and others concerned with rites of passage), and it is assumed that life under the new status grants one a higher social position. The individuals who struggle to achieve citizenship, and the groups and people who assist them (including me), anticipate such an outcome. When teaching citizenship classes, I hoped that the students would pass and that opportunities would expand for them. Thus, ultimately both the individuals desiring citizenship and I were constructing the new status as threshold to new and better possibilities.

I am not suggesting that the acquisition of citizenship is a negative end, since I know and have seen the benefits that accrue to individuals; rather, the discourse of citizenship silences the possibility that for some individuals, albeit most likely a small number, there may be disenchantment after its acquisition. Moreover, as has been documented by Isao Takei, Rogelio Saenz, and Jing Li (2005), there is a real cost to being a Mexican noncitizen in California and Texas, as well as in Arizona, particularly since 1996.[6] Noncitizens, especially in California, have a lower mean hourly wage in comparison to Mexican naturalized citizens.

The positive narrative about the acquisition of citizenship, while most likely true for the majority of persons who reach this important step, excludes other experiences. Academics, migrant advocates, and INS/CIS officials have overlooked these other experiences. It is one of the silences in the citizenship literature. This silence is not absolute, though researchers have overlooked some of the clues to the existence of apprehension in seeking citizenship and possible disenchantment with being a citizen. Helen Walker, for example, in her 1928–1929 article on Mexicans and naturalization, notes a comment by a Mexican migrant who presumably had considered naturalizing. She indicates that he "liked the United States better than his native Mexico" but was told, "And what is the use? They [the Americans] will call me a 'dirty greaser,' anyway" (468). A second individual, Señor Q., is quoted as saying, "What is the use anyway? Can't go around wearing papers on your sleeve. How does anybody know if you have had the examination? We would still have to go upstairs in the movie houses, live in the low parts of town, send our children to the old and ugly school. We are still Mexicans because we look the same" (469). Although she was not able to appreciate what they were saying regarding citizenship as being embedded in social relations (power relations) in the United States, specifically in reference to racial/ethnic hierarchies and class dimensions, she provides material that give readers clues about possible sources of dissatisfaction related to citizenship.

Shortly after Helen Walker's article appeared, Emory Bogardus, a well-known sociologist at the time, published *The Mexicans in the United States* (1934). In the chapter on "Citizenship and Adult Education," he points out apprehensions and disenchantments about citizenship. According to Bogardus, Mexicans in the late 1920s and early 1930s were not petitioning for citizenship because "naturalization does not make adequate changes in the status of the Mexican. Citizenship is disappointing to him, for he is still likely to be treated as a Mexican and a foreigner. Citizens in the United States as a rule do not distinguish between naturalized and unnaturalized Mexicans. 'They all look alike,' is the superficial explanation and inadequate justification. Since the naturalized Mexican is still treated as unnaturalized, he logically asks, 'Why become naturalized?'" (78). Bogardus then notes: "They prefer to live as self-respecting Mexicans than to live among 'holier-than-thou' citizens of the United States" (79). Drawing on interview data collected by Helen Walker, he writes: "They talk to us about becoming citizens, but if we become citizens we are still Mexicans. They look at our hair, and listen to our speech and call us Mexican. Even my boy who was born in the United States is a Mexican it seems. He has to go to the Mexican school. There is always a difference in the way he is treated" (79).

Subsequent research provides multiple statements by Mexican Americans who enlisted in World War II to assert their belonging and their desire for acceptance. Chicano/Mexican Americans can trace their roots to the Southwest prior to its annexation to the United States yet are still regarded as foreigners. This research has not explicitly linked statements like these to disenchantments related to citizenship. Feminist writings on women as second-class citizens make similar observations: women have had a long struggle to achieve parity, a struggle that will likely continue. The important point is that despite their possession of citizenship, their subject position as women shapes their position in society; thus citizenship is not a guarantor of parity or equality. Its enchanted quality holds out the promise that it can be the guarantor of equality, a guarantor that we have no second-class U.S. citizens.

Señora Galarza

Señora Galarza, a woman in her early fifties, has lived in the Austin, Texas, area since 1977. She came to Austin because one of her brothers had migrated to the area. She was able to take advantage of the IRCA legalization program, applied with the help of a notary public, and was granted temporary residency. In 1991 she was granted permanent residency and then citizenship in 1999. Between 1997 and 1999, she took several ESL classes (some of which she was not able to finish because of her work schedule), one of my citizenship classes, and two more classes after that. She is more comfortable with English now but still struggles to become proficient.

The main reason she pursued citizenship was to reunite with her son and daughter, both of whom are over eighteen. It was her understanding that it would be much easier to bring her children to the United States if she were a U.S. citizen. She has worked hard to survive economically, and she wants to get ahead and help her children. Their future is important to her, and she thinks that they will have more opportunities here than in Mexico to have stable economic lives. Currently, she works for a midsize company doing office maintenance. She starts her shift around 3:30 a.m., works for about three to four hours, gets a break, and then works for two more hours. Señora Galarza has been with the same employer for about ten years, though not always as an employee. At first she worked for the subcontractor, but later she was hired as an employee. She is particularly happy to work for the employer because of her access to health insurance and other benefits, benefits she did not have with the subcontractor.

However, her workday does not end with that job. She has a second job, a small retail business, where she has worked for sixteen years. She gets off that job at 6 p.m. Then she goes home, has dinner, and goes to bed at 8 p.m. She gets up at 3 a.m. the next day. This is her daily routine Monday through Friday. On Saturday, her light day, she only has to work at the retail store. Everything else has to be done on Sunday: attend mass, shop for groceries, do laundry, iron clothes, mend clothes, attend to car repairs, briefly visit her brother or some friends, and eat at one of the small Mexican restaurants near her apartment. Then she has to get to bed by 8 p.m.

For Señora Galarza, nothing much has changed since she obtained citizenship. She does not have economic independence (if we take this to mean a stable economic life). As a single woman with limited skills, she has to work two jobs to make ends meet. She does not have social equality (if we take this to mean a middle-class social life, occupation, or acceptance in the broader community). And the future does not look bright. She knows that she has to keep working at both jobs as long as she physically can. She indicated that perhaps when she reaches retirement age, she will only work at the retail store.

However, the above dream elements are not the main source of her disenchantment with citizenship. It is something closer to her original reason for seeking citizenship: the issue of wanting to formally reunite with her children. When she attended the citizenship promotion events or talked to other people, she was told that it would be easier to get permanent residency visas for her children as a U.S. citizen. However, in migration law and policy, details are critical—the cliché "the devil is in the details" is applicable here. It is indeed easier, but only if the children are under eighteen years old. Otherwise, it is not that easy.

Señora Galarza's disenchantment with her acquisition of citizenship is that it will take eight to ten years for her daughter and son to be formally admitted. She did not realize that the waiting period was this long, which is due to the preference system set up under the 1965 Immigration Act and some of its subsequent amendments that cap the number for each preference category. She still appreciates what she has been able to accomplish as a single woman in the United States, and she is proud that she was granted

U.S. citizenship, yet she sees that the whole application process, which she characterized as "un sacrificio para los hijos" (a sacrifice for my children), did not lead to what she ultimately desired. And while she never said that it was not worth it, she clearly was disenchanted that she had not yet been able to reach her ultimate dream: reuniting with her children.

Señora Galarza's story also points to the actions that individuals sometimes take in response to state policies in order to partially accomplish their goals, but these actions in turn place them in problematic circumstances. Señora Galarza's son (in his mid-twenties) has, rather than wait the eight to ten years, obtained a tourist visa and is temporarily living with his mother. He is also working in Austin. His lack of formal employment authorization is not a problem for his employer. As he noted, "los empleadores no preguntan mucho" (the employers don't ask very much). However, his acceptance of employment is a violation of the terms of the tourist visa, which makes him subject to removal. He can also be removed if he stays beyond the authorized period on his visa. Moreover, if he is apprehended, he cannot reenter the United States for about ten years (due to the Illegal Immigration Reform and Immigrant Responsibility Act of 1996), and that would also affect his position on the migration queue. The net effect is that the possibility of Señora Galarza uniting with her son—part of her dream of obtaining citizenship—would become a more costly and distant event if this were to happen. Señora Galarza's daughter still resides in Mexico and has no immediate plans to migrate to the United States.

The above is not to suggest that Señora Galarza would have been better off if she had remained a permanent resident, but rather that for her the acquisition of citizenship was part of a broader dream. It was not the end itself. The broader dream included her desire to reunite with her children. Her limited knowledge about the realities of rules and laws regarding sponsoring relatives by citizens reduced the value of her assessment of what she had accomplished: she struggled and eventually was granted citizenship. Part of the onus in fostering disenchantment also rests with migrant assistance organizations, which did not sufficiently clarify for her the limitations of family reunification when children reach the age of eighteen. Moreover, although she was granted citizenship and defined herself as a U.S. citizen (an important change), socioeconomic position and everyday life remain the same.

Señor Alvarez

When I first met Señor Alvarez in one of my early citizenship classes, he was quite jovial and talkative, never missed a class, and usually arrived ten to fifteen minutes early. Since I also arrived early, we often had a chance to talk about a broad range of topics, such as work, class topics, INS announcements, or some political news story (he had a keen interest in current events). During class he was quite willing to answer questions and to role-play an examiner questioning the other participants, or an applicant responding to an examiner's questions. He took the class seriously, studied the material we went over in class, completed homework assignments, and asked questions. It was always a pleasure to listen to his perspective on news items out of Washington or from Mexico City.

Now in his early fifties, Señor Alvarez has lived in the United States since 1970. He entered the country with a visa that granted him work authorization.[7] In 1973 he was able to petition for permanent residency based on the birth of his child within the United States. Prior to the late 1970s, it was possible for persons, including the informally authorized, to adjust their status based on U.S.-born children. A change in the law in 1978 mandated that parents could not apply directly to adjust their status but had to wait until their child turned eighteen. Then the child had to petition for the parents.[8]

Señor Alvarez held multiple jobs throughout his adult life, and through some of those experiences he picked up upholstery skills. He applied at a local college in Austin to work in the upholstery section and was successful in obtaining the job. He started working at that job in 1983 and held it for eighteen years (until 2001). In order to make ends meet and be a responsible father and wage earner, he converted his garage into an upholstery shop and began to take on jobs. Consequently, his workday started early in the morning at his college job and continued into the evening at his shop at home. The weekends were the light days. He only worked at his shop at home. The Alvarez family survived economically based on Señor Alvarez's two incomes and the income earned by Señora Alvarez. Their three incomes allowed them to purchase a modest home in a working-class neighborhood in East Austin, raise their family, pay the mortgage, buy supplies and equipment for the shop at home, take the family to local parks, and once in a while go out to eat as a family to a fast food restaurant or a small family-operated Mexican restaurant.

Señor Alvarez was granted U.S. citizenship in 2000. He is very proud of this achievement. After many years of studying English, taking citizenship classes, and obtaining his GED, he eventually reached his goal of obtaining citizenship. After obtaining citizenship, he thought of himself as a "U.S. citizen." However, identifications are relational. What one selects as an identification can be different from what others may attribute. At his college job, his coworkers were Euro-Americans and Mexican Americans. Señor Alvarez was the only *extranjero* (foreign born/stranger'); he was the "Mexican" (*el mexicano*). Señor Alvarez was assigned the heavy and difficult jobs, and the other men were assigned the lighter and easier jobs. Mexican Americans did the next lightest jobs; and the Euro-American workers did the very lightest jobs. For years Señor Alvarez accepted the division of labor, as that was how it was when he started. He took it for granted that since he was the only noncitizen, and the others were more proficient in English and were citizens, that is how it would probably continue.

He thought that when he became a U.S. citizen things might be a bit easier at work. He did not expect a complete reversal of the status quo, but he hoped he would have access to at least the kinds of jobs that the Mexican American coworkers had. Citizen or not, the social dynamic had already been established over seventeen years: he was still the Mexican. He continued to get the heavy and difficult jobs, apparently the jobs that are better assigned to Mexicans than to Mexican Americans or Euro-Americans.

Señor Alvarez was disappointed, but he appreciated the job—the low but good pay; the health, vacation, and sick leave benefits; and the long winter holiday. So he continued to do the best he could with the jobs he was assigned. Soon, however, things began to unravel. He lifted a heavy couch by himself and hurt his back. He was able to take some time off based on the Workers' Compensation insurance carried by the employer. When he returned to work he was again assigned to the large jobs, but he realized that he was not going to be able to do them, or at least not immediately. He talked to the shop manager and requested lighter projects, such as those assigned to his Mexican American coworkers, at least until he was able to recover. He was told that several of the large jobs were behind schedule and those were the items to which he was assigned. He pleaded with the supervisor about reconsidering. After all, he had been a good, loyal worker for seventeen years and he liked his job. He did not mind the hard work. The manager told Señor Alvarez that he had two choices: continue with the projects he was assigned or take disability retirement.

Señor Alvarez began taking strong pain medications, which helped temporarily, but one side effect of these is drowsiness. He used his sick leave days to see if could take the medication and rest, and perhaps get better. Unfortunately, the dosages of painkillers he was taking kept him in bed all day. After some time he realized that his hope of returning to work was not going to be possible, so he submitted his disability retirement. The injury not only affected his college job, but also his shop at home.

The back injury had an immediate economic impact (he now received about two-thirds of what he was earning at his college job, and he lost the income from his home shop), and it affected him psychologically. He spent long days in bed, with little motivation to do anything, and at times he wondered about the quality and value of his life. A storefront Baptist church, however, motivated him to do the best he could. He began to volunteer and later was ordained at the church.

At our last visit together, the jovial and talkative man I had originally met was gone. Señor Alvarez was now a serious, dour man with sad facial expressions. He valued his acquired citizenship, but now he simply wanted to serve God. I was interviewing a different man than the one I had originally met in my citizenship class. He was now a depressed man who seemed to have turned to a small church to insert some purpose into his life.

Promotions that encourage eligible persons to apply for citizenship by citing its benefits, such as the right to vote, greater freedom to travel, and the ability to sponsor a relative, seem to overlook the fact that the actual benefits and values of citizenship are embedded in broader social processes. The differences between the actions of Señor Alvarez and his Mexican American coworkers are not simply due to differences in their form of citizenship. They are shaped in sets of power relations and racial/ethnic hierarchies that define the process of citizenship. Citizenship integrates migrants into the circle of membership; it does not, however, erase the power relations, class differences, or racial/ethnic distinctions. The tensions within citizenship for Mexican migrants, as noted by Walker and Bogardus in the 1920s and 1930s, and based on Señor Alvarez's story, suggest that they are still with us.

Did Señor Alvarez reach the beacons enunciated by Aguirre—social equality, economic independence, and a bright future—after acquiring U.S. citizenship? The answer is no. He may have been a U.S. citizen (a category of social equality), but at the upholstery shop he never stopped being considered a Mexican, a subordinate who merited harder work. The shop manager's refusal to allow Señor Alvarez to temporarily perform non-Mexican work resulted in him having to leave the job he had held for eighteen years. This outcome did not lead to economic independence. Instead, it resulted in a substantial decrease in income (from his job and from his home shop).

The future does not seem bright. Señor Alvarez's wife now has to shoulder a greater part of the family income, yet because of the lower wage work she performs she cannot make up the difference in lost income. Life is harder for both, and they will have to depend more on their young-adult children. However, as their children start their own families, they may not be able to help as much.

Does Sr. Alvarez value his U.S. citizenship? Yes. He values it highly and is proud of the sacrifices that he made to obtain it (ESL classes, citizenship classes, studying at home, GED classes, etc.). Yet he also realizes from his college job experience that even though he knows that he is a U.S. citizen, others, including Mexican Americans, see him and label him a Mexican. It is ironic in the sense that he is proud of being born in Mexico, possessing Mexican culture, and of being a Mexican, but he does not like being labeled a Mexican in the pejorative sense because he is now a U.S. citizen.

The multidimensionality of citizenship emerges when we examine the differences between the social positions occupied by people like Señora Galarza and Señor Alvarez. The case of the late ABC news anchor Peter Jennings provides a useful comparison.[9] Jennings was born in Ottawa, Canada, in 1938 and was hired by ABC in 1964. On May 30, 2003, he was granted U.S. citizenship at a small, quiet ceremony with forty-nine other people in a federal building in New York.[10] Jennings's decision to naturalize was influenced by the September 11, 2001, events (though he did not specify what specifically related to that event or its aftermath motivated him). Few people knew about the naturalization ceremony. Jennings, after residing in the United States for close to forty years decided to file his N-400. After it was made public that he was now a U.S. citizen, some were apparently surprised to hear the news. They had taken it for granted that he was an American because they had seen him on television for so long.

Not everyone welcomed Jennings's announcement. Some conservative individuals found it insulting that he planned to maintain his Canadian citizenship (not unlike the response to Superman's announcement in an April 2011 comic book). They questioned how he could become an American and still have allegiance to Canada. One critic asked how Jennings planned on maintaining allegiance to Canada when he had to swear in the oath that he was giving up allegiances to other countries.

As a Euro-Canadian male of some means (i.e., the advantages of race, gender, class, and language), Jennings probably rarely had anyone question his right to be here. Señor Alvarez, on the other hand, was never thought of as an American. Even after he became an American, he was still a Mexican. Moreover, Jennings most likely did not have problems obtaining legal assistance to complete the N-400. And he did not take a citizenship class, though he noted that he studied the 100 Citizenship Questions. Finally, since he had been a news anchor at ABC since he was twenty-six years old, it is probably safe to conclude that he was not given the most menial or backbreaking jobs because he was a Canadian. The point here is that citizenship is not a uniform political status. It is a construct embedded in a social field, and the power relations within which it is enmeshed shape its form and its potential benefits.

The experiences of Señora Galarza and Señor Alvarez illustrate several important dimensions related to the acquisition of citizenship in the United States, at least for Mexican migrants with similar social positions. First, their stories make explicit what has been overlooked in the extensive literature on naturalization, that the acquisition of citizenship may lead to disenchantment. The present state of disenchantment could change in a positive direction in the future; however, I am not as optimistic about these specific cases. Their disenchantment, however, is separate from the value they place on citizenship. They both were proud of having been granted U.S. citizenship and of being citizens.

The source of disenchantment is not the same for both individuals. Señora Galarza was disenchanted by the lack of clear communication regarding permanent resident visas for children over eighteen. In the promotion of citizenship, simply telling eligible applicants about the benefits of

U.S. citizenship without also presenting the reality of what to expect can be readily remedied. Señora Galarza should have been told that she would have to wait eight to ten years before reuniting with her children.

The case of Señor Alvarez raises several important issues. One, it elucidates the theoretical point that citizenship is more than a juridical status; it is an "instituted process" (Polanyi 1957, 243–270). Citizenship is "embedded and enmeshed in institutions, economic and noneconomic" (250).[11] While Señor Alvarez was, and thought of himself as, a U.S. citizen (his subjectivity was that of a citizen, with its notions of equality), in the social setting at work, with its racial/ethnic hierarchy, his subjectivity and identification as a U.S. citizen could be accepted or rejected. In his case it was rejected. For his Mexican American and Euro-American coworkers, he remained what he was before, a Mexican (not unlike what was reported for the late 1920s and early 1930s). The juridical status of individuals is embedded and enmeshed in the power relations within which they operate, and so it must be negotiated. Most important is that to understand what citizenship is, researchers need to explore the social settings within which citizenship is negotiated and not simply formulate dichotomous variables of citizen and noncitizen and then assume that this captures the reality of a social situation.

Another important issue raised by Señor Alvarez's story is the presence of a strong desire to belong. Señor Alvarez's immediate family was already here; his motivation to obtain U.S. citizenship was not like that of Señora Galarza, who also wanted to belong but emphasized a stronger desire to live with her children. After all, she has lived apart from her children for most of their lives, and so I did not sense that she separated the desire to belong from wanting to reunite with her children; thus belonging, for her, would mean reuniting with her children. Once together as a family, they can live together and belong to the place where they live.

Señor Alvarez wanted to be a full member of the political community that he was part of. He knew that he was never going to return to Mexico, that this was his home. He appreciated the opportunities he found here, the schooling his children received, and the opportunities they will have here. They are U.S.-born citizens. Señor Alvarez mentioned all these things when I asked him about his experiences in the United States and his reasons for desiring citizenship. I interpret these as expressions of wanting to belong, of wanting to be a full member of what he has been a part of for over thirty years. His answers underscore the importance of the desire to belong. But belonging is also relational. The broader community has to accept the person as a full member, as belonging in the community. According to Alain Badiou (2004), it is important to recognize the distinction between membership and belonging (or between represented and included). For Señor Alvarez, the acquisition of citizenship represented a vehicle to acquire belonging, but it was not successful.

Señor Alvarez's story also illustrates the applicability of the concept of recognition (Kojève 1969, 2000). Drawing on the Hegelian dialectic in asymmetrical power relations (the master-servant dialectic), Kojève argues that a central factor during interactions is recognition (part of what he labels "anthropogenic desire"). Recognition can be applied to relations between dominant and dominated, or the state and individuals. According to Kojève, "It is the Citizen, and him only, who will be fully and definitely satisfied (*befriedigt*); for he alone will be recognized by one whom he himself recognizes and he will recognize the one who recognizes him. Therefore, it is only he who will be truly realized in actuality as a human being" (2000, 213). Although Kojève is here using "citizen" in a special sense in the context of his discussion, what is important is that in unequal power relations the less dominant party has a desire to be recognized for his or her humanity (coded here as an aspect of citizenship). What Karl Marx noted as "an individual man, in his everyday life, in his work, and in his relationships" ([1843] 1972, 44). It is a desire to be recognized as a human being (or citizen), not as a dominated category (alien, stranger, *extranjero,* Mexican). In my reading of Señor Alvarez's disenchantment, it is related to the absence of recognition of his subjectivity as a U.S. citizen; he wanted to be recognized as a citizen and an equal human being. Instead, after eighteen years as a loyal and dependable worker, his manager and coworkers recognized him only as a member of a subordinate sociopolitical category: Mexican. Señor Alvarez recognized the dominant Other, but that Other did not recognize him. In other words, the dominant remained dominant—or, more precisely, recognized as dominant—while the dominated remained unrecognized.

Conclusion

As evident from the controversy surrounding the legitimacy of Barack Obama's presidency, the debate on the meaning of the birth provision in the Fourteenth Amendment, the 2005–2011 efforts to pass a comprehensive immigration reform, and actions by state and local governments since the mid-1990s to exclude aliens from resources, citizenship is a contemporary concern. Herman van Gunsteren's (1978, 10) astute observation over three decades ago regarding citizenship as an essentially contested concept and conflictual practice is borne out by our contemporary experience. Citizenship, as argued here, is a Janus-faced process that simultaneously includes and excludes. Thus, its many positive elements should be viewed alongside its exclusionary elements and as dependent on the latter.

Debates regarding the boundaries of citizenship are not limited to political issues such as those noted above; they are also evident regarding statutory provisions, despite the likely assumption that Congress or the courts must have already addressed such citizenship issues. One example is the case of *United States v. Flores-Villar*, which concerns citizenship and gender differences in law. The contestation centers on whether the statute (8 U.S.C. §1409) can discriminate against a child born out of wedlock to a U.S. citizen parent, depending on whether the citizen parent is the mother or the father. The law requires additional restriction when the citizen parent is the father. In June 2011, on a 4–4 vote, the Supreme Court upheld a lower court's ruling that it is constitutional for U.S. law to discriminate in the granting of citizenship on the basis of gender.

The concepts of citizen and citizenship, both historically and contemporarily, are important in U.S. sociopolitical discourses. Citizenship is a fundamental construct within the power relations in the United States. It indexes a broad set of ideas, such as belonging, membership, and identification, and it supports and overlaps with discourses related to nationality, nationalism, patriotism, and loyalty. A central dimension of the concept is the notion of fidelity, principally fidelity toward the state and its institutions. Moreover, citizen and citizenship signify multiple meanings and thus lack cloture. This lack of cloture is part of the power of the concept; its very openness allows the state, interest groups, and individual actors to ground their actions on behalf of citizenship. Through a long list of struggles, white males without property, women, African Americans, Asians, Latinos, Native Americans, and others have succeeded in broadening the boundaries of belonging. Today citizenship in the United States represents a significantly more encompassing circle of membership—a circle that has added about 25 million new citizens since 1907, and over 500,000 in 2009–2010.

My central concern in this volume has been threefold: One, to expand our understanding of the history and contemporary dimensions of citizenship (including naturalization), particularly as they apply to, and are experienced by, lower-income Mexican migrants. Two, to contribute to the undertheorized issue of what makes discourses (more precisely, discursive formations) productive. Three, to foster a more complex understanding of what may accompany the acquisition of citizenship, the possibility of disenchantment with the new status. I suggest that it is not a disenchantment with the United States, its principles, its leaders, or the opportunities and benefits that it has provided migrants—migrants are quite grateful and respectful of these—but rather a disenchantment with other factors. In one case it was a disenchantment with what the individual thought would be possible, under migration laws, regarding her ability to reunite with her children. In the second it was a disenchantment with the fact that becoming a U.S. citizen did not erase his position as an alien. He was still seen by his coworkers as "the Mexican."

Returning to the issue raised in the introduction, in his case the alien number on his certificate of naturalization extended its power into his status as a citizen. His possession of the certificate did not erase the alienness ascribed to him. In my case, class and status differences appear to have allowed a greater erasure of my alienness. Though I was recently reminded that I have not lost all of my ascribed alienness. An administrator in my university included me in a memo informing the presumably foreign faculty that the university had put some money aside to assist in paying visa fees, green card fees, and adjustment application fees. My U.S. citizenship appears to have been temporarily set aside; my ascribed alienness had returned. I should not be surprised by this event. Friends whose ancestors settled in what is now New Mexico or Texas before 1835 have shared stories about how eight or more generations later they are still asked "Where are you from?"

The initial three chapters present a framework for thinking about the sizable literature on citizenship, and for recognizing the double process of inclusion and exclusion that is intrinsic to citizenship. As an effort to come to terms with the multiplicity of approaches and discussions of citizenship, I suggest that one avenue is to conceptualize them as part of three discursive fields, which together comprise a larger discourse of citizenship (or citizenships): juridical, sociopolitical, and everyday discourse of citizenship. Their division into three fields is not to suggest they are mutually exclusive fields; quite the opposite, each of the three fields overlaps with and draws from the others. Though the juridical use seems to hold some dominance, it seems to bleed into the others, even when the question is not strictly a formal question about juridical status. Among political scientists concerned with electoral citizenship participation and candidate polls, for example, articulate and insightful arguments are presented regarding the topics, yet the actual juridical citizenship status of those surveyed may not be verified. Thus the reader is left to assume that the citizens talked about are U.S. citizens/electors who actually have voting privileges. One unique contribution of the discussion is the bringing to the fore the importance of the everyday uses of "citizen/citizenship" and how these uses have become part of taken-for-granted phenomena. A small number of scholars have alluded to or suggested their presence but have not elaborated on it (e.g., Berlant 1993; Shklar 1991).

I also argue that scholars need to pay attention to the unique national trajectories and how they have formulated the nationality and citizenship dichotomy and have warned against universalizing assumption based on uses in the United States and Western European nations. Specifically, I suggest that in Mexico the historically dominant notion is nationality and nationalism, whereas in the United States citizenship occupies the dominant position. The result is that there are no citizen children in Mexico (since nationality is acquired at birth, citizenship at eighteen), and in the United States almost no one refers to or thinks of themselves as a national—an odd situation since all citizens are nationals (though a small number of nationals are not citizens). The point is that greater attention should be paid to how we apply concepts across states; a plea for allocating greater attention to the trans-state discursivity of fundamental concepts such as citizen/citizenship and not accepting linguistic glosses as unproblematic. My discussion also indexed a philosophical-political issue that needs to be more closely examined: What takes place conceptually when a person from a nation where nationality is the dominant paradigm acquires citizenship in the United States (where citizenship is the dominant paradigm)?

My argument about the Janus-faced dimension of citizenship is unique to the extent that its focus is citizenship itself. Other scholars have talked about how the policies of nations have the dual entanglement of exclusion and inclusion, or produce both solidarity and conflict (e.g., Coutin 2003; Turner 1986, 1993a). I sought to build on these by addressing the specific process as it relates to citizenship. My argument is also influenced by the perceptive discussion formulated by Alexander Kojève (1969) of Hegel's *herr-knecht* (master-servant, master-slave). In particular, it draws on the idea that there can be an oppositional determination within dichotomous factors. It is a process wherein one element is constitutive of the other and vice versa.[1] Consequently, the argument is that fostering solidarity and community oftentimes depends on the exclusion of a category of persons. Benedict Anderson's (2006) analysis of nationalism suggests that the development of the modern nation-state relied on such as construction, a construction of a We that stood in contrast to a Them. Judith Shklar (1991, 35) hinted at a parallel idea when she noted that "xenophobia is helpful" to citizenship.

In reference to broader theoretical concerns in anthropology and other social sciences, my analysis has sought to address an issue left unanswered in Michel Foucault's theoretical arguments. In several places, including in some of his posthumously released early writings, Foucault (e.g., 1989) argues that while it is well recognized that the state historically implements coercive measures (i.e., negative) to govern the population, measures that assert compliance through disciplinary tactics, he also notes the presence of positive measures. In other words, in society we are governed by power that is both negative and positive. Judith Butler summarized it well: "But if following Foucault, we understand power as forming the subject as well as providing the very condition of its existence and the trajectory of its desire, then power is not simply what we oppose but also . . . what we depend on for our existence . . . Subjection consists precisely in this fundamental dependency on a discourse we never chose but that, paradoxically, initiates and sustains our energy" (1997, 2). Stated differently, the positive forces are central to our formation as subjects (the process of subjectivization or subjection); they are part of what allows us to become the subjects we are.

What was left unanswered is how power and discourses accomplish their positive production. In the case discussed here, the question is how do the discourses of citizenship produce subjects who consider themselves citizens, more specifically good citizens. So while Foucault did a superb job in elucidating the disciplinary forces of power, he did not address the second part of his theoretical question before his death in 1984. I argue that this is made possible because the discourse on citizenship does not operate in a vacuum; it draws upon parallel content in other discourses, and the discourse comes to make sense to individuals (in the case examined, migrants desiring U.S. citizenship). It makes sense because it holds the possibility of meeting individual needs and desires. Moreover, becoming citizens allows subjects to meet their own needs and desires. These needs and desires encompass concrete activities such as the ability to petition for a family member and to vote, as well as affects related to the desire to be a full member in the sociopolitical community, to belong, and to be recognized.

I argue that the productive power of the discourse of citizenship is facilitated because it draws on other discourses that also rely on a notion of fidelity. Citizenship, in the context of the state, is a mechanism that fosters attachment and obedience to the state. Benedict Anderson calls this our willingness to kill and die for our nation. When death is the result of such service, we commonly refer to it as the ultimate sacrifice and highly valorize all the fallen soldiers. We can think of the ultimate sacrifice as the ultimate expression of fidelity, a fidelity that can also be labeled as patriotism, loyalty to one's nation. What I suggest is that the discourses of marriage and graduation contribute to the power of the discourse of citizenship. They also have many parallel concepts and practices to that of naturalization. Marriage, in particular, is a practice strongly grounded on a notion of fidelity—the absence of fidelity is a common reason for its dissolution. It also involves an oath (a vow), generally relies on a public event involving family and friends, and can lead to disenchantment. The discourse and practices of graduation are also important to the discourse of citizenship. Fidelity in this discourse is represented in the concept of "school spirit." It encompasses the creation of a circle of membership that excludes those not defined as members, involves a public event, and the symbolic giving of a certificate (i.e., diploma), and it can also lead to disenchantment.

The discursive union of elements gives discourses the ability to make sense to those desiring citizenship, thereby playing a role in our self-creation as subjects. Our wanting to be good citizens overlaps with our desire to be good spouses, good siblings, good children, good students, good workers, and good soldiers. Migrants seeking U.S. citizenship want to be good citizens. The elements in the discourse of citizenship make sense to Mexican migrants, and to us, because they validate the common sense that is part of our lived experience. They are essential to our lives, and because we perceive them as essential they go "without saying because they come without saying" (Bourdieu 1977, 167).

Moreover, our commonsense understanding of fidelity and its overlapping presence allows us to associate it with virtues that we want to possess. We both desire these and are disciplined in varying degrees to maintain them; our failure to adhere to demanded norms creates the space for the state to take action against us—for the force of law to emerge. The attributes of a good citizen (a person possessing the proper fidelities to the state and its institutions) are similar to categories such as the aforementioned; they contribute to the social lubrication of the state, the nation, the military, the workplace, the school, and the family.

Conceptually, this book uses the terms "informally authorized" and "formally authorized" instead of the commonly used "illegal/undocumented migrant" (see Plascencia 2009a). The alternatives terms bring the state back in by explicitly acknowledging the role of the state and its migration enforcement apparatus in actually fostering an unauthorized migration and employment, which is authorized (though not formally). Within my discussion, I offer a critique of the common Occidentalism of the concept of citizen/citizenship. Through a brief discussion of the *vecino*, national, and citizen in Mexico's legal-political history, I argue that researchers must pay attention to the commensurability of such fundamental concepts.

My discussion of the promotion, application, and oath-taking ceremonies sought to contribute to the understanding of naturalization. While the naturalization literature is small relative to the larger corpus on citizenship, it is now substantial, even without including congressional hearings and government reports (such as the 1905 Commission on Naturalization report). The literature spans from the 1890s to 2011, though a larger share has appeared since the 1990s. The literature is diverse, covering naturalization policies in the British colonies in North America; several analyses of large data sets, such as the Current Population Survey; discussion of the Bureau of Naturalization (the bureau that later became part of the INS); and several efforts to examine the electoral participation of new citizens. In addition, a small number of works have been published that have examined naturalization ceremonies, reported interviews with recent citizens, or compared naturalization patterns for particular groups (e.g., Alvarez 1987; Bloemraad 2006a, 2006c; Coutin 2003; DeSipio 1995, 1996; Félix 2008; Freeman et al. 2002; Gilbertson and Singer 2000, 2003; Michelson and Pallares 2001; North 1987; Portes 1987). All of these works were instrumental in approaching the material discussed in the chapters, and in shaping the questions in the project and/or the analysis of the materials and interviews.

An important difference between the material presented in the preceding chapters and the scholarly work cited here is my effort to present the broader naturalization spectrum: the promotion and application process, citizenship classes, naturalization ceremonies, and interviews with migrants who had achieved their dream of being granted U.S. citizenship. What is unique is the focus on persons who represent a special cohort of migrant. They are individuals who traversed the juridical-political categories from informally authorized migrants to temporary residents, permanent residents, and U.S. citizens. Another important difference is my role as researcher and citizenship class instructor during the research project. As an instructor, I sought to reciprocate their generosity with their time and their stories about their paths to citizenship.

Epilogue

THE BOUNDARIES OF BIRTH AND POWER

On April 27, 2011, a historically unique event took place. The White House posted the president's long-form birth certificate on its website and President Obama held a press conference to announce the action. The event, on its surface, appears mundane: an elected government official makes his birth certificate public. As such, it is an unremarkable event. However, the context of the event indexes something significantly different. The fact that President Obama decided to release the document in his third year in the Office of the President is remarkable. Its release had the aim of not only clarifying his place of birth, and thus reinforcing the fact that he met the constitutional requirement of being a "natural born Citizen," but also of asserting the legitimacy of his presidency based on his citizenship. According to a pre- and post-poll by Gallup, the release of the birth certificate apparently convinced some U.S. residents that he was born in the Unites States. Gallup reports that a few days before the release, 38 percent of respondents indicated that President Obama was "definitely born in U.S.," and by the first week of May, 47 percent reported the same opinion; those who felt that he was "probably" or "definitely born in another country" decreased from 24 to 13 percent (Morales 2011).

Irrespective of one's interpretation of Gallup poll data, the release of the birth certificate, the continuing doubts about the president's birthplace, and the ongoing debate regarding the legitimacy of his presidency bring to the fore the contemporary importance of the concept of citizenship in the United States. These issues also underscore the themes discussed here regarding citizenship as a central construct in U.S. sociopolitical discourses and its inherent contestability. Supporters of the "birther movement," for example, have been successful in invoking citizenship as an issue of overriding importance in their opposition to President Obama and his policy proposals. It is the core issue through which doubts about the legitimacy of the current president of the United States are being articulated. This is not a minor issue. President Obama's strategic release of his birth certificate was a political counterresponse to that position and represents an effort to displace its prominence in the media and general public.

The persistence of concerns regarding President Obama's birth certificate and his United States citizenship highlight the importance of the principle of jus soli, in contrast to jus sanguinis, and how the construct of citizenship plays a fundamental part in political struggles. In other words, debatable boundaries of birth—that is, whether the birthplace is acceptable or not—simultaneously invoke questions about belonging and membership and relate to power relations. This concern is not simply juridical. The discrediting of Obama's status as a natural-born citizen operates alongside questions about the legitimacy of his presidency and fosters opposition to policies of his administration. While previous presidents have also faced crises of legitimacy based on unpopular wars, corruption, violation of congressional mandates, marital infidelities, etc., what is unique in the present environment is the centrality of citizenship in the political debate.

Birth and citizenship are also part of two other contemporary political debates. The first is the question of whether the principle of jus soli should be applied to children born in the United States whose parents are subject to removal. The second issue is whether U.S.-born citizens labeled "enemy combatants" or "specially designated global terrorist" (SDGT) have the same constitutional protections as other citizens, or whether they fall within an extra-constitutional state of exception, as formulated by Giorgio Agamben (1998, 2000). The cases of Yasir Esam Hamdi and José Padilla as enemy combatants, and Anwar al-Awlaki as an SDGT, as noted in the introduction, pose concrete challenges to our understanding of the unalienable rights of a U.S. citizen. President Obama's April 2010 authorization of al-Awlaki's targeted killing by the military or CIA reveals that during times of heightened national security concerns the constitutional rights of citizens may be disregarded. The killing of al-Awlaki on September 30, 2011, by a drone attack in Yemen foregrounds the challenge to this understanding.[1]

The Birthright Citizenship Controversy

The issue of birth is paramount in the birthright citizenship debate. Over the past quarter of a century, academics, elected officials, and migrant advocates have been engaged in debating the intent of the authors of the Fourteenth Amendment, the authority of Congress to legislatively redefine constitutional provisions, and how precedent cases should be interpreted. At the core of the birthright citizenship debate is the question of the meaning of the first clause, the citizenship clause, of the Fourteenth Amendment: "All persons born or naturalized in the United States, and subject to the jurisdiction thereof, are citizens of the United States and of the State wherein they reside." More specifically, it is the question of whether the clause, particularly the section stipulating "subject to the jurisdiction," applies to children born in U.S. territory whose parents are labeled "illegal aliens" and are subject to removal (although it is commonly not specified who is included under the label).

Much of the debate and scholarship has focused on two fundamental elements. The first issue is whether parents deemed to be illegal aliens are subject to the jurisdiction of the United States as noted in the Fourteenth Amendment. There are two principal positions on this: those favoring the continuation of birthright citizenship for all persons assert that parents are subject to the jurisdiction as stipulated in the Fourteenth Amendment and over a century of Supreme Court decisions; those proposing its repeal argue that such parents are not subject to the jurisdiction. At the heart of the difference is a political philosophy question regarding the role of consent and allegiance in the formation of a political community, particularly the relationship between membership grounded on mutual consent between the state/broader community and the individual, and ascriptive membership, specifically the jus soli principle.

The second major concern is whether Congress can legislatively modify the provision in the Fourteenth Amendment in order to prohibit the granting of citizenship to children whose parents are subject to removal, or whether the change must be made through a constitutional amendment. From the 102nd (1991–1992) to the 112th (2011–2012) session of Congress, thirty-two bills have been introduced that seek to repeal the long-standing practice of granting citizenship to "all persons born ... in the United States." Only nine of these propose a constitutional amendment. The clear preference for a legislative option is a pragmatic political choice; it is a procedurally simpler process involving fewer actors. A constitutional amendment, on the other hand, requires a two-thirds majority in both houses, the approval of thirty-eight state legislatures, and can be a prolonged process. The recent experience with the last amendment to the Constitution, the Twenty-seventh Amendment, and the earlier proposed Equal Rights Amendment, foretell political difficulties in amending the Constitution. The latter was introduced in 1923, was approved by both houses of Congress in 1972, but failed to garnish the support of thirty-eight states by the June 30, 1982 deadline; thus, despite its laudable aims, the proposal to ensure equal rights was controversial in many states. The Twenty-seventh Amendment, related to the salaries of members of Congress (presumably not a controversial issue), was first introduced in 1789 but not ratified until over 200 years later: 1992.

The current debate on birthright citizenship has its intellectual origins in 1985. The publication of *Citizenship without Consent: Illegal Aliens in the American Polity* by Peter Schuck and Rogers Smith, both on the faculty at Yale University at the time, resulted in its becoming both a source of inspiration and object of sharp critiques. Professors Schuck, an established legal scholar, and Rogers Smith, a political scientist, produced an influential work that raises important political and philosophical questions about citizenship in the United States. Legislators, such as Congressman Elton Gallegly (R-CA), the author of numerous bills since 1991 that seek to repeal the birthright provision, as well as scholars concerned with the issue, commonly cite arguments in the book to assert their respective positions. The book's arguments have been the object of strong critiques on the part of legal scholars, particularly of its political philosophy arguments, its interpretation of the 1866 debates on the Fourteenth Amendment, and case law regarding key citizenship cases (e.g., Carens 1987; Gunlicks 1994–1995; Helton 1986–1987; Magliocca 2007–2008; Martin 1985–1986; Neuman 1987; Schwartz 1986). These, in turn, have produced lively and informative responses from the book's authors (Schuck 1994–1995; Schuck and Smith 1985–1986; Smith 2008–2009).

It is beyond the scope of this epilogue to present a detail summary of Professors Shuck and Smith's arguments regarding their interpretation of political theory, U.S. legal history, and case law, or the substantive critiques of these. However, it is worth outlining the core arguments raised in their book and how these have been incorporated by leading proponents of the repeal of the current application of the citizenship clause.

The three primary arguments put forth by Schuck and Smith can be summarized as follows. First, the authors trace elements in the development of British common law and suggest that the granting of subjectship was transformed into the granting of citizenship in U.S. jurisprudence. This is represented by the principle of jus soli, or citizenship based on birth in the territory under jurisdiction of the sovereign, and is characterized as an ascriptive form of membership. An individual who possesses the particular quality is ascribed as being a subject in the political community. Such individuals owe their allegiance to the state, and the state assumes a responsibility to the subject. This ascriptive principle is said to stand in direct tension with the liberal political principle of government by consent. For Schuck and Smith, mutual consent is the more important principle in U.S. policy. Consequently, citizenship should be based on the principle of mutual consent, and the granting of citizenship ascriptively weakens the principle of government by consent. The reinterpretation of the citizenship clause is a way to proactively correct the long-standing error in granting citizenship.

The second argument extends the notion of mutual consent to the concept of "subject to the jurisdiction" in the citizenship clause. Schuck and Smith argue that "subject to the jurisdiction" should be reinterpreted as requiring mutual consent. In their argument this means that the U.S. government does not consent to the presence of illegal aliens, and because state consent is absent, such persons are not under the jurisdiction of the United States. And because the adult parents are not "subject to the jurisdiction," the birth of their children excludes them from the privilege granted under the citizenship clause. An important part of their argument is that Supreme Court decisions in precedent cases such as *United States v. Wong Kim Ark,* 169 U.S. 649 (1898), are incorrect interpretations (critics strongly disagree with this position) and thus do not prohibit the repeal of the citizenship clause.

Schuck and Smith's third argument focuses on juridical procedure. They argue that Congress has the power to legislatively define whom the citizenship clause covers—that is, a constitutional amendment is not required. As noted, twenty-three of the thirty-two bills that have been introduced between 1991 and 2011 aim to legislatively accomplish this.

Schuck and Smith's arguments have not only stimulated much academic debate about all of the above issues, and many other legal and political theory questions, they also have become fundamental to members of Congress who have sought to repeal the citizenship clause. Congressman Gallegly, the leading sponsor of bills proposing such a repeal (he sponsored the first such bill in 1991, and seven of the thirty-two bills filed) drew inspiration from the two Yale scholars. On October 22, 1991, Congressman Gallegly spoke on the floor of the House of Representatives and asked his colleagues to support the two measure he was introducing to repeal the citizenship clause: one was a constitutional amendment (HJR 357) and the other a bill to legislatively change the interpretation of the citizenship clause (HR 3605). Much of his speech regarding the intent of the authors of the Fourteenth Amendment, the interpretation of the *Dred Scott* decision, and the *Wong Kim Ark* case, as well as the reference to consent, closely parallel the arguments in their book.[2] More concretely, Congressman Gallegly states the following:

> Some constitutional scholars, including Peter Schuck and Roger [*sic*] Smith of Yale University, have suggested that birthright citizenship is an anomaly in a nation that is based on the will of the people and government by consent and propose a reinterpretation of the 14th amendment's citizenship clause. They argue that its guarantee of citizenship to those born "subject to the jurisdiction" of the United States should be read to embody the public law's conception of consensual membership, and therefore to refer only to children of those legally admitted to permanent residence in the American community—that is, citizens and legal resident aliens. . . . It is difficult to defend a practice that automatically extends birthright citizenship to the native-born offspring of illegal aliens. The parents of such children are, by definition, individuals whose

presence within the jurisdiction of the United States is prohibited by law. If our society has refused explicitly to consent to their membership, it certainly cannot be said to have consented to that of their offspring merely because they happen to be born in this country. (Gallegly 1991)

Congressman Gallegly's statement leaves no doubt that Schuck and Smith's intellectual analysis provided a juridical and historical foundation for his proposals. What are absent in Congressman Gallegly's statement are the multiple critiques and counterinterpretations of Schuck and Smith's arguments (e.g., Eisgrubber 1997; Gotanda 1997; Meyler 2000–2001; Neuman 1996; Pettit 2006–2007; and Shulman 1994–95). He also ignores Schuck and Smith's own subsequent distancing from their arguments in the book: "while we do favor making choices governing citizenship more self-conscious and explicit, we also regard commitments to fundamental human rights as authoritative and would restrain consensualism to preserve them; . . . we do not advise Congress to adopt such a policy [the repeal of the citizenship clause]" (Schuck and Smith 1985–1986, 545, 547).

Further Limitations in Schuck and Smith's Analysis

Most critiques of Schuck and Smith's arguments, as well as discussion of birthright citizenship, have been written by legal scholars; consequently, much of the substantive criticism focuses on questions related to interpretations of landmark citizenship cases, the majority and dissenting opinions of Supreme Court justices, and congressional actions.[3] This has resulted in the absence of several important historical and policy dimensions, including some juridical issues, related to citizenship. Space does not allow a detail discussion of each, so I will outline some of the more important ones, particularly those that relate to common assumptions in proposals to repeal the citizenship clause.

Schuck and Smith's discussion of jus soli and jus sanguinis, as part of developing the notion of mutual consent, ignores two other mechanisms through which citizenship is granted in the United States: collective citizenship and private bills. While a historically smaller number of individuals have been granted citizenship through these, they nonetheless are state actions that grant citizenship and thus should be included in discussions that examine citizenship. Neither of these two mechanisms gives much support to the thesis of mutual consent in forming a political community. Senators and representatives filing private bills argue for "relief" for an individual and direct the granting of citizenship, but no indicator or requirement of consent on the part of the individual is specified or required. Moreover, the fact that the person sought relief through a private bill implies that the normal migrant adjustment and naturalization processes apparently were not available to them. Congress continues to grant citizenship through private bills without specifying a threshold or evidence of explicit or tacit consent on the part of the individual.

The case of collective citizenship is even more problematic to the mutual consent and is subject to jurisdiction arguments. When the United States, for example, acquired through conquest the ceded territory from Mexico, the approximately 100,000 Mexican nationals that remained in the territory were granted de jure U.S. citizenship through the Treaty of Guadalupe Hidalgo (1848). Consent was unilateral. The state consented to acquire the territory and assumed jurisdiction; it did not ask the residents for explicit consent. Those who did not leave their homes, ranches, livestock, and other property and remained in the ceded territory were granted citizenship collectively. The tacit consent in this case was based on residence in the territory. The unprincipled acquisition of Hawaii (through the Treaty of Annexation of Hawaii of 1897) also presents similar problems to the mutual consent argument. It could be argued that the since the treaty has yet to be ratified by Congress, the granting of citizenship to native Hawaiians is even more problematic to Shuck and Smith's arguments about consent. This represents the odd situation of a community that was granted citizenship through treaty, and Congress consented to their inclusion (and granted representation in Congress), yet never formally consented to the acquisition of the territory where the citizens live—a kind of quasi consent. Moreover, the history of a movement in Hawaii for Hawaiian sovereignty suggests a more complex picture of the role of mutual consent in political communities. The case of Puerto Rico, also acquired by conquest and dubious politics in 1898, presents a further problem related to the fact the even though Puerto Ricans were granted citizenship in 1917, U.S. citizenship for those who reside on the island is different from the citizenship of those who reside in continental territory. U.S. citizens on the island are not represented in Congress, nor can they vote for president. Consequently, the idealized notion of government by consent adopted by Schuck and Smith in their policy proposal is not as straightforward as they assume.

An odd limitation in Shuck and Smith's book is the repeated reference to illegal aliens, including in the subtitle, yet the label is never defined. It is odd because Shuck as a legal scholar must be aware that illegal alien, under the Immigration and Nationality Act (INA), has a specific juridical meaning: "any alien convicted of a felony who is in the United States unlawfully" (8 U.S.C. §1365). Yet the repeated use of the term is based on a popular definition, what most individuals associate with those who are believed to have entered the country without authorization, particularly from Mexico (Plascencia 2009a). The lack of clarity about the population being discussed also contributes to the common oversight regarding the fact that the "subject to removal" population is comprised of visa violators and individuals who entered without formal authorization—though estimates vary, each cohort makes up about 50 percent of the total population subject to removal. Despite this, the national preoccupation with "securing the border" and "illegal aliens" assumes that the problem is almost exclusively about unauthorized entry from Mexico. Migrants from Canada, Ireland, Poland, and other nations who are residing in the United States in violation of their visas or without formal authorization, and therefore subject to removal, are a minor concern to policy makers focused on solving the nation's "immigration crisis" through a secured Mexico–United States border.

Moreover, their deployment of the popular label "illegal alien" represents a subtle discursive register that dates back to the 1930s but became solidified in the early 1970s: "Mexican immigrant" and "illegal alien/undocumented migrant" have become largely synonymous in the public imagination and debate on migration. Consequently, I suggest that their argument about repealing the citizenship clause for "illegal aliens," should be read as a proposal to repeal the application of the clause to Mexican migrants deemed to be subject to removal. The bills to legislatively alter the clause or amend the Constitution can be read as deploying the same register and seeking the same aim.

Law professor Michael Olivas's astute observation regarding state and local efforts to exclude noncitizens from local resources also applies to efforts to repeal the citizenship clause: "I believe that most of the current local and state ordinances, even as they are sometimes undifferentiated and aimed in a vague way at perceived 'foreigners,' are primarily aimed at excluding and stigmatizing immigrants of Mexican heritage, whether citizen, undocumented, or ascribed-undocumented. . . . I believe such prejudice is clearly aimed at Mexicans, real or imagined" (2008, 104). Legal scholars (e.g., Gotanda 1997; Haney López 1996; Hing 1993; Johnson 1995–1996; Neuman 1996), as well as numerous historians and social scientists, have written extensively on the inherent dimension of race in migration and citizenship policies in the United States. As discussed here, race remained an ascriptive exclusion to naturalization for 162 years (1790 to 1952).

Historian Natalia Molina has recently offered an insightful examination of what can be interpreted as a prequel to the contemporary birthright debate (2010). Professor Molina examines the organized efforts in the 1920s to make Mexicans "ineligible to U.S. citizenship," similar to what was in place for Chinese, Japanese, and other Asians. Nativist and eugenics-oriented groups lobbied strongly to prohibit the naturalization of Mexicans, despite the 1897 case of In re Rodríguez in San Antonio, Texas, that ruled that Mexicans were eligible to acquire U.S. citizenship through naturalization. Mexicans living in other federal districts were denied this opportunity by federal offices and courts. Efforts to make Mexicans ineligible to citizenship achieved some success.

Lastly, the argument that "illegal aliens" are not subject to the jurisdiction of the state because the United States did not authorize their entry is not supported by actual juridical practices. Over the past eight decades, Congress has approved measures that recognize the presence of person who may have entered without authorization, and it has provided a path to citizenship for them (Plascencia n.d.b.). Some of these actions include the adoption of the 1929 registry provision (8 U.S.C. §1259) that allows those who are subject to removal to be granted lawful permanent residency if they remain undetected for the specified period of time (currently the date is set at January 1, 1972). After meeting the required period of residency, they can petition to be naturalized. The current military provision, based on the language adopted in 1940, allows the granting of citizenship to "an alien or a noncitizen national . . . whether or not he has been legally admitted to the United States for permanent residency" (8 U.S.C §1440), who performs military work during a defined conflict period. Congressional action allows a migrant to be reclassified from illegal alien to U.S. citizen on the basis of military work.

Between 1976 and 1982 Congress added the concept of permanently residing under color of law (PRUCOL) to several statutes, though it left it to be defined by the courts. In *Holley v. Lavine* (1977), the court of appeals determined that a migrant subject to removal could remain in the United States and receive public benefits because INS knew the individual's identity and residence, but it invoked their discretion not to deport the individual. The administrative inaction resulted in the granting of PRUCOL status. These examples, and multiple federal administrative policies, such as the issuance of the individual taxpayer identification number (ITIN) by the Internal Revenue Service, demonstrate that Congress and federal agencies have enacted multiple laws and rules that recognize the presence of persons who may have violated their visa or entered without formal authorization. Such policies allow their transition to citizens and help them meet federal tax and other laws that apply to all residents—citizen and noncitizen. The enactment of state policies for a particular population that facilitates their presence, grants them citizenship whether or not they have been admitted for permanent residency, or makes them subject to removal indicates that the population is subject to the jurisdiction of the state. Moreover, if one accepts residence and abiding by all laws as tacit forms of consent, and combines this with the above state actions, the clear implication is that there is mutual consent and that migrants are subject to the jurisdiction of the United States.

Interpreting the Birthright Citizenship Debate

The more than two-decade debate on the interpretation of the citizenship clause has been dominated by discussions of juridical matters such as the correct reading of the 1866 debate on the Fourteenth Amendment. The focus on juridical issues has been of great importance in assessing Schuck and Smith's policy proposal; however, it has not fostered a broader discussion of its context—in particular, the set of parallel actions of states and municipalities to regulate migration and migrants through ordinances that exclude informally authorized migrants from a broad set of resources, and whose ultimate aim is to foster a set of social conditions so inhospitable that human life becomes intolerable. Michel Foucault and Giorgio Agamben refer to such actions as biopolitics. The grave sense of personal and economic insecurity created by attrition through enforcement is intended to lead to self-deportation (Plascencia, in press).

Two years after the first congressional proposal to repeal the citizenship clause (1991), antimigrant groups in California launched what became Proposition 187, which voters approved in 1994. Since the early 1990s, states and municipalities have been engaged in intense policy debates regarding the presence and impact of migrants, particularly individuals imagined as illegal/undocumented migrants. A wide spectrum of exclusionary ordinances such as English-only legislation, restricted marriage licenses, landlord verification of the migration status of renters, elimination of in-state tuition for students without a social security number, restricted drive licenses, and others have been enacted. According to the National Conference of State Legislatures, in 2007 all fifty states considered and adopted efforts to control migration, principally through efforts aimed at migrants.

Efforts to repeal the citizenship clause are part and parcel of state and local efforts to regulate migration. While the latter restrict access to resources deemed to properly belong to citizens and taxpayers, the former restricts access to a paramount political and economic resource: citizenship. Both efforts are targeted explicitly at illegal aliens and implicitly at Mexicans (though contextually this label encompasses other Latino groups). In this context, Mexicans have come to be imagined, to borrow Charles Loring Brace's term, as a "dangerous class," one that needs to be eliminated. State and local efforts to restrict access to resources and criminalize migrants, and proposals to repeal the citizenship clause, share a common aim: to eliminate illegal immigration.

Attrition through enforcement, including efforts to repeal the citizenship clause, appear to be motivated by three factors: economic insecurity (particularly in the context of the Great Recession), demographical/race concerns, and political concerns. The Great Recession has made the majority of U.S. residents apprehensive about their own and their children's economic well-being. And as with the Great Depression, illegal immigrants are the usual suspects for the cyclical crises of capitalism. Since the 1980s, particularly in light of "the Decade of the Hispanic," the release of decennial census estimates has repeatedly highlighted a future United States that will be increasingly multicultural; specifically, projections that by 2050 Latinos will make up 24.4 percent of the population.

The birther movement—a specific concern about the first nonwhite president—and proposals to repeal the citizenship clause cannot be extricated from their racialized discourses, even if they are explicitly about President Obama, or illegal aliens. The linguistic markers "Obama" and "illegal aliens" respectively index an African American male and Mexicans. Consequently, the demographic consternation is about a nation where "whites" will be an increasingly smaller component of the total population. The third factor is related to the second. It is a concern about the political status of "nonwhites," particularly Latinos in the nation. The inevitable growth of the Latino population will lead to an increasing potential to shape the state and national political environment. From the perspective of the broader European-descent population, this may represent a troubling future, a future of potential uncertainty. If this is a correct assessment, proposals to repeal the citizenship clause are a political strategy to reduce the growth of a feared future elector base, a racialized base.

In summary, this discussion highlights several of the conceptual contributions in this volume. First, the birther movement, proposals to repeal the citizenship clause, and the discussion regarding the registry provision, PRUCOL, and the granting of citizenship based on military work underscore the Janus-faced dimension of citizenship, which simultaneously includes and excludes. Repealing the citizenship clause includes citizens who can access jus soli while excluding those who do not have the consent of the broader community to enter the circle of membership. The acrimonious debate stimulated by the birther movement and proposals to repeal the current application of the principle of jus soli make clearly evident the contestability of the concept of citizenship. President Obama's presidency has been facing a crisis of legitimacy principally based on citizenship. His decision to release his birth certificate in April 2011 was a political countermove to a critique dating back to the 2008 campaign. Lastly, this book has sought to highlight the prime importance of the notion of citizenship to the sociopolitical discourse in the United States. The efforts since 1991 to reinterpret the more than century-long accepted jurisprudence of the citizenship clause in the Fourteenth Amendment give ample prominence to that suggestion.

Notes

1. The exception to this are individuals born in some U.S. possessions, such as American Samoa and Swains Island, who are U.S. nationals but not U.S. citizens; otherwise, all U.S. citizens are U.S. nationals.

2. See http://i2.cdn.turner.com/cnn/2010/images/08/04/rel10k.pdf.

3. I use the terms "migration" and "migrants" in place of "immigration" and "immigrants." This usage is based on the recognition by migration scholars over the past several decades that migration is not always a planned one-way movement from one nation to another; instead, migration can take several forms, such as circular migration, return to nation of birth after retirement, and others.

4. The concept of "juridical," as used here, follows the use invoked by Pierre Bourdieu (1986–1987). It refers to state-initiated action framed as part of "law"—i.e., actions that have the "force of law" (Bourdieu 1986–1987). This use is broader than that found in standard legal research and analysis, which generally limits it to actions related to a legal court.

5. See *Korematsu v. United States*, 323 U.S. 214 (1944); other parallel cases, such as *Hirabayashi v. United States* 320 U.S. 81 (1943), and *Yasui v. United States* 320 U.S. 114 (1943), challenged the constitutionality of the curfew order imposed on Japanese Americans.

6. See *Rumsfeld v. Padilla*, 542 U.S. 426 (2004), and *Hamdi v. Rumsfeld*, 542 U.S. 507 (2004).

7. The most prominent anthropologists that have contributed to this literature are Renato Rosaldo, Aihwa Ong, and Michel Laguerre. Several recent dissertations have focused on citizenship-related issues.

8. Pierre Bourdieu (1999) refers to this general process as the "abdication of the state" and sees it as resulting in "la grande misère" (or "la misère du monde") at the level of society, and in "positional suffering" at the individual level.

9. See table 20 for 2010, http://www.dhs.gov/files/statistics/publications/YrBk10Na .shtm.

10. In the survey reported by Freeman, Plascencia, González Baker, and Orozco (2002) of individuals participating in English-as-a-second-language/citizenship courses and had applied for citizenship, 38 percent had been granted permanent resident status through the legalization programs under the 1986 Immigration Reform and Control Act.

11. Fuller descriptions of IRCA and the legalization provisions are found in Plascencia (2000). Although the term "perishable crop" would seem to need no explanation or comment, the opposite is true. It is a good example of the political nature of naming. Under the administrative rules written by the U.S. Department of Agriculture, and based on the political strength of crop production associations, some crops that the average person would regard as a perishable crop were not included, and others that most individuals would likely never regard as a perishable crop, such as grass sod, became such.

12. The final number that will have been legalized under IRCA is still not determined. Two class-action suits filed on behalf of persons eligible to apply but were not allowed to apply by the Immigration and Naturalization Service (INS) led to an agreement signed by Secretary Tom Ridge (Department of Homeland Security) that will allow between 60,000 and 400,000 of those individuals, seventeen years later, to apply for temporary residence, later permanent residency, and eventually U.S. citizenship. See *Catholic Social Services v. Tom Ridge, et al.*, and *Felicity Mary Newman et al. v. U.S. Citizenship and Immigration Services (CIS)*. The CIS estimates the lower number and migrant-advocates the higher total.

13. See 66 Stat. 163.

14. The reasons for not aggressively pursuing the enforcement of employer sanctions have varied since IRCA's enactment. Under President Reagan's regime, the priority was fighting Communism (primarily in Central America) and the War on Drugs; President George H. W. Bush's regime, while continuing some of President Reagan's interest, shifted the national priority to Iraq; under President Clinton, controlling the border and ending welfare as we know it became major concerns; and under President George W. Bush, the War on Terrorism and the Iraq War have come to dominate U.S. policy concerns. In its first two and a half years, the Obama administration has removed a larger number of informally authorized migrants, but these were not related to the enforcement of the nation's employer sanctions law. Thus, despite the recognition that the availability of U.S. jobs is a major stimulus to unauthorized migration and repeated calls to fix the problem, the assertive application of the rule of law among employers has not been a priority from the Reagan to the Obama administrations.

15. Substantial scholarship has examined the philosophical and sociological limitations of Weber's terse formulation of the idea that the world is disenchanted—*die Entzauberung der Weldt*. An idea that is said Weber drew from Friedrich Schiller, specifically his statement of "*die Entgötterrung der Natur*" (the "disgodding" of nature). Substantial discussion of Weber's formulation of disenchantment can be found in Bennett (2003); Germanin (1993); Greisman (1976); Koshul (2005); Saler (2003).

16. See Saler (2003) for the suggestion that enchantment and disenchantment may operate simultaneously.

17. The reference to a "real green card" is simply to point out that at the time that I possessed a green card, the card was actually green. A few years after obtaining my naturalization certificate, the Immigration and Naturalization Service changed the color of the card. Since then it has changed color about four or five times, yet the old name stuck—people, including officials, still talk about the green card.

18. A Roman god of beginnings and transitions, Janus is generally represented as possessing two heads, each one gazing in opposite directions. He is also associated with thresholds/doorways, gates, and doors. January, the first month of a new year, is thus appropriately based on Janus.

19. The line is from the lyrics to "No Soy de Aquí" by Alberto Cortez (1989). The phrase can be translated as "I'm not from here, nor am I from there," "there" referring to the place of one's origin.

20. My involvement with CASA allowed me the opportunity to work with the late Rudy Lozano. Rudy was active in organizing workers, principally informally authorized, at local *tortillerias* (tortilla production businesses). He also assisted the late Mayor Harold Washington in building a strong coalition between African Americans, "ethnic-Whites," and Latinos in Chicago. Rudy was assassinated. His murder is still a mystery, though some suspect that it was politically motivated— either by the *tortilleria* owners or someone within Chicago's political machine.

21. It should be pointed out that Mr. Nelson was one of the authors of Proposition 187 in California; the second key author was a former INS district director of the Los Angels office: Howard Ezell.

22. The reason why unemployment insurance (UI) benefits were illogical in INS's strategy was simply that UI is not a state-funded program, and so any reduction would not result in saving state monies. It is hard to explain why Nelson would have been so uninformed about this particular part of his promotion. The UI program is an employer-funded program: employers that carry UI insurance pay a quarterly amount to the federal government based on the number of employees. The funds then return to the state via the Department of Labor to cover the UI benefits received by workers. The funds never become part of the general revenue funds of the state.

23. The first project was carried out while affiliated with the Center for the Study of Human Resources (now named the Ray Marshall Center for Human Resources), part of the LBJ School of Public Affairs. The second was carried out under the direction of Professors Gary P. Freeman and Rodolfo O. de la Garza, directors of the Public Policy Center (now the Public Policy Institute), affiliated with the Department of Government. The second project was partially funded by the Texas Department of Human Services, as part of a project that examined local efforts in several cities in Texas that had funding to promote citizenship.

CHAPTER 1 — FIELDS OF CITIZENSHIP

1. The discussion of the importance of foundational concepts for understanding society draws upon the work of the historian Reinhart Koselleck (1982, 1985, 2002).

2. The U.S. Supreme Court issued its opinion on June 13, 2011, on *U.S. v. Ruben Flores-Villar*. The case is a challenge to the gendered distinction in law regarding the parent of a child born out of wedlock. The statute has different criteria based on whether the citizen parent is the father or the mother of the child. As a result of Justice Kagan's recusal from the case, the resulting 4–4 vote meant that the appellate court's opinion on the acceptability of the gender distinction was allowed to stand.

3. In an example of a recent effort to move away from a rights versus obligation characterization of citizenship, Peter Kistivo and Thomas Faist (2007) suggest a framework of themes: inclusion, erosion, withdrawal, and expansion.

4. See, for example, Aleinikoff (1990); Aleinikoff and Klusmeyer (2000, 2001); Bosniak (2000a, 2000b, 2001, 2002, 2006); Hing (2007); Johnson (2007); Knapp (1996); Knop (2001); Legomsky (1994); Motomura (2006); Neuman 1996; Saito 1997; and Schuck 1998.

5. See Beiner (1995); Brubacker (1992); DeSipio and de la Garza (1998); Isin and Turner (2002); and Pickus (1998).

6. See McGovney (1923, 1934).

7. See Alvarez (1987); Bogardus (1934); DeSipio (1995, 1996); Félix (2008); Félix, González, and Ramírez (2008); Freeman, Plascencia, Baker, and Orozco (2002); García (1981); Gilbertson and Singer (2000); Portes and Curtis (1987); and Walker 1928–1929.

8. See Bernard (1936).

9. See Bloemraad (2006a, 2006b, 2006c); Bloemraad and Ueda (2006); Bueker (2006); DeSipio (1987); Gordon (2007); Liang (1994); North (1987); Van Hook, Brown, and Bean (2006); Woodrow-Lafield et al. 2004; and Yang (1994).

10. The initial naturalization guidelines were enacted in the 1790 Naturalization Act.

11. Of secondary relevance here, though important in highlighting the limitation in translation, is the Chinese concepts of *guomin, gongmin,* and *shimin;* all three are represented by a different character, have a distinct translation and political meaning, yet all three are translated as "citizen" or "citizenship."

12. The summary is based on the following: *Constitución de Cadiz de 1812;* Annino (1999); Becerra Ramírez (2000); Escalante Gonzalbo (1992); Joseph and Nugent (1994); Lomnitz (1993, 1996, 1999); Mallon (1994, 1995); Wil Panster (1997); and EZLN documents (http://ezln.org).

13. "Supuesto que la guerra que nos hacen los norteamericanos, tienen por objeto la dominación y despojo de nuestro territorio, el cual no puede recobrarse sin la cooperación de todos los mexicanos; se declara: que todas las propriedades territoriales serán comunes a todos los ciudadanos de la República."

14. See "Declaración de la Selva Lancadona," http://ezln.org/documentos/1994/199312xx.es.htm.

15. "No son únicamente los que portan espadas que chorrean sangre y despiden rayos fugaces de gloria militar, los escogidos a designar el personal del gobierno de un pueblo que quiere democratizarse; ese derdho lo tienen tambíen los ciudadanos que han luchado en la prensa y en la tribuna, que están identificados con los ideales de la Revolucion." See "Segunda declaración de la Selva Lancadona," http://ezln.org/documentos/1994/19940610.es.htm.

16. Because of the age of the individuals and because not all finished *secundaria,* they were not exposed to the new curriculum. With reference to the first issue, they have not been part of the political movement promoting the external vote, though most were aware of it. Chapter 6 touches on this issue.

17. An important addition to the literature on citizenship is the contribution of scholars who have examined the topic in the context of Australia, Egypt, Japan, Korea, Germany and Israel, Syria and Lebanon, and the broader Middle East.

18. Max Weber offers an earlier tripartite scheme for the historical meanings of citizenship, although T. H. Marshall does not cite him. According to Weber, citizenship (*Bürgertum*) has had three sociohistorical significations: economic, political, and class (1927, 315).

19. For example, Joao Carlos Espada's *Social Citizenship Rights* (1996) and Thomas Faist's *Social Citizenship for Whom?* (1995).

20. Cited and also referred to in Levinson (2004). The phrase is taken from Enrique Krauze's *Por una democracia sin adjetivos* (1988).

21. Prior to the nineteenth century there were important feminist writings such as those of Mary Wollstonecraft. Her book *A Vindication of the Rights of Women* was published in 1792.

22. See Benhabib and Cornell (1987). In this thin but dense book, the contributors (including important writers such as Iris Marion Young, Judith Butler, and Nancy Fraser) explore the limitations, particularly the masculinist orientations, of figures such as Marx, Habermas, and Foucault. More recently, Seyla Benhabib and Judith Resnik edited a superb volume that integrates citizenship, migration, and gender (2009).

23. See Brown (1988). Well-known thinkers such as Hannah Arendt, Aristotle, Machiavelli, and Weber are critically examined in terms of their perspectives, specifically their androcentric political philosophies.

24. See Butler and Scott (1992). The edited volume encompasses a broad topical and geographic terrain and disciplines (including a contribution by anthropologist Ana María Alonso). Chantal Mouffe's contribution specifically addresses citizenship. Her understanding of citizenship is presented in contrast to the model offered by Carole Pateman and Iris Marion Young (Mouffe 1992b, 369–384).

25. See Dietz (1992). Mary Dietz's essay aims to formulate a critique of liberalist, Marxist feminist, and "maternalist" feminist conceptions of citizenship. She offers an alternative to these (Dietz 1992, 63–85).

26. See Mouffe (1992a, 1992b, 1993).

27. See Shanley and Pateman (1991); Pateman comments on the topic of citizenship and gender in several places throughout *The Disorder of Women* (1998a). Her observation regarding the "Wollstonecraft Dilemma" is found in her "The Patriarchal Welfare State" essay (1989b, 179–209).

28. Marvin Harris refers to Brinton as "one of the most influential anthropologists among Boas' contemporaries" (1968, 255).

29. The expression is not limited to Brazil; it also can be found in Mexico and other Latin American nations. Though not elaborated by Da Matta, my own personal observation of its use has been more with female spouses of influential

males, who after asking the question will add, "Soy la esposa de X (I am wife of X)." The expected response on the part of the person being asked the question is to immediately apologize and then grant to the wife the special privilege (e.g., entry to a building, office, or parking lot; make a table available at a restaurant).

30. The working titles of the film were "The Devil Inside," "Meet Ruth Stoops," and "Precious," and the story line is about the exaggerated and parodied actions between pro-choice and anti-abortion groups.

31. See http://www.citizenwatch.com. The Citizen Watch Company is a multinational Japanese company with offices in Canada, England, and the United States.

32. I thank Dr. De Ann Pendry for sharing her accidental discovery of the "Model Citizens" show with me.

33. See   http://superman.bz/mike-huckabees-kryptonite-superman-goes-international/, and http://www.youtube.com/watch?v=pPfOAHoLrMI.

34. See http://scans-daily.dreamwidth.org/2941226.html.

35. I am drawing upon Reinhart Koselleck's important discussion of asymmetric counterconcepts (1982). See also his related elaboration on the importance of understanding the historical development of foundational concepts (1985, 2002).

CHAPTER 2 — THE JANUS FACE OF CITIZENSHIP:
THE SIDE OF INCLUSION

1. In general, the Americanization movement was an effort involving federal, state, and local government and multiple nonprofit organizations that surfaced between 1910 and 1930. The dominant aim of most efforts was to transform migrants and other minority communities into "Americans." The social change (assimilation) envisioned was for migrants and the other communities to leave behind all traces of difference regarding language, cultural practices, and ways of interacting, and to model themselves into visions of middle-class Euro-American residents. While the various efforts had some impact on some individuals, overall they did not succeed as planned. An underlying assumption in the programs was that the broader society would embrace the converts and converts would have equal access to all opportunities; it assumed that broader racialized perspectives would somehow disappear.

2. H. Mark Roelofs observes: "The shelves of any public library . . . will confirm that the literature on 'good' citizenship is extensive. . . . The Schools of Education have made the propagation of the ideal of good citizenship a cardinal mission, and have spread their message through textbook after textbook, lecture after lecture, thesis after thesis" (1957, 2).

3. Some of the other textbooks that examined what made citizenship a central theme were Griscom (1921); and Parker, Patterson, and McAllister (1939).

4. Other notable reports include those of the National Foundation for Education in American Citizenship (Burdette 1942); National Task Force on Citizenship Education (Brown 1977), National Center for Learning and Citizenship (2001).

5. See, e.g., Riordon (1963). The author's discussion of Tammany Hall illustrates the political importance of naturalization to local bosses.

6. For some examples of discussions on the parallelism between war, battering of females, and sport, see McBride (1995). See also Walvin (1987) for a discussion of the link in Britain between slavery and sport. It should also be noted that sport/game metaphors are also found in war; thus the two fields complement each other.

7. The Girl Scout Gold Award is the highest award given, and although it is not labeled a citizenship bade, the award notes that it encompasses evidence of "leadership and citizenship skills."

8. "Metic," as suggested by Max Weber (1958), refers to aliens who resided in Athens but did not have full citizenship; in other words, they occupied a midpoint sociopolitical position between being an outsider and a citizen.

CHAPTER 3 —— THE JANUS FACE OF CITIZENSHIP:
THE SIDE OF EXCLUSION

1. Several writers have expressed a similar idea regarding the dual dimensions of inclusion and exclusion within citizenship, such as Ruth Lister (1997, 42) who notes, for example, that "inclusion and exclusion represent the two sides of citizenship's coin." And although she notes that exclusion and inclusion are "more of a continuum" (1997, 43), she ultimately stresses the effect on the person being excluded. In the context of her book, these individuals are primarily women and secondarily migrants. Thus, ultimately she does not specifically address the issue of how individuals are simultaneously included and excluded, nor how inclusion is created for those individuals defined to be included. It should be noted that although the focus here is on juridical citizenship, exclusion and inclusion also affect the sociopolitical and everyday forms of citizenship. For example, a person excluded from a particular occupation because of lack of U.S. citizenship can be included in an occupation not restricted to citizens.

2. Holston's focus, however, is more with how economically marginalized communities have been taking actions to improve their sociopolitical position through efforts that rely on the national discourse of citizenship.

3. At times people involved in struggles to attain full citizenship rights for themselves have expressed their opposition to granting those rights to others defined as "aliens." For example, in the woman's suffrage movement in the late 1800s and early 1900s, some of the leadership expressed xenophobic concerns with the "ignorant foreign vote"—that is, the male migrant. Thus, their position was based on both wanting the vote in order to include the enlightened white woman and wanting to exclude migrant males from suffrage. However, this raised questions about the race/ethnic and class contradictions among women: what position should be taken on the migrant woman? Did they represent the same "ignorant foreign vote," or should they, as women, be included in woman's suffrage? See, for example, Kraditor (1981, 123–162). An observation also noted by Shklar (1991).

4. Ronald Hayduk (2006) provides an excellent discussion of the history of noncitizen voting; see also Renshon (2009) for a more contemporary discussion of noncitizen voting in local elections.

5. The summary of the historical material relies principally on the following works: Bernard (1950); Bishop (1893); Divine (1972); Higham (1981); Hutchinson (1981); Jones (1992). Konvitz (1946); and Reisler (1976).

6. The original "registry" provision of the 1929 Registry Act set the threshold date as July 1, 1924. The date was subsequently updated to 1948, and the 1986 IRCA further updated the date from June 30, 1948, to January 1, 1972.

7. The list with several additions is based on DeSipio and de la Garza (1998, 67).

8. Although the 1848 Treaty provided collective U.S. citizenship for "Mexicans," it was at times contested within states. See, for example, the case of Pablo de la Guerra in the 1870s in California (Menchaca 1995, 22). See also Tenorio, Menchaca, and Montejano (1999). For a fuller discussion of the treaty, see Griswold del Castillo (1990).

9. The INA allows exceptions for persons with physical and mental limitations.

10. My guess is that many U.S. citizens would probably provide a wrong answer by listing four branches: Air Force, Army, Marines, Navy. There are only three branches, as the Marines are a unit of the Navy.

11. The discussion here draws upon the following general works: Bishop (1893), Keyssar (2000), Kraditor (1981), Ogden (1958), and Williamson (1960). Kessar's discussion is particularly useful because of its comprehensiveness in terms of time span and topics.

12. The Supreme Court has upheld the power of states to disenfranchise "felons" (*Richardson v. Ramirez*). For a useful summary, see Uggen, Behrens, and Manza (2005).

13. See Fecteau (2000).

14. This section relies on Avila (2003), Aylsworth (1931), Hayduk (2006), Keyssar (2000), Moulier-Boutang (1985), Raskin (1993a, 1993b), Renshon (2009), Rosberg (1977), Smith (1932), Tung (1985).

15. Based on a telephone conversation with Michael Jones-Correa, 2003.

16. In general, a monopoly involves control over the supply of a product. A special-privilege monopoly involves a legislative enactment granted to a private entity (Sloan and Zurcher 1964).

17. The observation that it may change is based on efforts supporting former California governor Arnold Schwarzenegger to allow naturalized citizens to occupy the presidency.

18. See *Truax v. Raich, 239* U.S. 33 (1915).

19. The discussion here relies on Curry (1921), Ferguson (1947), Lazarus (1989), Lowe (1976), McGovney (1947), Price (2000), Roodner (1964), Sandmeyer (1936), Shapiro (1993), and Weisman (1980).

20. Chin Lungs story is found in Chan (1986); though not much is said about the land laws.

CHAPTER 4 — THE MAKING OF CITIZENS

1. A similar argument is made by Aihwa Ong (1995, 1996) in discussing, for example, the relationship between the biopolitics of medicine and the treatment of Khmer refugees in northern California, specifically in the treatment of mental health conditions. Ong argues that the biomedical gaze, with its good intentions to

help and desire to control, is both accepted and rejected by Khmer patients. Thus, Khmer refugees become governable subjects, but not to the degree desired by the medical institutions.

2. See *Catholic Social Services, et al. v. Tom Ridge, et al.*, CIV-S-86–1343 LKK/JFM (E.D. Cal) (2004), and *Felicity Mary Newman et al. v. U.S. Citizenship and Immigration Services*, CIV. No. 87–4757-WDK (C.D. Cal) (2004).

3. The National Organization of Latino Elected and Appointed Officials Educational Fund is the principal Latino organization that has focused on the promotion of citizenship. It was established in 1976, has its headquarters in Los Angeles, and operates offices in Houston, New York, and Washington, D.C. The organization has received significant support from major foundations and corporations over the years to address its mission of civic empowerment. Since its inception it has implemented major efforts to promote citizenship and provide direct assistance in the application process. For more information, see http://www.naleo.org.

4. I also should note that I have not found an explanation for what occurred in 2000 in Arizona when 10,755 migrants were granted citizenship.

5. The names of the organizations and individuals mentioned in this chapter are pseudonyms.

6. I taught citizenship classes on a volunteer basis at two community-based organizations in Austin. One is located in East Austin, the other in South Austin. I taught six classes by myself, and co-taught classes in 1997–1998 and 2003–2004. I interacted with a combined total of about 100 students. I also observed English/civics classes (SLIAG funded classes) in 1990 in Lubbock, Amarillo, Waco, San Antonio, Houston, and Dallas. Additional data includes observations made in Austin, El Paso, Houston, and San Antonio in 1997 as part of a research project that involved visits to ESL/civics and citizenship classes (see Freeman, de la Garza, Plascencia, González Baker, and Orozco 1997).

CHAPTER 5 — BEARING TRUE FAITH AND ALLEGIANCE

1. *Siskind's Immigration Bulletin*, June 2, 2000. http://www.visalaw.com/00jun1/14jun100.html.

2. Bourdieu's concept of instituting draws upon the earlier work of Karl Polanyi (1971), particularly chapter 13, "The Economy as Institute Process," (243–270).

3. The 1906 act set up the basic rules and forms for naturalization.

4. I am borrowing this phrase from the title of John Gavit's *Americans by Choice* (1971).

5. Some of the past problems of granting citizenship are described in Gavit (1971).

6. Coutin (2003) provides an insightful description and analysis of the ten ceremonies she attended at the Los Angeles Convention Center.

7. Letter sent to those who took the Oath in San Antonio, Texas, 2004.

8. This is one of the vows listed under "Traditional Wedding Vows" at the Wedding Network website, http://www.theweddingnetwork.com.au.

9. The text of a suggested Christian wedding ceremony notes: "Marriage is a meaningful word, meaningful because it means the end of your search for that

special person you looked forward to (and prayed about) to complete your life" (http://www.aspecialmemmory.com).

10. See "Mexican Marriage Vows," http://www.suite101.com.

11. Office of Citizenship brochure M-602(06/04). The quotation is taken from Title IV, Subtitle E, Section 451 of the Homeland Security Act of 2002.

12. Office of Citizenship brochure M-602(06/04).

CHAPTER 6 — DESIRE, SACRIFICE, AND DISENCHANTMENT

1. Although the distinction made by Ramon may sound odd, it is a distinction that others have made in the United States. Timothy McVeigh, for example, defined himself as a true patriot who loved his country and had served in the military; however, after the violent confrontation that took place in Waco in 1993, resulting in the death of over 70 individuals, McVeigh became angry against the U.S. government. His anger expressed itself in the bombing of the Alfred P. Murrah Federal building in Oklahoma City; 168 individuals were killed. In his mind he was able to reconcile both perspectives.

2. See, for example, Barreto and Muñoz (2003), Bass and Casper (2001a, 2001b), DeSipio (1995), Leal (2002), Michelson and Pallares (2001), Pantoja, Ramirez, and Segura (2001).

3. In the late 1990s, the *New Americans Guide* could be found in community-based organizations, churches, school districts, community colleges, and many other places. I saw copies of the booklet available in multiple organizations in various Texas cities. The addition of the "100 Questions" as an insert inside the back cover probably attracted service providers to make it available. The Fannie May Foundation also sent out copies to organizations that requested it.

4. The 2011 revised toolkit sells for forty-nine dollars.

5. See CIS, Press Office (www.uscis.gov).

6. The year 1996 marks the start of multiple state and local actions seeking to exclude informally authorized migrants from a broad range of resources: driver license, bail bond, in-state tuition at public colleges and universities, etc. The enactment of SB1070 in 2010 is one such action.

7. Although he did not explicitly indicate it, and I did not want to be pushy on the point, I suspect that the visa may have expired by the time his first child was born in 1973.

8. For families with U.S.-born children who were apprehended after about 1978, this was a de facto deportation of citizens, since few parents were willing to leave their children behind. The choices were to turn the child over to the state for placement in a foster home, to leave the child with a relative or friend, or to leave the country with their children. As expected, though INS chose not to keep track of the number of such cases, most appeared to have selected to leave with their children. As reported in Plascencia (2000), some of the U.S.-born children later surfaced as undocumented citizens, meaning they grew up in Mexico and were socialized as Mexican. Some of these individuals later entered the United States without authorization and applied for legalization under IRCA, though they were U.S. citizens.

9. Several other celebrities could substitute for Jennings, including Pamela Anderson and Jim Carrey. Other celebrities are in the process of petitioning for citizenship (e.g., Salma Hayek).

10. See "Peter Jennings Is a U.S. Citizen," *CBS News*, July 9, 2003; Peter Johnson, "Canadian Peter Jennings Becomes a U.S. citizen," *USA Today*, July 8, 2003; J. Freedom du Lac, "Jennings Brings Quest for Knowledge to California," *Sacramento Bee*, May 21, 2003; "Peter Jennings: 'I Feel at the Top of the World,'" *Ottawa Citizen*, May 1, 2004.

11. The link between the Polanyi's notion of "instituted process" and citizenship is borrowed from the excellent sociohistorical essay by sociologist Margaret Somers (1993).

CONCLUSION

1. It is a process that is also incorporated in linguistics and applies to basic concepts such as cold-hot—the idea that humans have to possess both terms in order to make sense of the two concepts, and that each depends on the other.

EPILOGUE

1. As noted in the introduction, the 1942 executive order to intern Japanese-descent citizens and noncitizens, as well as the arranged deportation of Japanese-descent individuals from Peru and other Latin American countries to the United States for their internment in U.S. camps, also represent similar moments when state-of-emergency policies were adopted in violation of what we assume are the inalienable rights of U.S. citizenship and what constitutes national sovereignty.

2. Although the discussion here focuses on Schuck and Smith's position on birthright citizenship, and the majority of legal scholars who examine their arguments disagree with them, there are other scholars who propose similar positions—for example, Eastman (2007), Erler (1996), Graglia (2009–2010), Ho (2007–2008), and Wood (1998–1999). Moreover, more recently Ayelet Shachar (2009) offers a critique of birthright citizenship but on different grounds. She argues that the granting of birthright citizenship unfairly privileges those fortunate enough to be born in the United States and other wealthy nations. Thus she argues that birthright citizenship should be reduced in importance in order to foster greater equality in the globalized world we live in. A central mechanism introduced is the birthright privilege levy—a tax on persons acquiring birthright citizenship in wealthy countries that would be distributed to poor nations.

3. Some exceptions to this are the essays by political scientist Joseph Carens (1987) and historian Mae Ngai (2006–2007).

Works Cited

Agamben, Giorgio. 1998. *Homo Sacer: Sovereign Power and Bare Life*. Palo Alto, CA: Stanford University Press.

———. 2000. *Means without End: Notes on Politics*. Minneapolis: University of Minnesota Press.

Aleinikoff, T. Alexander. 1990. "Citizens, Aliens, Membership and the Constitution." *Constitutional Commentary* 7 (1): 9–34.

Aleinikoff, T. Alexander, and Douglas Klusmeyer, eds. 2000. *From Migrants to Citizens: Membership in a Changing World*. Washington, DC: Carnegie Endowment for International Peace.

———. 2001. *Citizenship Today: Global Perspectives and Practices*. Washington, DC: Carnegie Endowment for International Peace.

Althusser, Louis. 1971. *Lenin and Philosophy and Other Essays*. Translated by Ben Brewster. New York: Monthly Review Press.

Alvarez, Robert R. 1987. "A Profile of the Citizenship Process among Hispanics in the United States." *International Migration Review* 21 (2): 327–351.

Anderson, Benedict. 2006. *Imagined Communities: Reflections on the Origin and Spread of Nationalism*. London: Verso.

Annino, Antonio. 1999. "Ciudadanía 'versus' gobernabilidad republicana en México: Los orígines de un dilema." In *Ciudadanía política y formación de las naciones: Perspectivas históricas de América Latina,* edited by Hilda Sabato, 62–93. Mexico City: El Colegio de México.

Anthropological Society of Washington. 1894. "Citizenship Prize Essays." *American Anthropologist* 7 (4): 343–357.

Avila, Joaquin. 2003. *Political Apartheid in California: Consequences of Excluding a Growing Noncitizen Population*. Latino Policy and Issues Brief. Los Angeles: UCLA Chicano Studies.

Aylsworth, Leon E. 1931. "The Passing of Alien Suffrage." *American Political Science Review* 25: 114–116.

Baden-Powell, Robert. 2004. *Scouting for Boys: A Handbook for Instruction in Good Citizenship*. New York: Oxford University Press.

Bader, Veit. 1997. "The Cultural Conditions of Transnational Citizenship: On Interpretation of Political and Ethnic Cultures." *Political Theory* 25 (6): 771–813.

Badiou, Alain. 2004. *Infinite Thought: Truth and the Return of Philosophy*. Translated and edited by Oliver Feltham and Justin Clemens. London: Continuum Books.

Baker, Bryan. 2010. *Naturalization Rates among IRCA Immigrants: A 2009 Update*. Fact Sheet. Department of Homeland Security. http://www.dhs.gov/xlibrary/assets/statistics/publications/irca-natz-fs-2009.pdf.

Barbalet, J. M. 1988. *Citizenship: Rights, Struggle and Class Inequality*. Minneapolis: University of Minnesota Press.

Barone, Michael, and John Fonte. 2000. "Does America Have an Assimilation Problem?" *American Enterprise*. December. http://www.theamericanenterprise.org

Barreto, Matt A., and José A. Muñoz. 2003. "Reexamining the 'Politics of In-Between': Political Participation among Mexican Immigrants in the United States." *Hispanic Journal of Behavioral Sciences* 25 (4): 427–447.

Bass, Loretta E., and Lynne M. Casper. 2001a. "Differences in Registering and Voting between Native-Born and Naturalized Americans." *Population Research and Policy Review* 20: 483–511.

———. 2001b. "Impacting the Political Landscape: Who Registers and Votes among Naturalized Americans." *Political Behavior* 23 (2): 103–130.

Bateman, Thomas S., and Dennis W. Organ. 1983. "Job Satisfaction and the Good Soldier: The Relationship between Affect and Employee 'Citizenship.'" *Academy of Management Journal* 26 (4): 587–595.

Bauböck, Rainer. 1994. *Transnational Citizenship: Membership and Rights in International Migration*. London: Edward Elgar.

Becerra Ramírez, Manuel. 2000. "Nationality in Mexico." In *From Migrants to Citizens: Membership in a Changing World*, edited by T. Alexander Aleinikoff and Douglas Klusmeyer, 312–341. Washington, DC: Carnegie Endowment for International Peace.

Beckman, Ludvig. 2006. "Citizenship and Voting Rights: Should Resident Aliens Vote?" *Citizenship Studies* 10 (2): 153–165.

Beiner, Ronald, ed. 1995. *Theorizing Citizenship*. Albany: State University of New York Press.

Benhabib, Seyla, and Drucilla Cornell, eds. 1987. *Feminism as Critique: On the Politics of Gender*. Minneapolis: University of Minnesota Press.

Benmayor, Rina. 2002. "Narrating Cultural Citizenship: Oral Histories of First-Generation College Students of Mexican Origin." *Social Justice* 29 (4): 96–121.

Benmayor, Rina, Rosa M. Torruellas, and Ana L. Juarbe. 1992. *Response to Poverty among Puerto Rican Women: Identity, Community, and Cultural Citizenship*. Report to the Joint Committee for Public Policy Research on Contemporary Hispanic Issues of the Inter-University Program for Latino Research and the Social Science Research Council.

Bennett, Jane. 2001. *The Enchantment of Modern Life: Attachments, Crossing, and Ethics*. Princeton: Princeton University Press.

Berlant, Lauren E. 1993. "The Theory of Infantile Citizenship." *Public Culture* 5: 395–410.

Bernard, William S. 1936. "Cultural Determinants of Naturalization." *American Sociological Review* 1 (6): 943–953.

———, ed. 1950. *American Immigration Policy: A Reappraisal.* New York: Harper & Brothers.

Bishop, Cortland F. 1893. "History of Elections in the American Colonies." *Studies in History, Economics and Public Law* 3: 1–297.

Bloemraad, Irene. 2006a. "Citizenship Lessons from the Past: The Contours of Immigrant Naturalization in the Early 20th Century." *Social Science Quarterly* 87 (5): 927–953.

———. 2006b. "Becoming a Citizen in the United States and Canada: Structured Mobilization and Immigrant Political Incorporation." *Social Forces* 85 (2): 667–695.

———. 2006c. *Becoming a Citizen: Incorporating Immigrants and Refugees in the United States and Canada.* Berkeley: University of California Press.

Bloemraad, Irene, and Reed Ueda. 2006. "Naturalization and Nationality." In *A Companion to American Immigration*, edited by Reed Ueda, 36–57. Malden: Blackwell Publishing.

Bogardus, Emory S. 1919. *Essentials of Americanization.* Los Angeles: University of Southern California Press

———. 1934. *The Mexican in the United States.* Los Angeles: University of Southern California.

Bosniak, Linda S. 2000a. "Citizenship Denationalized." *Indiana Journal of Global Law Studies* 7:447–509.

———. 2000b. "Universal Citizenship and the Problem of Alienage." *Northwestern Law Review* 94 (3): 963–984.

Bosniak, Linda S. 2001. "Denationalizing Citizenship." In *Citizenship Today: Global Perspectives and Practices,* edited by T. Alexander Aleinikoff and Douglas Klusmeyer, 237–252. Washington, DC: Carnegie Endowment for International Peace.

———. 2002. "Constitutional Citizenship through the Prism of Alienage." *Ohio State Law Journal* 63 (5): 1285.

———. 2006. *The Citizen and the Alien: Dilemmas of Contemporary Membership.* Princeton: Princeton University Press.

Bourdieu, Pierre. 1977. *Outline of a Theory of Practice.* Translated by Richard Nice. Cambridge: Cambridge University Press.

———. 1986–1987. "The Force of Law: Toward a Sociology of the Juridical Field." *Hastings Law Journal* 38: 814–853.

———. 1992. "Rites as Acts of Institution." In *Honor and Grace in Anthropology,* edited by J. G. Peristiany and Julian Pitt-Rivers, 79–89. England: Cambridge University Press.

———, et al. 1999. *The Weight of the World: Social Suffering in Contemporary Society.* Palo Alto, CA: Stanford University Press.

Bredbenner, Candice Lewis. 1998. *A Nationality of Her Own: Women, Marriage, and the Law of Citizenship.* Berkeley: University of California Press.

Brimelow, Peter. 1995. *Alien Nation: Common Sense About America's Immigration Disaster.* New York: Random House.

Brow, James. 1996. *Demons and Development: The Struggle for Community in a Sri Lankan Village*. Tucson: University of Arizona Press.

Brown, B. Frank, ed. 1977. *Education for Responsible Citizenship: The Report of the National Task Force on Citizenship Education*. New York: McGraw-Hill Book Co.

Brown, Wendy. 1988. *Manhood and Politics: A Feminist Reading in Political Theory*. Totowa: Rowman & Littlefield.

Brubacker, Rogers. 1992. *Citizenship and Nationhood in France and Germany*. Cambridge: Harvard University Press.

Buchan, Morag. 1999. *Women in Plato's Political Theory*. New York: Macmillan.

Bueker, Catherine Simpson. 2006. *From Immigrant to Naturalized Citizen: Political Incorporation in the United States*. New York: LFB Scholarly Publishing.

Burdette, Franklin L. 1942. *Education for Citizen Responsibilities: The Role of Anthropology, Economics, Geography, History, Philosophy, Political Science, Psychology, Sociology*. Princeton: Princeton University Press.

Burgett, Bruce. 1998. *Sentimental Bodies: Sex, Gender, and Citizenship in the Early Republic*. Princeton: Princeton University Press.

Butler, Judith. 1997. *The Psychic Life of Power: Theories of Subjection*. Palo Alto, CA: Stanford University Press.

Butler, Judith, and Joan W. Scott, eds. 1992. *Feminist Theorize the Political*. New York: Routledge.

Camargo, Carlos Fernando. 2003. "Immigrant Subjectivities and Commodity Culture: Cultural Citizenship, Americanization and Immigrant Autobiographies." Ph.D. diss., University of California, Berkeley.

Capen, Louise I., and Melchor D. Montfort. 1937. *My Worth to the World: Studies in Citizenship*. New York: American Book Co.

Carens, Joseph H. 1987. "Who Belongs? Theoretical and Legal Questions about Birthright Citizenship in the United States." *University of Toronto Law Journal* 37: 413–443.

Carroll, James T. 1997. "Americanization or Indoctrination: Catholic Indian Boarding Schools, 1874–1926." Ph.D. diss., University of Notre Dame.

Castañeda, Alejandra. 2006. *The Politics of Citizenship of Mexican Migrants*. New York: LFB Scholarly Publishing

Castoriadis, Cornelius. 1987. *The Imaginary Institution of Society*. Translated by Kathleen Blamey. Cambridge: Polity Press.

Castronovo, Russ. 2001. *Necro Citizenship: Death, Eroticism, and the Public Sphere in the Nineteenth Century United States*. Durham: Duke University Press.

Caute, David. 1978. *The Great Fear: The Anti-Communist Purge under Truman and Eisenhower*. New York: Touchstone / Simon & Schuster.

Center for Information and Research on Civic Learning and Engagement and Carnegie Corporation. 2003. *Civic Mission of Schools*. http://www.civicmissionof-schools.org.

Chan, Sucheng. 1986. *This Bitter-Sweet Soil: The Chinese in California Agriculture, 1860–1910*. Berkeley: University of California Press.

Chávez, Leo R. 2001. *Covering Immigration: Popular Images and the Politics of the Nation*. Berkeley: University of California Press.

———. 2008. *The Latino Threat: Constructing Immigrants, Citizens, and the Nation*. Palo Alto, CA: Stanford University Press.

Clarke, Paul Barry. 1996. *Deep Citizenship*. London: Pluto Press.

Commission on Naturalization. 1905. *Report to the President of the Commission on Naturalization*. 59th Cong., 1st sess., Doc. 46. Washington, DC: Government Printing Office.

Constable, Marianne. 1994. *The Law of the Other: The Mixed Jury and Changing Conceptions of Citizenship, Law, and Knowledge*. Chicago: University of Chicago Press.

Constitución de Cadiz de 1812. http://www.valvanera.com/constitucion1812.htm.

Cooper, Tova Tracy. 2005. "Educational Curricula, Americanization and the Autobiography of a New Citizenry, 1880–1920." Ph.D. diss., University of California, Irvine.

Cortéz, Alberto. 1989. "No Soy de Aquí." *12 Grandes Exitos*. Nashville: EMI Capitol Records.

Coutin, Susan Bibler. 2003. "Cultural Logics of Belonging and Movement: Transnationalism, Naturalization, and U.S. Immigration Politics." *American Ethnologist* 30 (4): 508–526.

Courtney, Heather. 2001. *Los Trabajadores/The Workers*. Documentary.

Curry, Charles F. 1921. *Alien Land Laws and Alien Rights*. 67th Cong., 1st sess., H.R. Doc. 89. Washington, DC: Government Printing Office.

DaMatta, Roberto. 1991. "Do You Know Who You're Talking To?" In *Carnivals, Rogues, and Heroes: An Interpretation of the Brazilian Dilemma*. Edited by Roberto DaMatta and translated by John Drury, 137–197. Notre Dame: University of Notre Dame Press.

———. 1985. *A casa y a rua: Espaço, cidadania, mulher e morte no Brasil*. São Paulo: Editora Brasiliense.

de Crèvecoeur, J. Hector St. John. (1782) 1963. *Letters from an American Farmer and Sketchers of Eighteenth-Century America*. New York: New American Library.

DeSipio, Louis. 1987. "Social Science Literature and the Naturalization Process." *International Migration Review* 21 (2): 390–405.

———. 1995. "Making Citizens or Good Citizens? Naturalization as a Predictor of Organizational and Electoral Behavior among Latino Immigrants." Paper presented at the American Political Science Association meeting, August 31–September 3, Chicago.

———. 1996. "After Proposition 187, the Deluge: Reforming Naturalization Administration While Making Good Citizens." *Harvard Journal of Hispanic Policy* 7–24.

DeSipio, Louis, and Rodolfo O. de la Garza. 1998. *Making Americans, Remaking America: Immigration and Immigrant Policy*. Boulder: Westview Press.

Dietz, Mary. 1992. "Context Is All: Feminism and Theories of Citizenship." In *Dimensions of Radical Democracy*, edited by Chantal Mouffe, 63–85. London: Verso.

Divine, Robert A. 1972. *American Immigration Policy, 1924–1952*. New York: Da Capo Press.

Du Bois, W.E.B. 1961. *The Souls of Black Folk: Essays and Sketches.* Greenwich: Fawcett Publications.

Durkheim, Emile. (1893) 1964. *The Division of Labor in Society.* New York: Free Press.

Eastman, John C. 2007. "Born in the U.S.A.? Rethinking Birthright Citizenship in the Wake of 9/11." *Texas Review of Law and Politics* 12:167–179.

Eisgruber, Christopher L. 1997. "Birthright Citizenship and the Constitution." *New York University Law Review* 72:54–96.

Elkin, Adolphus Peter. 1944. *Citizenship for the Aborigines: A National Aboriginal Policy.* Sydney: Australian Publishing Co.

Ellis, Richard J. 2005. *To the Flag: The Unlikely History of the Pledge of Allegiance.* Lawrence: University Press of Kansas.

Erler, Edward J. 1996. *Societal and Legal Issues Surrounding Children Born in the United States to Illegal Alien Parents.* Hearing, Subcommittee on Immigration and Claims, and Subcommittee on the Constitution, of the Committee on the Judiciary, House of Representatives. 104th Cong., sess., H.R. Doc., pp. 113–115. Washington, DC: Government Printing Office.

Escalante Gonzalbo, Fernando. 1992. *Ciudadanos imaginarios: Memorial de los afanes y desventuras de la virtud y apología del Vicio Triunfante en La República Mexicana—Tratado de moral pública.* Mexico: Colegio de México.

Escalante Gonzalbo, Fernando. 1995. "El Ciudadano." In *Mitos Mexicanos*, edited by Enrique Florescano, 185–188. México: Nuevo Siglo.

Espada, Joao Carlos. 1996. *Social Citizenship Rights: A Critique of F. A. Hayek and Raymond Plant.* New York: Macmillan.

Evans, David T. 1993. *Sexual Citizenship: The Material Construction of Sexualities.* London: Routledge.

Faist, Thomas. 1995. *Social Citizenship for Whom? Young Turks in Germany and Mexican Americans in the United States.* Aldershot, UK: Avebury.

Fannie May Foundation and National Immigration Forum. 1996. *New Americans Guide.* Washington, DC: Fannie May Foundation.

Farh, Jiing-Lih, P. Christopher Earley, and Shu-Chi Lin. 1997. "Impetus for Action: A Cultural Analysis of Justice and Organizational Citizenship Behavior in Chinese Society." *Administrative Science Quarterly* 42 (3): 421–444.

Fecteau, Loie. 2000. "NM State Supreme Court: Language No Barrier for Jury Duty." *Albuquerque Journal,* January 20.

Félix, Adrián. 2008. "New Americans or Diasporic Nationalists? Mexican Migrant Responses to Naturalization and Implications for Political Participation." *American Quarterly* 60 (3): 601–624.

Félix, Adrián, Carmen González, and Ricardo Ramírez. 2008. "Political Protest, Ethnic Media, and Latino Naturalization." *American Behavioral Scientist* 52 (4): 618–634.

Ferguson, Edwin E. 1947. "The California Alien Land Law and the Fourteenth Amendment." *California Law Review* 35: 61–90.

Ferguson, Kathy E., and Phyllis Turnbull. 1999. *Oh Say, Can You See? The Semiotics of the Military in Hawaii.* Minneapolis: University of Minnesota Press.

Fields, Harold. 1935. "Making Naturalization Administrative." *Boston University Law Review* 15:260–270.

Flores, William V., and Rina Benmayor, eds. 1997. *Latino Cultural Citizenship: Claiming Identity, Space, and Rights.* Boston: Beacon Press.

Foley, Douglas E. 1990. *Learning Capitalist Culture: Deep in the Heart of Tejas.* Philadelphia: University of Pennsylvania Press.

Foucault, Michel. 1980a. "Two Lectures." In *Power/Knowledge: Selected Interviews and Other Writings, 1972–1978,* edited by Colin Gordon, 78–108. New York: Pantheon Books.

———. 1980b. "Truth and Power." In *Power/Knowledge: Selected Interviews and Other Writings, 1972–1978,* edited by Colin Gordon, 109–133. New York: Pantheon Books.

———. 1989. "The Subject and Power." In *Michel Foucault: Beyond Structuralism and Hermeneutics,* edited by H. L. Dreyfus and P. Rabinow, 208–228. Chicago: University of Chicago Press.

———. 1990. *The History of Sexuality: Volume 1,* An Introduction. Translated by Robert Hurley. New York: Vintage Books.

———. 2000. *Power: Essential Works of Foucault, 1954–1984.* Vol. 3. Edited by James D. Faubion. New York: New Press.

Freeman, Gary P., Rodolfo O. de la Garza, Luis F. B. Plascencia, Susan González Baker, and Manuel Orozco. 1997. *The Texas Citizenship Initiative: Final Report.* Austin: Public Policy Clinic, University of Texas.

Freeman, Gary P., Luis F. B. Plascencia, Susan González Baker, and Manuel Orozco. 2002. "Explaining the Surge in Citizenship Applications in the 1990s: Lawful Permanent Residents in Texas." *Social Science Quarterly* 83 (4): 1013–1025.

Freeman, Gary P., David L. Leal, and Luis F. B. Plascencia. 2003. "The Business of the Future: Banks, Latinos and the Changing Financial Borders." *Texas Business Review* (April).

García, Alma M. 2002. *The Mexican Americans.* Westport, CT: Greenwood Press.

Garcia, John A. 1981. "Political Integration of Mexican Immigrants: Exploration into the Naturalization Process." *International Migration Review* 15 (4): 611–624.

García, Mario T. 1978. "Americanization and the Mexican Immigrant, 1880–1930." *Journal of Ethnic Studies* 6 (2): 19–34.

Gardner, Martha. 2005. *The Qualities of a Citizen: Women, Immigration, and Citizenship, 1870–1965.* Princeton: Princeton University Press.

Gavit, John Palmer. (1922) 1971. *Americanization Studies: The Acculturation of Immigrant Groups into American Society.* Americans By Choice Series, edited by William S. Publication No. 125, Patterson Smith Reprint Series in Criminology, Law Enforcement, and Social Problems. Bernard. Montclair, NJ: Patterson Smith.

Germain, Gilbert G. 1993. *A Discourse on Disenchantment: Reflections on Politics and Technology.* Albany: State University of New York Press.

Geyer, Georgie Anne. 1996. *Americans No More.* New York: Atlantic Monthly Press.

Gilbertson, Greta, and Audrey Singer. 2000. "Naturalization under Changing Conditions of Membership: Dominican Immigrants in New York City." In

Immigration Research for a New Century: Multidisciplinary Perspectives, edited by Nancy Foner, Rubén G. Rumbaut, and Steven Gold, 157–186. New York: Russell Sage Foundation.

———. 2003. "The Emergence of Protective Citizenship in the USA: Naturalization among Dominican Immigrants in the Post-1996 Welfare Reform Era." *Ethnic and Racial Studies* 26 (1): 25–51.

Gobé, Marc. 2002. *Citizen Brand: 10 Commandments for Transforming Brands in a Consumer Society.* New York: Allworth Press.

González, Nancie L. 1988. *Sojourners of the Caribbean: Ethnogenesis and Ethnohistory of the Garifuna.* Urbana: University of Illinois Press.

Gordon, Susan M. 2007. "Integrating Immigrants: Morality and Loyalty in US Naturalization Practice." *Citizenship Studies* 11 (4): 367–382.

Gotanda, Neil. 1997. "Race, Citizenship, and the Search of Political Community among 'We the People.'" *Oregon Law Review* 76: 233–259.

Goyer, David. 2011. "The Incident." In *Action Comics #900.* Art by Miguel Sepulveda. June.

Graglia, Lino A. 2009–2010. "Birthright Citizenship for Children of Illegal Aliens: An Irrational Public Policy." *Texas Review of Law and Policy* 14: 1–14.

Gramsci, Antonio. 1971. *Selections from the Prison Notebooks.* Edited and translated by Quintin Hoare and Geoffrey Nowell Smith. New York: International Publishers.

Greisman, H. C. 1976. "'Disenchanting of the World': Romanticism, Aesthetics and Sociological Theory." *British Journal of Sociology* 27 (4): 495–507.

Griscom, Ellwood, Jr. 1921. *Americanization: A School Reader and Speaker.* New York: Macmillan.

Griswold de Castillo, Richard. 1990. *The Treaty of Guadalupe Hidalgo: A Legacy of Conflict.* Norman: University of Oklahoma Press.

Gunlicks, Michael. 1994–1995. "Citizenship as a Weapon in Controlling the Flow of Undocumented Aliens: Evaluation of Proposed Denials of Citizenship to Children of Undocumented Aliens Born in the United States." *George Washington Law Review* 63: 551–584.

Hall, Stuart, and David Held. 1990. "Citizens and Citizenship." In *New Times: The Changing Face of Politics in the 1990s,* edited by Stuart Hall and Martin Jacques, 173–188. London: Verso.

Haney López, Ian F. 1996. *White by Law: The Legal Construction of Race.* New York: New York University Press.

Harris, Marvin. 1968. *The Rise of Anthropological Theory: A History of Theories of Culture.* New York: Thomas Y. Crowell Co.

Hartmann, Edward G. 1967. *The Movement to Americanize the Immigrant.* New York: AMS Press.

Hayduk, Ron. 2006. *Democracy for All: Restoring Immigrant Voting Rights in the United States.* New York: Routledge.

Heater, Derek. 2004. *A History of Education for Citizenship.* London: Routledge Falmer.

Helton, Arthur C. 1986–1987. "Book Review: Citizenship without Consent." *New York University Journal of International Law* 19: 221–226.

Higashi, Julie. 2002. "Scouting in the United States: Cultivating Civic Mindedness and National Identity." In *We the People" in the Global Age: Re-examination of Nationalism and Citizenship,* edited by Ryo Oshiba, Edward Rhodes, and Chieko Kitagawa Otsuru, 229–248. Osaka: Japan Center for Area Studies, National Museum of Ethnology.

Higgs, Robert J. 1987. "Yale and the Heroic Ideal, Götterämmerung and Paligenesis, 1865–1914," In *Manliness and Morality: Middle-Class Masculinity in Britain and America, 1800–1940,* edited by J. A. Mangan and James Walvin, 160–175. New York: St. Martin's Press.

Higham, John. 1981. *Strangers in the Land: Patterns of American Nativism, 1860–1925.* New York: Atheneum.

Hing, Bill Ong. 1993. *Making and Remaking Asian America through Immigration Policy, 1850–1990.* Palo Alto, CA: Stanford University Press.

———. 2007. "Immigration Policy: Thinking Outside the (Big) Box." *Connecticut Law Review* 30 (4): 1401–1441.

Ho, James C. 2007–2008. "Birthright Citizenship, the Fourteenth Amendment, and the Texas Legislature." *Texas Review of Law and Policy* 12: 161–165.

Hodson, Randy. 2002. "Management Citizenship Behavior and Its Consequences." *Work and Occupation* 29 (1): 64–96.

Hoffman, Abraham. 1974. *Unwanted Mexican Americans in the Great Depression: Repatriation Pressures, 1929–1939.* Tucson: University of Arizona Press.

Holston, James. 2008. *Insurgent Citizenship: Disjunctions of Democracy and Modernity in Brazil.* Princeton: Princeton University Press.

Hutchinson, E. P. 1981. *Legislative History of American Immigration Policy, 1798–1965.* Philadelphia: University of Pennsylvania Press.

Ichilov, Orit, and Nisan Nave. 1981. "'The Good Citizen' As Viewed by Israeli Adolescents." *Comparative Politics* 13 (4): 361–376.

Intercollegiate Studies Institute. 2006. *The Coming Crisis in Citizenship: Higher Education's Failure to Teach America's History and Institutions.* Wilmington, DE: Intercollegiate Studies Institute.

Isin, Engin F. 2002. *Being Political: Genealogies of Citizenship.* Minneapolis: University of Minnesota Press.

Isin, Engin F., and Bryan S. Turner, eds. 2002. *Handbook of Citizenship Studies.* London: Sage Publications.

Johnson, Kevin R. 1995–1996. "Fear of an 'Alien Nation': Race, Immigration, and Immigrants." *Stanford Law and Policy Review* 7: 111–126.

———. 2007. *Opening the Floodgates: Why America Needs to Rethink Its Borders and Immigration Laws.* New York: New York University Press.

Jones, Maldwyn Allen. 1992. *American Immigration.* 2nd ed. Chicago: University of Chicago Press.

Joseph, Gilbert M., and Daniel Nugent, eds. 1994. *Everyday Forms of State Formation: Revolution and the Negotiation of Rule in Modern Mexico.* Durham: Duke University Press.

Kalnay, Francis. 1941. *The New American: A Handbook of Necessary Information for Aliens, Refugees and New Citizens.* New York: Greenberg Publisher.

Kalt, Brian C. 2004. "The Exclusion of Felons from Jury Service." Public Law and Legal Theory, Working Paper Series, Research Paper No. 01–04.

Kann, Mark E. 1991. *On the Man Question: Gender and Civic Virtue in America.* Philadelphia: Temple University Press.

———. 1998. *A Republic of Men: The American Founders, Gendered Language, and Patriarchal Politics.* New York: New York University Press.

Kearney, Michael. 1986. "From the Invisible Hand to the Visible Feet: Anthropological Studies of Migration and Development." *Annual Review of Anthropology* 15: 331–361.

———. 1995. "The Local and the Global: The Anthropology of Globalization and Transnationalism." *Annual Review of Anthropology* 24: 547–565.

Kerber, Linda K. 1998. *No Constitutional Right to Be Ladies: Women and the Obligations of Citizenship.* New York: Hill & Wang.

Kettner, James H. 1978. *The Development of American Citizenship, 1608–1870.* Chapel Hill: University of North Carolina Press.

Keyssar, Alexander. 2000. *The Right to Vote: The Contested History of Democracy in the United States.* New York: Basic Books.

Kivisto, Peter, and Thomas Faist. 2007. *Citizenship: Discourse, Theory, and Transnational Prospects.* Malden: Blackwell Publishing.

Knapp, Kiyoko Kamio. 1996. "The Rhetoric of Exclusion: The Art of Drawing a Line between Aliens and Citizens." *Georgetown Immigration Law Journal* 10: 401–440.

Knop, Karen. 2001. "Relational Nationality: On Gender and Nationality in International Law." In *Citizenship Today: Global Perspectives and Practices,* edited by T. Aleinikoff and Douglas Klusmeyer, pp. 89–124. Washington, DC: Carnegie Endowment for International Peace.

Kojève, Alexander. 1969. *Introduction to the Reading of Hegel.* Edited by Allan Bloom, Translated by James H. Nichols Jr. New York: Basic Books.

Kojève, Alexander. 2000. *Outline of a Phenomenology of Right.* Edited by Bryan-Paul Frost, translated by Bryan-Paul Frost and Robert Howe. Lanham: Rowman & Littlefield.

Konvitz, Milton R. 1946. *The Alien and the Asiatic in American Law.* Ithaca: Cornell University Press.

Koselleck, Reinhart. 1982. "*Begriffsgeschichte* and Social History." *Economy and Society* 11 (4): 409–427.

———. 1985. *Futures Past: On the Semantics of Historical Time.* Translated by Keith Tribe. Cambridge: MIT Press.

———. 2002. *The Practice of Conceptual History: Timing History, Spacing Concepts.* Translated by Todd Samuel Presner. Palo Alto, CA: Stanford University Press.

Koshul, Basit Bilal. 2005. *The Postmodern Significance of Max Weber's Legacy: Disenchanting Disenchantment.* New York: Palgrave.

Kraditor, Aileen S. 1981. *The Idea of the Woman Suffrage Movement, 1890–1920.* New York: W. W. Norton & Co.

Krauze, Enrique. 1986. *Por Una Democracia sin Adjetivos.* México: Joaquin Mortiz-Planeta.

Krikorian, Mark. 2004. "Don't Give Noncitizens the Vote: Recent Proposals to Relax Election Requirements Would Ill Serve the National Interest." *Newsday*, April 26. http://www.cis.org/node/378.

Kymlicka, Will, and Wayne Norman. 1994. "Return of the Citizens: A Survey of Recent Work on Citizenship Theory." *Ethics* 104 (2): 352–381.

Laguerre, Michel. 1996. "Transnational Diasporic Citizenship." Working Paper 96–13, Institute of Governmental Studies, Berkeley, CA.

———. 1998. *Diasporic Citizenship: Haitian Americans in Transnational America.* New York: St. Martin's Press.

Lazarus, Mark L. 1989. "An Historical Analysis of Alien Land Law: Washington Territory and State, 1853–1889." *University of Puget Sound Law Review* 12: 197–246.

Leal, David L. 2002. "Political Participation by Latino Non-Citizens in the United States." *British Journal of Political Science* 32: 353–370.

Legomsky, Stephen H. 1994. 'Why Citizenship?" *Virginia Journal of International Law* 35: 279–300.

Levinson, Bradley A. U. 2004. "Hopes and Challenges for the New Civic Education in Mexico: Toward a Democratic Citizen without Adjectives." *International Journal of Educational Development* 24: 269–282.

Levinson, Bradley A. U., Douglas E. Foley, and Dorothy C. Holland, eds. 1996. *The Cultural Production of the Educated Person: Critical Ethnographies of Schooling and Local Practice.* Albany: State University of New York Press.

Liang, Zai. 1994. "Social Contact, Social Capital, and the Naturalization Process: Evidence from Six Immigrant Groups." *Social Science Research* 23: 407–437.

Lister, Ruth. 1997. *Citizenship: Feminist Perspectives.* Washington Square: New York University Press.

Lomnitz, Claudio. 1993. "Hacia una antropología de la nacionalidad mexicana." *Revista Mexicana de Sociología* 55 (1): 169–195.

———. 1996. "Fissures in Contemporary Mexican Nationalism." *Public Culture* 9 (1): 55–68.

———. 1999. "Models of Citizenship in Mexico." *Public Culture* 11 (1): 269–293.

Lopreato, Joseph. 1970. *Italian Americans.* New York: Random House.

Lowe, Lisa. 1996. *Immigrant Acts: On Asian American Cultural Politics.* Durham: Duke University Press.

Lowe, Ronald E. 1976. "The Arizona Alien Land Law: Its Meaning and Constitutional Validity." *Arizona State University Law Journal* (2): 253–276.

Luykz, Aurolyn. 1999. *The Citizen Factory: Schooling and Cultural Production in Bolivia.* Albany: State University of New York.

Magliocca, Gerard N. 2007–2008. "Indians and Invaders: The Citizenship Clause and Illegal Aliens." *Pennsylvania Journal of Constitutional Law* 10: 499–526.

Mallon, Florencia. 1994. "Reflections on the Ruins: Everyday Forms of State Formation in Nineteenth Century Mexico." In *Everyday Forms of State Formation: Revolution and the Negotiation of Rule in Modern Mexico,* edited by Gilbert M. Joseph and Daniel Nugent, 69–106. Durham: Duke University Press.

———. 1995. *Peasant and Nation: The Making of Postcolonial Mexico and Peru.* Berkeley: University of California Press.

Mann, Michael. 1987. "Ruling Class Strategies and Citizenship." *Sociology* 21 (3): 339–354.

Marshall, T. H. 1950. *Citizenship and Social Class.* Cambridge: Cambridge University Press.

Martin, David A. 1985–1986. "Membership and Consent: Abstract or Organic?" *Yale Journal of International Law* 11: 278–296.

Marx, Karl. (1843) 1972. "On the Jewish Question." In *The Marx-Engels Reader,* edited by Robert C. Tucker, 24–51. New York: W. W. Norton & Co.

Mason, Carol. 2000. "Cracked Babies and the Partial Birth of a Nation: Millennialism and Fetal Citizenship." *Cultural Studies* 14 (1): 35–60.

McBride, James. 1995. *War, Battering, and Other Sports: The Gulf between American Men and Women.* Atlantic Highlands, NJ: Humanities Press.

McConnell, Stuart. 1996. "Reading the Flag: A Reconsideration of the Patriotic Cults of the 1890s." In *Bonds of Affection: Americans Define their Patriotism,* edited by John Bodnar, 102–119. Princeton: Princeton University Press.

McGovney, Dudley O. 1923. "Race Discrimination in Naturalization, Part I." *Iowa Law Bulletin* 8 (3): 129–161.

———. 1934. "Naturalization of the Mixed-Blood—A Dictum." *California Law Review* 22 (4): 377–391.

———. 1947. "The Anti-Japanese Land Laws of California and Ten Other States." *California Law Review* 35: 7–60.

Meeks, Eric V. 2007. *Border Citizens: The Making of Indians, Mexican, and Anglos in Arizona.* Austin: University of Texas Press.

Melzer, Sara E., and Leslie W. Rabine, eds. 1992. *Rebel Daughters: Women and the French Revolution.* New York: Oxford University Press.

Melzer, Sara E., and Kathryn Norberg, eds. 1998. *From the Royal to the Republican Body: Incorporating the Political in Seventeenth-and Eighteenth-Century France.* Berkeley: University of California Press.

Menchaca, Martha. 1995. *The Mexican Outsiders: A Community History of Marginalization and Discrimination in California.* Austin: University of Texas Press.

Meyler, Bernadette. 2000–2001. "The Gestation of Birthright Citizenship, 1868–1898 States' Rights, the Law of Nations, and Mutual Consent." *Georgetown Immigration Law Journal* 15: 519–562.

Michelson, Melissa R., and Amalia Pallares. 2001. "The Politicization of Chicago Mexican Americans: Naturalization, the Vote, and Perceptions of Discrimination." *Aztlán* 26 (2): 63–85.

Molina, Natalia. 2010. "'In a Race All Their Own': The Quest to Make Mexicans Ineligible for U.S. Citizenship." *Pacific Historical Review* 79 (2): 167–201.

Morales, Lymari. 2011. "Obama's Birth Certificate Convinces Some, but Not All, Skeptics." *Gallup.* May 13. http://www.gallup.com/poll/147530/Obama-Birth-Certificate-Convinces-Not-Skeptics.aspx.

Mosse, George L. 1989. "National Anthems: The National Militant." In *From Ode to Anthem: Problems of Lyric Poetry,* edited by Reinhold Grimm and Jost Hermand, 86–99. Madison: University of Wisconsin Press.

Motomura, Hiroshi. 2006. *Americans in Waiting: The Lost Story of Immigration and Citizenship in the United States.* New York: Oxford University Press.

Mouffe, Chantal. 1992a. "Democratic Citizenship and the Political Community." In *Dimensions of Radical Democracy,* edited by C. Mouffe. London: Verso.

———. 1992b. "Feminism, Citizenship and Radical Democratic Politics." In *Feminist Theorize the Political Butler,* edited by Judith Scott and Joan W. Scott, 369–384. New York: Routledge.

———. 1993. *The Return of the Political.* London: Verso.

Moullier-Boutang, Yann. 1985. "Resistance to the Political Representation of Alien Populations: The European Paradox." *International Migration Review* 19 (3): 485–492.

Myer, Walter, and Clay Coss. 1952. *America's Greatest Challenge.* Washington, DC: Civic Education Service.

National Center for Learning and Citizenship, Education Commission of the States. 2001. *Every Student a Citizen: Creating the Democratic Self.* http://www.ecs.org.

National Conference of State Legislatures. 2011. 2011 *Immigration-Related Laws, Bills and Resolutions in the States: Jan. 1—March 31, 2011.* http://ncls.org/default.aspx? yabid=13114.

Nelson, Dana D. 1998. *National Manhood: Capitalist Citizenship and the Imagined Fraternity of White Men.* Durham: Duke University Press.

Neuman, Gerald L. 1987. "Back to Dred Scott?" *San Diego Law Review* 24: 485–500.

———. 1996. *Strangers to the Constitution: Immigrants, Borders, and Fundamental Law.* Princeton: Princeton University Press.

Ngai, Mae M. 2006–2007. "Birthright Citizenship and the Alien Citizen." *Fordham Law Review* 75: 2521–2530.

Niemi, Richard G., and Jane Junn. 1998. *Civic Education: What Makes Students Learn.* New Haven: Yale University Press.

North, David S. 1987. "The Long Grey Welcome: A Study of the American Naturalization Program." *International Migration Review* 21 (2): 311–326.

Ogden, Frederic D. 1958. *The Poll Tax in the South.* Tuscaloosa: University of Alabama.

Olivas, Michael A. 2008. "Lawmakers Gone Wild? College Residency and Response to Professor Kobach." *Southern Methodist Law Review* 61: 99–132.

Ong, Aihwa. 1993. "On the Edge of Empire: Flexible Citizenship among Chinese in Diaspora." *Positions* 1: 745–778.

———. 1995. "Making the Biopolitical Subject: Cambodian Immigrants, Refugee Medicine and Cultural Citizenship in California." *Social Science and Medicine* 40 (9): 1243–1257.

———. 1996. "Cultural Citizenship as Subject-Making." *Current Anthropology* 37 (5): 737–751.

———. 1999. *Flexible Citizenship: The Cultural Logics of Transnationality.* Durham: Duke University Press.

———. 2006. *Neoliberalism as Exception: Mutations in Citizenship and Sovereignty.* Durham: Duke University Press.

Organ, Dennis W. 1988. *Organizational Citizenship Behavior: The Good Soldier Syndrome.* Lexington: Lexington Books.

Organ, Dennis W., and Katherine Ryan. 1995. "A Meta-Analytic Review of Attitudinal and Dispositional Predictors of Organizational Citizenship Behavior." *Personnel Psychology* 48: 775–802.

Pak, Katherine Tegtmeyer. 2001. "Towards Local Citizenship: Japanese Cities Respond to International Migration." Working Paper No. 30. Center for Comparative Immigration Studies, University of California, San Diego.

Panster, Wil G., ed. 1997. *Citizens of the Pyramid: Essays on Mexican Political Culture.* Amsterdam: Thela Publishers.

Pantoja, Adrian D., Ricardo Ramirez, and Gary M. Segura. 2001. "Citizens by Choice, Voters by Necessity: Patterns of Political Mobilization by Naturalized Latinos." *Political Research Quarterly* 54 (4): 729–750.

Parker, J. Cecil, C. Perry Patterson, and Samuel B. McAlister. 1939. *Citizenship in Our Democracy.* New York: D. C. Heath and Co.

Pateman, Carole. 1989a. *The Disorder of Women: Democracy, Feminism and Political Theory.* Cambridge: Polity Press.

———. 1989b. "The Patriarchal Welfare State." In *The Disorder of Women: Democracy, Feminism and Political Theory,* edited by Carole Pateman, 179–209. Cambridge: Polity Press.

Perin, Constance. 1998. *Belonging in America: Reading between the Lines.* Madison: University of Wisconsin Press.

Pettit, Katherine. 2006–2007. "Addressing the Call for the Elimination of Birthright Citizenship in the United States Constitutional and Pragmatic Reasons to Keep Birthright Citizenship Intact." *Tulane Journal of International and Comparative Law* 15: 265–289.

Pickus, Noah M. J., ed. 1998. *Immigration and Citizenship in the Twenty-First Century.* Lanham, MD: Rowman & Littlefield.

Pitkin, Hanna Fenichel. 1984. *Fortune Is a Woman: Gender and Politics in the Thought of Niccolò Machiavelli.* Berkeley: University of California Press.

Plascencia, Luis F. B. 2000. *From Undocumented to Documented: Transmigrants that Applied for "Legalization" under IRCA in Texas.* M.A. report, University of Texas, Austin.

———. 2001. "State, County and Municipal Legislation." In *Encyclopedia of American Immigration,* ed. James Ciment Armonk, 2:518–522. New York: M. E. Sharpe.

———. 2009a. "The 'Undocumented' Mexican Migrant Question: Re-examining the Framing of Law and Illegalization in the United States." *Urban Anthropology* 38 (2–4): 375–434.

———. 2009b. "Citizenship through Veteranship: Latino Migrants Defend the U.S. 'Homeland.'" *Anthropology News* 50 (5): 8–9.

———. 2010. "'Civil Death' and Latino Veterans: The Deportation/Removal of Non-Citizen Veterans." Paper presented at the American Anthropological Association annual conference, November 17–21, New Orleans.

———. 2011. "State and Local Regulation of Migration and Migrants." In *Anti-Immigration in the United States: A Historical Encyclopedia,* edited by Kathleen Arnold, 451–455. Santa Barbara, CA: Greenwood Press.

————. In press. "Attrition through Enforcement and the Elimination of a 'Dangerous Class.'" In *Latino Politics and International Relations: The Case of Arizona's Immigration Law SB1070*, edited by Lisa Magaña. New York: Springer.

————. n.d.a. "The Military Gates of Citizenship: Latino 'Aliens and Noncitizen Nationals' Performing Military Work in the United States."

————. n.d.b. "The Web of Exception: The State Construction and Erasure of the Migrant Legal/Illegal Divide in the United States."

Plascencia, Luis F. B., Gary P. Freeman, and Mark Setzler. 2003. "The Decline of Barriers to Immigrant Economic and Political Rights in the American States, 1977–2001." *International Migration Review* 37 (1): 5–23.

Polanyi, Karl. 1971. "The Economy as Instituted Process." In *Trade and Market in Early Empires: Economies in History and Theory*, edited by Karl Polanyi, Conrad M. Arensberg, and Harry W. Pearson, 243–270. Chicago: Henry Regnery Co.

Portes, Alejandro, and John Curtis. 1987. "Changing Flags: Naturalization and Its Determinants among Mexican Immigrants." *International Migration Review* 21 (2): 352–371.

Press, John. 2009. "Frances Kellor, Americanization, and the Quest for Participatory Democracy." Ph.D. diss., New York University.

Price, Polly. 2000. "Alien Land Restrictions in the American Common Law: Exploring the Relative Autonomy Paradigm." Stanford/Yale Junior Faculty Forum, Research Paper 00–04. Social Science Research Network Electronic Paper Collection. http://papers.ssnr.com.

Prucha, Francis Paul, ed. 1973. *Americanizing the American Indians: Writings by the 'Friends of the Indian' 1880–1900*. Lincoln: University of Nebraska Press.

Putnam, Robert D. 1995. "Bowling Alone: America's Declining Social Capital." *Journal of Democracy* 6 (1): 65–78.

————. 2000. *Bowling Alone: The Collapse and Revival of American Community*. New York: Simon & Schuster.

Raskin, Jamin B. 1993a. "Legal Aliens, Local Citizens: The Historical Constitutional and Theoretical Meaning of Alien Suffrage." *University of Pennsylvania Law Review* 141: 1391–1470.

————. 1993b. "Time to Give Aliens the Vote (Again)." *Nation* 256 (13): 433–434.

Reisler, Mark. 1976. *By the Sweat of Their Brow: Mexican Immigrant Labor in the United States, 1900–1940*. Westport: Greenwood Press.

Renshon, Stanley. 2009. *Noncitizen Voting and American Democracy*. Lanham, MD: Rowman & Littlefield.

Riesberg, Peter. 1992. *Citizenship in the Western Tradition: Plato to Rousseau*. Chapel Hill: University of North Carolina Press.

Riordon, William L. 1963. *Plunkitt of Tammany Hall*. New York: E. P. Dutton & Co.

Ritter, Gretchen. 2000. "Gender and Citizenship after the Nineteenth Amendment." *Polity* 32 (3): 345–375.

————. 2006. *The Constitution as Social Design: Gender and Civic Membership in the American Constitutional Order*. Palo Alto, CA: Stanford University Press.

Roelofs, H. Mark. 1957. *The Tension of Citizenship: Private Man and Public Duty*. New York: Rinehart & Co.

Roodner, Theodore. 1964. "Washington's Alien Land Law—Its Constitutionality." *Washington Law Review* 39: 115–133.

Roosevelt, Theodore. 1956. *The Free Citizen: A Summons to Service of the Democratic Ideal.* Edited by Herman Hagerdorn. New York: Macmillan.

Rosaldo, Renato. 1992. "Cultural Citizenship: Attempting to Enfranchise Latinos." In *La Nueva Visión*, 7. Palo Alto: Stanford Center for Chicano Research, Stanford University.

———. 1994. "Cultural Citizenship and Educational Democracy." *Cultural Anthropology* 9 (3): 402–411.

Rosaldo, Renato, William Flores, and Blanca Silvestrini. 1994. "Identity, Conflict, and Evolving Latino Communities: Cultural Citizenship in San Jose, California." Working Paper Series, No. 47. Palo Alto, CA: Stanford Center for Chicano Research, Stanford University.

Rosberg, Gerald M. 1977. "Aliens and Equal Protection: Why Not the Right to Vote?" *Michigan Law Review* 75: 1092–1136.

Ross Pineda, Raúl. 2000. "Derechos políticos en el extranjero: Balance y perspectivas ante el nuevo gobierno Mexicano." Unpublished manuscript.

Rouse, Roger. 1992. "Making Sense of Settlement: Class Transformation among Mexican Migrants in the United States." *Annals of the New York Academy of Science* 645: 25–52.

Saito, Natsu Taylot. 1997. "Alien and Non-Alien Alike: Citizenship, 'Foreignness,' and Racial Hierarchy in American Law." *Oregon Law Review* 76: 261–346.

Salas, Elizabeth. 1990. *Soldaderas: In the Mexican Military.* Austin: University of Texas Press.

Saler, Michael. 2003. "'Clap If You Believe in Sherlock Holmes': Mass Culture and the Re-Enchantment of Modernity, c. 1890–c. 1940." *Historical Journal* 46 (3): 599–622.

Sánchez, George J. 1990. "'Go After the Women': Americanization and the Mexican Immigrant Woman, 1915–1929." In *Unequal Sisters: A Multicultural Reader in U.S. Women's History*, edited by Ellen Carol Du Bois and Vicki L. Ruiz, 250–263. New York: Routledge.

San Miguel, Guadalupe, Jr. 1987. *"Let All of Them Take Heed": Mexican Americans and the Campaign for Educational Equality in Texas, 1910–1981.* Austin: University of Texas Press.

Sandmeyer, Elmer C. 1936. "California Anti-Chinese Legislation and the Federal Courts: A Study in Federal Relations." *Pacific Historical Review* 5 (3): 189–211.

Schlesinger, Arthur, Jr. 1992. *The Disuniting of America: Reflections on a Multicultural Society.* New York: W. W. Norton & Co.

Schneider, Dorothee. 2000. "Symbolic Citizenship, Nationalism and the Distant State: The United States Congress in the 1996 Debate on Immigration Reform." *Citizenship Studies* 4 (3): 255–273.

Schuck, Peter H. 1989. "Membership in the Liberal Polity: The Devaluation of American Citizenship." In *Immigration and the Politics of Citizenship in Europe and North America*, edited by William Rogers Brubacker, 51–65. Lanham, MD: University Press of America.

———. 1994–1995. "Whose Membership Is It, Anyway? Comments on Gerald Neuman." *Virginia Journal of International Law* 35: 321–331.

———. 1998. *Citizens, Strangers, and In-Betweens: Essays on Immigration and Citizenship*. Boulder: Westview Press.

Schuck, Peter H., and Rogers M. Smith. 1985. *Citizenship without Consent: Illegal Aliens in the American Polity*. New Haven: Yale University Press.

———. 1985–1986. "Membership and Consent: Actual or Mythic? A Reply to David A. Martin." *Yale Journal of International Law* 11:545–552.

Schudson, Michael. 1998. *The Good Citizen: A History of American Civic Life*. New York: Free Press.

Schwartz, David S. 1986. "Book Review: The Amorality of Consent." *California Law Review* 74: 2143–2171.

Shachar, Ayelet. 2009. *The Birthright Lottery: Citizenship and Global Inequality*. Cambridge, MA: Harvard University Press.

Shanks, Cheryl. 2001. *Immigration and the Politics of American Sovereignty, 1890–1990*. Ann Arbor: University of Michigan Press.

Shanley, Mary Lyndon, and Carole Pateman, eds. 1991. *Feminist Interpretations and Political Theory*. University Park: Pennsylvania State University Press.

Shapiro, Mark. 1993. "The Dormant Commerce Clause: A Limit on Alien Land Laws." *Brooklyn Journal of International Law* 20: 217–253.

Shaver, Annis North. 2004. "Americanization: The Immigrant's Bridge to Assimilation." Ph.D. diss., University of Miami.

Sheridan, Clare. 1999. "A Genealogy of Citizenship: Mexican Americans, Race and National Identity." Ph.D. diss., University of Texas, Austin.

Shimberg, Benjamin, Barbara F. Esser, and Daniel H. Kruger. 1973. *Occupational Licensing: Practices and Policies*. Washington, DC: Public Affairs Press.

Shklar, Judith N. 1991. *American Citizenship: The Quest for Inclusion (Tanner Lecture on Human Values)*. Cambridge: Harvard University Press.

Shulman, Robert J. 1994–1995. "Children of a Lesser God: Should the Fourteenth Amendment Be Altered or Repealed to Deny Automatic Citizenship Rights and Privileges to American Born Children of Illegal Aliens?" *Pepperdine Law Review* 22: 669–725.

Simmel, Georg. 1950. "The Stranger." In *The Sociology of Georg Simmel*, edited and translated by Kurt H. Wolff, 402–408. New York: Free Press.

Siu, Lok. 2001. "Diasporic Cultural Citizenship: Chineseness and Belonging in Central America and Panama." *Social Text* 19 (4): 7–28.

Sloan, Harold S., and Arnold J. Zurcher. 1964. *A Dictionary of Economics*. 4th ed. New York: Barnes & Noble.

Smith, Donnal V. 1932. "The Influence of the Foreign-Born of the Northwest in the Election of 1860." *Mississippi Valley Historical Review* 19 (2): 192–204.

Smith, Rogers M. 2008–2009. "Birthright Citizenship and the Fourteenth Amendment in 1868 and 2008." *University of Pennsylvania Journal of Constitutional Law* 11: 1329–1335.

Snyder, R. Claire. 1999. *Citizen-Soldiers and Manly Warriors: Military Service and Gender in the Civic Republican Tradition*. Lanham, MD: Rowman & Littlefield.

———. 2003. "The Citizen-Soldier Tradition and Gender Integration of the U.S. Military." *Armed Forces and Society* 29 (2): 185–204.

Somers, Margaret R. 1993. "Citizenship and the Place of the Public Sphere: Law, Community, and Political Culture in the Transition to Democracy." *American Sociological Review* 58 (October): 587–620.

Stewart, Susan. 1984. *On Longing: Narratives of the Miniature, the Gigantic, the Souvenir, the Collection.* Baltimore: Johns Hopkins University Press.

Strong, Pauline Turner. 2004. "The Mascot Slot: Cultural Citizenship, Political Correctness, and Pseudo-Indian Sports Symbols." *Journal of Sport and Social Issues* 28 (1): 79–87.

Summers, Clyde W. 1946. "Admission Policies of Labor Unions." *Quarterly Journal of Economics* 61 (1): 66–107.

Takei, Isao, Rogelio Saenz, and Jing Li. 2005. "Cost of Being a Mexican Immigrant and Being a Mexican Non-Citizen in California and Texas." Unpublished manuscript. Last modified March 1. Photocopy.

Tambini, Damian. 2001. "Post-national Citizenship." *Ethnic and Racial Studies* 24 (2): 195–217.

Tenorio, Mauricio, Martha Menchaca, and David Montejano. 1999. "On the 150th Anniversary of the Treaty of Guadalupe Hidalgo." *Reflexiones 1998: New Directions in Mexican American Studies*, edited by Yolanda C. Padilla, 45–51. Austin: Center for Mexican American Studies and University of Texas, Austin.

Trend, David, ed. 1996. *Radical Democracy: Identity, Citizenship, and the State.* New York: Routledge.

Tung, Ko-Chih R. 1985. "Voting Rights for Alien Residents—Who Wants It?" *International Migration Review* 19 (3): 451–467.

Turner, Brian S. 1986. *Citizenship and Capitalism: The Debate Over Reformism.* London: Allen & Unwin.

———. 1993a. Preface to *Citizenship and Social Theory*, edited by B. S. Turner, vii–xii. London: Sage Publications.

———. 1993b. "Contemporary Problems in the Theory of Citizenship." In *Citizenship and Social Theory Turner*, edited by B. S. Turner, 1–18. London: Sage Publications.

Uggen, Christopher, Angela Behrens, and Jeff Manza. 2005. "Criminal Disenfranchisement." *Annual Review of Law and Social Science* 1: 307–322.

U.S. Citizenship and Immigration Services (CIS). 2005. *USCIS Strategic Plan: Securing America's Promise* (M-634). Washington, DC: U.S. Government Printing Office.

U.S. Department of Homeland Security, Office of Immigration Statistics. 2011. *2010 Yearbook of Immigration Statistics.* Washington, DC: U.S. Government Printing Office.

U.S. Department of Justice, Immigration and Naturalization Service. 2000. *1998 Statistical Yearbook of the Immigration and Naturalization Service.* Washington, DC: U.S. Government Printing Office.

———. 2002. *2000 Statistical Yearbook of the Immigration and Naturalization Service.* Washington, DC: U.S. Government Printing Office.

U.S. Immigration and Naturalization Service. 1990. Status of Eligible Phase II Applicants by State and County, Listed Number of Outstanding Applications. March 4. Unpublished memo.

U.S. Personnel Management Office. 2001. *Citizenship Laws of the World*. http://www .opm.gov/extra/investigate/is-01.pdf.

Valencia, Richard R., ed. 1991. *Chicano School Failure and Success: Research and Policy Agenda for the 1990s*. London: Falmer Press.

———. 2008. *Chicano Students and the Courts: The Mexican American Legal Struggle for Educational Equality*. New York: New York University Press.

van Gunsteren, Herman. 1978. "Notes on a Theory of Citizenship." In *Democracy, Consensus, and Social Contract*, edited by Pierre Birnbaum, Jack Lively, and Geraine Parry, 9–35. London: Sage Publications.

———. 1998. *A Theory of Citizenship: Organizing Plurality in Contemporary Democracies*. Boulder: Westview Press.

Van Hook, Jennifer, Susan K. Brown, and Frank D. Bean. 2006. "For Love or Money? Welfare Reform and Immigrant Naturalization." *Social Forces* 85 (2): 643–666.

Van Nuys, Frank. 2002. *Americanizing the West: Race, Immigrants, and Citizenship, 1890–1930*. Lawrence: University of Kansas.

Visweswaran, Kamala. 1997. "Diaspora by Design: Flexible Citizenship and South Asians in U.S. Racial Formations." *Diaspora* 6 (1): 5–29.

Walker, Helen. 1928–1929. "Mexican Immigrants and American Citizenship." *Sociology and Social Research* 13: 464–471.

Wallerstein, Immanuel. 2003. "Citizens All? Citizens Some! The Making of the Citizen." *Comparative Studies of Society and History* 45 (4): 650–679.

Walsh, Ellen. 2008. "'Advancing the Kingdom': Missionaries and Americanization in Puerto Rico, 1898–1930s." Ph.D. diss., University of Pittsburgh.

Walvin, James. 1987. "Symbols of Moral Superiority: Slavery, Sport and the Changing World Order, 1800–1950." In *Manliness and Morality: Middle-Class Masculinity in Britain and America, 1800–1940*, edited by J. A. Mangan and James Walvin, 242–260. New York: St. Martin's Press.

Warren, Allen. 1987. "Popular Manliness: Baden-Powell, Scouting, and the Development of Manly Character." In *Manliness and Morality: Middle-Class Masculinity in Britain and America, 1800–1940*, edited by J. A. Mangan and James Walvin, 199–219. New York: St. Martin's Press.

Weber, Max. 1927. "Citizenship." Chapter 28 in *General and Economic History*, translated by Frank H. Knight, 315–337. New York: Greenberg Publishers.

———. 1958. *The City*. Translated and edited by Don Martindale and Gertrund Neuwirth. New York: Free Press.

Weisman, Joshua. 1980. "Restrictions on the Acquisition of Land By Aliens." *American Journal of Comparative Law* 28 (1): 39–66.

Williamson, Chilton. 1960. *American Suffrage: From Property to Democracy, 1760–1860*. Princeton: Princeton University Press.

Willis, Paul. 1977. *Learning to Labour: How Working Class Kids Get Working Class Jobs*. New York: Columbia University Press.

Wood, Charles. 1998–1999. "Losing Control of America's Future—The Census, Birthright Citizenship, and Illegal Aliens." *Harvard Journal of Law and Public Policy* 22: 465–522.

Woodrow-Lafield, Karen, Xiaohe Xu, Thomas Kersen, and Bunnak Poch. 2004. "Naturalization of U.S. Immigrants: Highlights from Ten Countries." *Population Research and Policy* 23: 187–218.

Yang, Philip Q. 1994. "Explaining Immigrant Naturalization." *International Migration Review* 28 (3): 449–477.

Ziegler-McPherson, Christina A. 2000. Americanization: The California Plan; The Commission of Immigration and Housing of California and Public Policy, 1913–1923. Ph.D. diss., University of California, Santa Barbara.

LEGAL CASES CITED (CHRONOLOGICAL ORDER)

Scott v. Sanford, 60 U.S. 393 (1857).

Yick Wo v. Hopkins, 118 U.S. 356 (1886).

United States v. Wong Kim Ark, 169 U.S. (1898)

Patsone v. Pennsylvania, 232 U.S. 138 (1914).

Crane v. New York, 239 U.S. 195 (1915).

Heim v. McCall, 239 U.S. 175 (1915).

Truax v. Raich, 239 U.S. 33 (1915).

Asakura v. Seattle, 265 U.S. 332 (1924).

Clarke v. Deckenbach, 274 U.S. 392 (1927).

Hirabayashi v. United States, 320 U.S. 81 (1943).

Yasui v. United States, 320 U.S. 114 (1943).

Korematsu v. United States, 323 U.S. 214 (1944).

Takahashi v. Fish Commission, 334 U.S. 410 (1948).

Hernández v. Texas, 347 U.S. 475 (1954).

Graham v. Richardson, 403 U.S. 365 (1971).

Sugarman v. Dougall, 413 U.S. 634 (1973).

In re Griffiths, 413 U.S. 717 (1973).

Richardson v. Ramírez, 418 U.S. 24 (1974).

Re Examining Board v. Flores de Otero, 426 U.S. 572 (1976).

Holley v. Lavine, 553 F.2d 845 (2d Cir. 1977).

Nyquist v. Mauclet, 432 U.S. 1 (1977).

Foley v. Connelie, 435 U.S. 291 (1978).

Ambach v. Norwick, 441 U.S. 68 (1979).

Cabell v. Chávez-Salido, 454 U.S. 432 (1982).

Plyler v. Doe, 457 U.S. 202 (1982).

Bernal v. Fainter, 467 U.S. 216 (1984).

Ibarra et al. v. Texas Employment Commission, 823 F. 2nd 873 (5th Circuit, 1987).

Catholic Social Services, et al. v. Tom Ridge, et al., CIV-S-86–1343 LKK/JFM (E.D. Cal) (2004).

Felicity Mary Newman et al. v. U.S. Citizenship and Immigration Services, CIV. NO. 87–4757-WDK (C.D. Cal) (2004).

Hamdi v. Rumsfeld, 542 U.S. 507 (2004).

Rumsfeld v. Padilla, 542 U.S. 426 (2004).
United States v. Flores-Villar, 09–5801 (2010).

STATUTES CITED

1790 Naturalization Act, 1 Stat. 103.
1870 Naturalization Act, 16 Stat. 254.
1922 Cable Act, 42 Stat. 1021.
1924 Indian Citizenship Act, 43 Stat. 253.
1929 Registry Act, 45 Stat. 1512.
1952 McCarran-Walter Act, 66 Stat. 163.
1986 Immigration Reform and Control Act, 100 Stat. 3359.
1990 Immigration Act, 104 Stat. 4978.

Index

About the Author

Luis F. B. Plascencia is an assistant professor of anthropology in the Social and Behavioral Division and an affiliated professor in the School of Transborder Studies, and the School of Public Affairs at Arizona State University. His scholarship and engagement with migration issues encompasses local migrant rights efforts, policy analysis in state government, research in public policy centers, and university teaching and research.

9 780813 552804